Assessment Skills for Paramedics

Assessment Skills for Paramedics

Edited by
Amanda Blaber and
Graham Harris

Open University Press

Open University Press
McGraw-Hill Education
McGraw-Hill House
Shoppenhangers Road
Maidenhead
Berkshire
England
SL6 2QL

email: enquiries@openup.co.uk
world wide web: www.openup.co.uk

and Two Penn Plaza, New York, NY 10121-2289, USA

First published 2011

A catalogue record of this book is available from the British Library

ISBN-13: 978-0-33-524199-6 (pb)
ISBN-10: 0-33-524199-9 (pb)
e-ISBN: 978-0-33-524201-6

Library of Congress Cataloging-in-Publication Data
CIP data applied for

Typesetting and e-book compilations by
RefineCatch Limited, Bungay, Suffolk
Printed in the UK by Bell and Bain Ltd, Glasgow.

Fictitious names of companies, products, people, characters and/or data that may be used herein (in case studies or in examples) are not intended to represent any real individual, company, product or event.

The McGraw·Hill Companies

To the patience of our friends and family and Rachel – thank you.

For Lorna.

Contents

About the contributors

Denise Aspland RGN, Dip Child Health
Advanced Life Support Group Generic Instructor, Advanced Paediatric Life Support Instructor, Senior Sister/Practice Development Nurse, Darent Valley Hospital NHS Trust

Denise qualified as a Registered General Nurse in 1993 and worked at Leicester Royal Infirmary in Trauma Orthopaedics for 6 months.

Following her time at Leicester Royal Infirmary she travelled to Australia where she worked for a year, initially as a general nurse on Whitsunday Islands and subsequently at the Camperdown Children's Hospital in Sydney where she was introduced to paediatric nursing. This is where her passion for paediatrics started.

Returning to the UK in 1996 she undertook the paediatric nursing qualification at Great Ormond Street Hospital and specialised in paediatric gastric surgery.

In 1998 she moved to Dorset and worked in the A&E department at Poole Hospital. It was here she found her niche and was able to develop skills and knowledge in both adult and paediatric emergency medicine. As Poole hospital was the Major Trauma Centre for East Dorset she was able to experience emergency work under the direction of skilled professionals.

On relocating back to London she was employed at Lewisham children's A&E as a sister. It was here she became an APLS instructor in 2004 and has been teaching on this course ever since. She also tutors on a variety of courses at University of Greenwich. This has enabled her to share her knowledge and experience of paediatric emergency nursing. Her specialties are paediatric trauma and paediatric resuscitation. She hopes that you gain some valuable information on the management of paediatric emergencies from her chapter and that the scary world of the little folk does not perturb you from managing them in the pre-hospital setting.

Chris Baker MSc, BSc (Hons) with Emergency Care Practice, CertEd, HPC Registered Paramedic, Ambulance Clinical and Driving Tutor
Clinical Tutor/Link Tutor, University Team (Saint George's University of London Honorary contract), London Ambulance Service

Chris joined the London Ambulance Service in 1994 as a direct entry technician, and progressed to paramedic at the earliest possible opportunity, completing his training in 1996. During his career in the service he has practised in various areas of London, including both central and suburban areas. In 1999 he trained to be a Duty Officer, and then progressed to Clinical Tutor later that year. He has remained in training to the present day, with the exception of a year's secondment to the Professional Standards Unit. He has taught on technician, paramedic and advanced practitioner courses, as well as driving tuition, and is now part of the Higher Education Training Team. He hopes to commence a doctorate in education later this year.

His special interests include being both a member and directing staff on the Medical Response Team covering events throughout London, and a member of the Public Order Team. He has undertaken the National Bronze Officer course, and is due to undertake the Public Order Bronze Officer course. He is a specialist in 12 lead ECGs, mental health, manual handling and advanced life support.

Chris believes that assessment of the gastro-intestinal and urinary system still presents a grey area to many of us as out-of-hospital practitioners, and hopes that his chapter goes some way to simplifying this issue. He wishes all readers (and their patients!) good health, and safe practice.

Amanda Blaber PG (Dip)Ed, MSc Sociology of Health and Welfare, BSc (Hons) Health and Community Studies, Dip HE (Accident & Emergency), RGN
Senior Lecturer, University of Brighton

Amanda has a background in acute medical and emergency care nursing. This area of expertise naturally lends itself to partnerships and teamwork with ambulance service colleagues. After 12 years working at the level of senior sister, Amanda decided to accept the new challenge of higher education. Whilst working at the University of Hertfordshire, Amanda taught student nurses and paramedics, on both pre- and post-qualifying pathways. After moving to the University of Greenwich in 2003, Amanda led the curriculum development with the London Ambulance Service to achieve approval of the Foundation Degree (FdSc) in 2006. Amanda is now teaching student paramedics and nurses at the University of Brighton. Amanda is pleased to be able to assist Graham in the editing of this assessment text.

Kevin Dark BSc (Hons), PGCE, MCPara
Paramedic Tutor/Training Officer, London Ambulance Service NHS Trust

Kevin joined the London Ambulance Service in February 1996 after serving with the British Army as a Combat Medical Technician Class 1. Following successful completion of the IHCD Paramedic award in 1998 he continued his clinical and educational development completing elements of the Emergency Care Practitioner programme and the IHCD Tutor Training programme. The move of paramedic education and training into higher education (HE) establishments, enabled partnership working between NHS Ambulance Trusts and their local HE institution. His specialties and interests include cardiology and alternative response out-of-hospital care where he is an active member of the trust's CBRN, Medical Response and Public order teams in response to large-scale incidents or public events. Most recently he has begun to develop within the role as a Motorcycle Responder and looks forward to continuing with this element of paramedic practice.

Graham Harris BSc Paramedic Science, PGCE, MSc Education Management, Chartered MCIPD, MC Para
Senior Lecturer/Programme Leader, Paramedic Science Department of Acute and Continuing Care, School of Health and Social Care, Avery Hill Campus, University of Greenwich

Graham has a long background as a paramedic, with 16 years as a Combat Medical Sergeant and a further 25 years with the London Ambulance Service prior to moving full-time into higher education. He has been involved with teaching on paramedic higher education programmes for over five years, the past two years as Programme Leader for students undertaking the FdSc Paramedic Science programme at the University of Greenwich. Graham is the College of Paramedic's Council Member for the London region, and a faculty instructor for pre-hospital obstetric emergency training. He passionately believes in the development of the paramedic profession through higher education and continuing professional development. Graham believes that paramedics need to constantly develop and update their patient assessment skills as our role expands and develops. He hopes that this book will assist paramedics in achieving this and by doing so improve the quality of the care we provide to patients.

David Kerr MA, BSc (Hons), CertEd, MCPara
Senior Lecturer/Programme Leader Paramedic Science
Department of Acute and Continuing Healthcare, School of Health and Social Care, Medway Campus, University of Greenwich

David joined the London Ambulance Service in August 1986 on the Patient Transport Service which gave him a great insight into dealing with the older person.

In 1988 he re-graded to accident and emergency work, qualifying as a paramedic in 1992. After some time as a motorcycle response paramedic David left the London Ambulance Service to take up the role of paramedic team leader in the Kent Ambulance NHS Trust where he went on to qualify as an ambulance aid tutor before returning to the London Ambulance Service in 2003 as a training officer until 2010. David is now the programme leader for the BSc (Hons) Paramedic Science programme at the University of Greenwich, Medway campus. He firmly believes in the developing scope of paramedic practice through higher education and continuing professional development and hopes this book supports both the pre-registration student and the existing practitioner.

Rehan-Uddin Khan BSc (Clinical Sciences), MBBS, MRCOG
Consultant in Obstetrics and Gynaecology (Specialist in Maternal Medicine and Medical Education), RCOG tutor, Barts and the London NHS Trust

Rehan has a special interest in interdisciplinary learning and training. He is a faculty member at the Barts and the London Medical Simulation Centre.

Matthew Lane PGCHE, BSc (Hons) Money, Banking and Finance, FdSc Paramedic Science, IHCD Paramedic
Senior Lecturer in Emergency Care, University of Greenwich; Paramedic, London Ambulance Service NHS Trust

Matthew currently holds the position of Senior Lecturer in Emergency Care within the Department of Acute and Continuing Care at the University of Greenwich. His time at university is spent teaching a range of health care professionals including paramedics and nurses across the department. He is Course Coordinator for six courses across the FdSc Paramedic Science, BSc (Hons) Paramedic Science and BSc Nursing programmes where he fulfils a full range of teaching and assessing duties.

He is Personal Tutor Group Leader and endeavours to provide the important link between the university and partnering trusts to ensure the needs of the students are met. He is a Link Lecturer at Lewisham Hospital and Queen Elizabeth Hospital where he supplies student and mentor support within Accident and Emergency.

He also maintains clinical practice hours as a fully operational paramedic on an ambulance responding to emergency calls. He is a qualified Practice Placement Educator and as such facilitates learning and mentors paramedic science students from in-service training schools and higher education institutes.

Jaqualline Lindridge MA, DipHE (Emergency Care Practitioner), CertLegalStud, PGCE, MCPara
Training Officer, London Ambulance Service NHS Trust

Jaqualine joined the London Ambulance Service in January 2000 and has practised both as a paramedic and an emergency care practitioner. During her career in London she has enjoyed the challenge of working in both central and suburban areas of the city and in addition to frontline duties has practised in other acute settings including GP out-of-hours services, minor injury units, walk-in centres and the A&E department. She is now in a teaching role, educating student paramedics.

Her occupational special interests include the 12 lead ECG, physical assessment and medical ethics and law. Physical examination is an area of patient assessment which is both fascinating and essential to excellent patient care. She has enjoyed the challenge of assessing the neurological system in particular, and wanted to write this chapter to provide a simplified account of pre-hospital neurological evaluation which will allow the paramedic to assess their patients more effectively and in doing so match their skills to the developing scope of practice of the profession.

She hopes you enjoy the chapter and that it helps to demystify a daunting system; as one of her teachers once observed: 'feel the fear, and then do it anyway!'

Mathew Millman BSc (Hons), MCPara
Lecturer in Pre-hospital Medicine, Sheffield Hallam University

Mathew joined West Midlands Ambulance Service as an ambulance cadet in 1989, progressing through ambulance education, before qualifying as a paramedic in 1994. He joined Derbyshire Ambulance Service as a clinical supervisor in 1996, before its merger into East Midlands Ambulance Service, and has become involved in the education and training of ambulance staff in the practice environment since 2000. He entered into the Emergency Practitioner programme and qualified in 2006 and has since worked in the pre-hospital arena, primary care and emergency department settings, before joining Sheffield Hallam University in 2010.

His professional and academic areas of interest are firmly set into the evidence based practice principles of paramedic and ambulance staff and how the profession can develop from within. The area of assessment and support to some of the patients we meet with mental health concerns is rarely discussed in any detail from a paramedic viewpoint, but has just as much importance as the utilisation of advanced life support skills; therefore he hopes the chapter he has been involved in constructing is both helpful and informative, but also prompts those who read it to continue their education and understanding to help those who they serve.

Nandiran Ratnavel MBBS, MRCPCH

Consultant Neonatologist, Barts and The London Children's Hospital; Clinical Lead, London Neonatal Transfer Service; Chair, UK Neonatal Transport Interest Group; Chair, Thames Regional Perinatal Group, Barts and the London NHS Trust

Nandiran's undergraduate medical training took place at St. George's Hospital Medical School. During the latter part of his degree he identified a particular interest in paediatrics. Following his medical and surgical house jobs he entered postgraduate paediatric training. Then followed a very interesting training pathway that took him through general paediatrics, paediatric emergency medicine, paediatric cardiology, renal medicine and paediatric intensive care.

He then commenced subspecialty training in neonatology and neonatal transport. He took up the position of consultant at the Royal London Hospital in 2005 and works between the neonatal medical and surgical service, a tertiary referral service for north-east London and the London Neonatal Transfer Service. This service provides critical care stabilisation and transport for babies in hospitals across London and south-east England.

James Rouse BSc, DipIMC, RCSEd, MCPara

Paramedic, London Ambulance Service NHS Trust / London Air Ambulance

James began his career with the Great Western Ambulance Service (GWAS) in 2003 and made the move to the London Ambulance Service (LAS) in 2006. He currently fulfils his role as a paramedic with both the London Ambulance Service and London Air Ambulance. His operational duties on the London Air Ambulance require him to work on the Physician Response Unit (PRU) and the helicopter. In his work with the PRU, he treats patients with acute and chronic medical conditions and puts into practice the Quality CPR (QCPR) programme, which he hopes will improve cardiac arrest survival rates. On the helicopter his duties include operating as a flight paramedic attending trauma calls and working in the emergency operation centre triaging and dispatching the trauma team to appropriate patients.

He currently represents the College of Paramedics (CoP) and the London Ambulance Service in partnership with the Department of Health, National Innovation Centre. In his work he is required to help support a project team in the design, production and implementation of innovative equipment that will aid in improving existing pre-hospital patient care.

He has been awarded the Diploma in Immediate Medical Care by the Royal College of Surgeons, Edinburgh, and has successfully completed the advanced 12 lead ECG module at the University of Hertfordshire. He is currently on the MSc Health Sciences programme hoping to combine his operational experience with both education and research

Nigel Ward Dip HE (Paramedic Science), MCPara
Paramedic Team Leader, London Ambulance Service NHS Trust

Nigel joined the London Ambulance Service in May 1996 and practised as an ambulance technician until qualifying as a paramedic in April 2000. His first posting was to Camden Ambulance Station and he has worked from there in front-line duties ever since. He attended the London bombings in July 2005 and treated passengers at Kings Cross station on that day. Later that year he qualified as an Ambulance Aid tutor and although he sees himself predominantly as a front-line paramedic, he is occasionally seconded to education and development in the London Ambulance Service.

On match days he works for Queens Park Rangers FC in the stadium paramedic role, working with the physiotherapist and club doctor in the event of player injury. One of his heroes is the late Jackie Robinson, baseball player with the Brooklyn Dodgers, who once said 'a life is not important except in the impact it has on other lives', his favourite quote and a great philosophy for life.

Mark Whitbread MSc
Clinical Practice Manager/Paramedic/Cardiac Care Lead, Medical Directorate, London Ambulance Service NHS Trust

Mark has had over 29 years of working within the NHS, all in the area of acute care. He was one of the first Resuscitation Officers in the UK and developed the largest resuscitation service in the UK.

Within the ambulance service he was the leader in moving forward the concept of Primary PCI for patients presenting with an acute STEMI. He is a keen and motivated lecturer.

He also holds the position of Honorary Senior Clinical Fellow at the University of Hertfordshire where he has developed a unique advanced 12 lead ECG course for the pre-hospital care setting.

Mark's main area of research is acute cardiac care with specialist knowledge in ACS/arrhythmias and cardiac arrest management. He remains an 'on the road' paramedic undertaking regular operational shifts.

Acknowledgements

We would like to thank all of the contributors for giving their time and expertise to make this project possible. Thanks to Paul for his camera expertise and for the *models* (not that we are sure they would wish to be called this) who gave up their time.

How to use this book

This book is about 'Assessment' skills for paramedics and the chapters have been written utilising the *primary* and *secondary* survey format of assessment. Each chapter covers a particular area of assessment. However, due to the nature of some circumstances, for example, a newly born baby, resuscitation care is also addressed:

■ Respiratory assessment
■ Cardiovascular assessment
■ Assessment and care of the neonate.

Each chapter commences with a brief description of the area of assessment and where applicable, a **'Scene assessment'** appropriate to the particular theme.

The **'Primary survey'** configuration covers the **DR ABCDE** framework where appropriate and incorporates:

■ D – Danger
■ R – Response
■ A – Airway
■ B – Breathing
■ C – Circulation
■ D – Disability
■ E – Expose, Examine and Evaluate.

This presents a structured systematic format to follow which provides the paramedic/clinician with the opportunity to review the evidence provided in the primary survey in the **DR ABCDE** arrangement. Where appropriate this includes illnesses and injuries relevant to that particular area of assessment or specialty, which could potentially cause a life threatening problem to the patient.

Things to note:

■ The **'Trauma'** Chapter includes the additional **'C'** ABC element, which incorporates **'Catastrophic haemorrhage'**.
■ The **'Obstetric'** Chapter includes the additional **'F'** and **'G'** elements, which incorporate **'Fundus'** and **'Get to the point quickly'**.

- The 'Child assessment' Chapter relates to the use of the ABC 'DEFG' format, the latter specifically relating to 'Don't ever forget glucose'.

If on completing the primary survey elements of your assessment you identify that the patient does have a *'time critical'* condition then you will need to manage the respective element/s accordingly and convey the patient to the appropriate place of care.

However, if your assessment has clearly identified that the patient **DOES NOT** have a time critical condition then your assessment of the patient should continue by implementing and conducting a 'secondary survey'.

The chapters continue with a description of the assessment/examination for that particular area or specialty of the secondary survey followed by information on conditions specific to that system or area of speciality, which where appropriate adheres to the following structure:

HISTORY

- *Presenting complaint*   *(PC)*
- *History of presenting complaint* *(HPC)*
- *Past medical history*   *(PMH)*
- *Drug/medication history*   *(DMH)*
- *Social/family history*   *(SFH)*

REVIEW OF SYSTEMS

This affords a continuation of the structured arrangement which provides a systematic format of obtaining the *'history'* of the patient in relation to their presenting complaint and the area or systems affected. Following this structure whilst performing the secondary survey will enable the paramedic/clinician to obtain all of the elements of a focused history, which include:

- History
- Vital signs
- Physical assessment.

These elements enable the paramedic/clinician to identify illnesses or injuries not ascertained during the primary survey. They simultaneously provide the opportunity of detecting less obvious illnesses/injuries and/or signs and symptoms of underlying medical conditions.

Throughout the chapter there are **action boxes**, which include a summary of the key points of the **'Possible actions to be taken'** for the respective element of the survey. Depending on your findings from the assessment you will decide whether or not the action or actions are appropriate to the respective patient, and therefore whether they need to be addressed or not. As stated if the patient has a 'time critical' condition identified in the 'primary survey' then the paramedic/clinician will need to manage this accordingly; alternatively it may be a 'possible action that they consider'.

If you feel that your subject knowledge and/or relevant skills of assessing a particular area requires updating or refreshing then turn to the appropriate chapter, review the evidence provided and if and where applicable appraise the subject knowledge and practise the skills/techniques identified. As and when applicable you should implement these into practice through your future patient assessments.

Remember that with many patients and their presenting conditions you may be assessing two or more systems, and in certain instances two or more patients simultaneously. Paramedics as registered Health Professions Council (HPC) practitioners are required to maintain their knowledge and competency of skills. Whether you are an experienced paramedic/clinician or another health care professional, the information provided in this book will assist you in obtaining a structured assessment of the patient, and will hopefully assist you in maintaining your knowledge and competency of assessment skills.

1 General principles of assessment

Graham Harris

This chapter will provide a brief overview of the general principles of assessment. It will include how to undertake an *assessment* of the scene, conducting a primary and secondary survey, and the evidence that the paramedic/clinician needs to obtain whilst performing the assessment.

SCENE ASSESSMENT

As with any situation the attending paramedic/clinician can obtain a wealth of information and details from assessing the scene of the incident: these include safety and the situation.

Safety

When approaching any scene/incident consideration should be given to the following:

- Safety for self, colleague/s, patient/s and other persons on scene
- Are other emergency services present on scene; are they required?
- Can the scene be secured? Rescue attempts should only be undertaken by trained personnel (*rescue and fire service staff with breathing apparatus*)
- If the situation is hazardous can the patients be moved to safe area?
- Consider the possibility of further threat to self, colleague or patient from either
  - fire
  - blood or other body fluids
  - weapons
  - traffic
  - environmental conditions (*floods and snow are some recent causes in the UK*).

SITUATION

Whilst the situation itself is assessed following the safety assessment, in essence they tend to have significant overlap, as certain situations pose differing safety hazards:

- What has taken place at the scene?
- What is the type of incident/illness (*road traffic collision (RTC), medical emergency or exacerbation of existing condition*)?
- What is the mechanism of injury (MOI) (*fall, blunt or penetrating trauma*)?
- How many patients are there, and what are their ages?
- Do you require specialist resources (*helicopter emergency medical services (HEMS), hazardous area response team (HART)*?

PRIMARY SURVEY

The purpose of conducting a primary survey is to identify if there are any life-threatening problems, and manage accordingly whilst determining if early transportation is required. As with any situation, the paramedic/clinician conducts a primary survey utilising the **DR ABCDE** framework (Resuscitation Council (UK) ALS, 2011, p16). In essence, the primary survey is undertaken with an instantaneous overview of all elements in relation to the patient's respective system conditions.

Element	System
D – Danger	
R – Response	(Neurological system)
A – Airway/including 'C' spine immobilisation	(Respiratory system)
B – Breathing/severe illness/chest injuries	(Respiratory system)
C – Circulation/haemorrhage/shock	(Cardiovascular system)
D – Disability	(Neurological system)
E – Expose/Examine/Environment	

DANGER

This covers the safety of the paramedic/clinician, colleagues and then the patient. It is simultaneously ascertained as part of the scene assessment. The reasoning for this is that if the health care professional(s) are overcome or overwhelmed by the incident/circumstances of the incident, they will be of no benefit to the patient. There is therefore always a need for the paramedic/clinician to differentiate between the actual and potential aspects of danger of any incident they attend. This could incorporate anything from:

- positioning of the vehicle to provide protection at the scene of a road traffic collision
- approaching fire/hazmat/chemical incidents safely
- requesting that pets are secured in another room
- requesting the attendance of police at a possible crime scene
- ensuring that appropriate personal protective equipment (PPE) is worn in relation to the incident, for example, hi-visibility jackets when attending a road traffic incident.

Possible actions to be taken:

- Ensure personal protective equipment (PPE) is worn
- Request fire/police service assistance
- Request hazardous area response team (HART)
- Request mobile medical team (BASICS etc.)

RESPONSE

This provides the paramedic/clinician with the opportunity to introduce themselves and obtain an initial assessment of the patient's ability to respond to verbal communication. The paramedic/clinician introduces themselves and asks the patient what happened. How the patient responds (or does not respond) will provide significant information as to their level of consciousness. In the primary survey the **AVPU** framework is utilised:

- **A** – The patient is Alert, conscious and responds directly and appropriately to the paramedic/clinician's question/s.
- **V** – The patient responds to Vocal commands (verbally), which may be a grunt or groan.
- **P** – The patient responds only to Painful stimuli.
- **U** – The patient is Unresponsive.

Possible actions to be taken:

- Record the patient's level of consciousness (LOC)
- Record any period of unconsciousness (*it may be part of the patient's lucid interval*)

AIRWAY

- Does the patient have a patent airway and are they able to maintain it for themselves?
- The patient who responds A on the AVPU scale is described above as Alert. This can be considered to be the case if the patient is talking, therefore the airway is open. However, the patient may be making unusual sounds such as snoring or making gurgling sounds, a stridor or wheezing may be heard, all of which could indicate there is some form of airway obstruction.
- Gurgling indicates that there is fluid in the airway and there is a need for suction.
- Snoring may indicate a soft tissue problem either with the tongue, swelling or foreign body obstruction.
- Stridor indicates a problem above the vocal cords in the upper airway, whereas wheezing indicates the problem below the vocal cords in the lower airways.
- If the patient is unresponsive, open the airway (with the appropriate 'C' spine manoeuvre); ascertain if there are fluids or foreign bodies and manage accordingly.

Possible actions to be taken:

- Use 'C' spine airway manoeuvre if appropriate
- Ensure airway is patent and secure before proceeding to next element

---

BREATHING

- Look to see that the patient is breathing. If *apnoeic* then commence immediate ventilations using bag-valve-mask (BVM) and supplemental oxygen before continuing with the next element of the assessment.
- Look to see if the patient is using accessory muscles.
- Is there any flaring of nostrils?
- Look for sucking chest wounds, flail segments, paradoxical breathing, bruising and deformity of the thorax.
- If the patient is breathing assess their respiratory rate and effort and ensure that this is adequate enough to ensure oxygenation. If available, measure the oxygen saturation (SpO_2) and ensure an inspired oxygen concentration of 94% or more. If not, maintain this in keeping with the recommendations for acutely ill (94%–98%) or for chronic obstructive pulmonary disease (COPD) patients (88%–92%) (BTS 2008, p1).

- Listen to the patient talking and assess if they are able to complete a sentence in one breath.
- Auscultate the chest and listen for abnormal breath sounds over a minimum of five positions on each lung (Bickley and Szilagyi 2007, p125, 130). A wheeze indicates bronchospasm, whereas coarse sounds indicate pulmonary oedema. Feel the patient's chest for expansion, irregularity and tenderness.
- A patient with a respiratory rate of <10 or >29 breaths per minute may potentially require ventilatory support, as both rates are indicative of inadequate minute volumes and respiratory failure.

Possible actions to be taken:

- If patient is not responding: look, listen and feel for breathing for 10 seconds
- Ensure that the patient is not hypoxic
- Manage breathing/hypoxia effectively before moving to the next element

CIRCULATION

- Look to see if the patient has any form of haemorrhage, internal or external. Manage the haemorrhage accordingly (see *Trauma Assessment*: Chapter 7).
- Assessment of the patient's circulatory system includes palpating and recording the radial pulse, note the rate and volume/character:
  - Is it tachycardic or bradycardic? Is it full and bounding or weak, regular or irregular. If the radial pulse cannot be palpated, can the femoral or carotid pulses be palpated? A palpable peripheral pulse can provide the paramedic clinician with a rough estimate of blood pressure, radial = a systolic of 80mmHg, femoral = a systolic of 70mmHg and carotid = a systolic of 60mmHg (Salomone and Pons 2007).
- Assess the colour of the skin, is it pale indicating poor perfusion? This indicates partial oxygenation. Assess the temperature and the moisture of the skin: normal skin temperature is warm to touch, whereas cool skin indicates poor perfusion. Is the patient cyanosed? Are they jaundiced? (Longmore *et al.* 2004, p38). The paramedic/clinician should also assess and examine the patient's skin turgor to ensure the patient is hydrated (Schilling McCann 2008, p74).
- Check the capillary bed refill (CBR) by pressing over the nail beds: normal refill should occur within two seconds, an alternative location is the patient's sternum or forehead.

Possible actions to be taken:

- Control external haemorrhage
- Manage shock accordingly (see *Trauma Assessment: Chapter 7*)
- Palpate, assess and record pulse rate and rhythm

DISABILITY

- Assess the patient's level of consciousness (LOC). The Glasgow Coma Scale (GCS) provides an assessment of three specific key areas, Best Eye (4), Best Motor (5), and Best Verbal (6), with a respective maximum score of 15, and minimum score of 3.
- Record **T** if an endotracheal (ET) tube is inserted when scoring Best Verbal (Smith *et al.* 2008, p293).
- A GCS score of 3–8 may indicate that the patient has sustained either a severe head injury or a major cerebral insult.
- A GCS score of 14–15 is mild.
- A GCS score of 15 is normal.
- A GCS score of 8 defines coma (Kaplan and Roesler 2008).
- Remember to assess both the patient's posture and pupillary response. In patients who are comatose (GCS 8), note any decerebrate or decorticate posture and pupillary responses to light (normal response is constriction).
- Remember that the AVPU scale utilised in the response element is accepted as a quicker tool for use within the primary survey.
- Assess the patient's pupils for size, reaction and accommodation (*occurs when the patient converges their eyes and constricts their pupils to a near object*). The use of the following framework will assist the paramedic/clinician: **P**upils **E**qual and **R**ound; **R**eact to **L**ight and **A**ccommodation (PERRLA).
- Assess blood glucose levels (*hypo/hyperglycaemia may be the cause of altered levels of consciousness*).

Possible actions to be taken:

- Assess and document LOC
- Note abnormal postures (decerebrate/decorticate)
- Assess and document size, equality and accommodation of pupils
- Assess blood glucose levels

EXPOSE/ENVIRONMENT/EVALUATE

- Expose the patient's injury/injuries, e.g. on a trauma patient completely remove all clothing but remember to consider the environment and ensure that the patient is covered to prevent hypothermia and maintain dignity, as far as possible. Look for medical alert tag; this will often reveal information about the patient's past medical history or supply a telephone number where this information can be obtained. (See Chapter 5.)
- Consider consent; where and if applicable. Remember, not every patient is unconscious.
- Crime scene: if the call you are attending is or has the possibility of being a crime scene then make a note of the clothing before removal, the scene and people/vehicles/positioning etc. on arrival.
- Evaluate the findings within the primary survey that you have just completed and if you have identified any time critical problems within any of the elements then consider the need to transport and transfer immediately to an appropriate treatment centre, or remain on scene and conduct a secondary survey.

Possible actions to be taken:

- Expose the patient's affected area/s and examine
- Ascertain if the patient has medical alert tag/bracelet
- Remember patient dignity and possible hypothermia
- Evaluate – transfer or move onto secondary survey?

SECONDARY SURVEY

A focused history and physical examination to identify injuries or problems not identified during the primary survey. It provides the paramedic/clinician the opportunity of detecting less obvious injuries and/or signs and symptoms of underlying medical conditions. There are three key elements to the secondary survey:

- history
- vital signs
- the physical assessment.

HISTORY

The key elements of obtaining a patient history are described and an example of how the element/s could be recorded is described:

- PC: 48 ♀ C/O difficulty in breathing (DIB) (*dyspnoea*)
- HPC: History of feeling unwell for several days, developing a productive cough for 3/7, yellowish green in colour according to the patient, and today they feel unable to cope with the dyspnoea.

Presenting complaint (PC)

The following are examples of questions you might ask yourself. See the appropriate chapter for specific questions related to each area of assessment.

- What is the presenting complaint? (*This may be due to an illness (abdominal pain), or a specific injury (fell over and hurt my ankle).*)
- Is it because the patient has difficulty in breathing?
- Involved in a motor vehicle collision? or,
- They have severe abdominal pain.
- The paramedic/clinician needs to clearly identify the reason(s) why the patient or caller has requested their attendance; this includes ascertaining the mechanism of injury (MOI) in patients who have suffered trauma (Bledsoe and Benner 2006, p196).

History of presenting complaint (HPC)

- What is the history of the presenting complaint? If you have good questioning skills, further history may become available. For example, a patient who is complaining of difficulty in breathing (DIB) (dyspnoea). On questioning, it becomes apparent that they have a history of feeling unwell for several days, developing a productive cough over the past three days and today finds it extremely difficult to breathe.
- The above example explains why the history leading up to the presenting complaint is extremely important and can assist the paramedic/clinician to make a provisional diagnosis, instigate appropriate, timely treatment and management of the patient's problems (Limmer and O'Keefe 2009, p294).

Past medical history (PMH)

- What is the patient's past medical history?
- Have they had similar episodes previously?
- Do they have any other medical conditions?
- Are they diabetic? If so, what type; I or II? Are they asthmatic? Or suffer from either respiratory diseases and/or conditions such as chronic obstructive pulmonary disease (COPD), emphysema or chronic bronchitis?

- Do they have a cardiac condition such as hypertension, angina, left ventricular failure (LVF)?
- Consider patients' presenting with DIB and have an inhaler, or chest pain and have a GTN spray, or those with an allergic reaction and have an Epipen. These patients have been prescribed these for an existing medical condition (Limmer and O'Keefe 2009, p295).
- Have they ever been hospitalised or had any operations? If so, what for?

Drug/medication history (DMH)(to include prescribed, over the counter (OTC) and other health products)

- Is the patient currently prescribed medications for any pre-existing condition(s)? If so, what medications are they?
- Using the patient's medications, ask the patient to explain to you why they take each medication. This will help you to explore the patient's knowledge and understanding of their prescribed medications.
- Are they compliant with their medications?
- Have they purchased any OTC medications to relieve their symptoms?
- Has the patient taken any analgesics for any pain they may be suffering? If so, what time did they take the medicines?
- Are they taking or undergoing any courses of complimentary therapy medicines?

Possible actions to be taken:

- If transporting the patient, best practice dictates taking their medications with them, as the receiving unit may not stock particular medicines
- This also enables the receiving unit to record medicines, dosages and establish patient compliance

---

Social/family medical history (S/FMH)

- Depending upon the age of the patient, ascertain if they live alone or have relatives/carers or external agency input (social service input, meal deliveries etc.).
- Consider the activities of daily living (ADL), what can the patient do or not do for themselves? Has this changed?
- Remember to differentiate between *Physical* activities such as bathing, dressing and feeding, and *Instrumental* activities such as shopping, housekeeping and taking medications (Bickley and Szilagyi 2007, p405).
- Depending on the presenting medical condition, do other members of the patient's family also suffer from the condition/illness? Familial history is

often a factor in patients presenting with many conditions, for example, cardiac conditions.

REVIEW OF SYSTEMS (ROS)

- The signs and symptoms are ascertained as part of the physical assessment, as the paramedic/clinician conducts a review of the patient's major systems: respiratory, cardiovascular, neurological, gastro-intestinal (GI) etc.
- Modify questions to the system: Respiratory – Are you asthmatic? A patient complaining of difficulty in breathing may have a productive cough, ask the patient about the colour and quantity of the sputum/phlegm.
- On auscultation are there adventitious sounds? Is there pain on inspiration?
- When assessing a patient's pain use the OPQRSTA framework (Limmer and O'Keefe 2009, p436):

  O – *onset, when did the pain commence?*
  P – *pain, what provokes or relieves it?*
  Q – *quality, is it constant, colicky, sharp or heavy?*
  R – *radiate, any radiation from site?*
  S – *severity, any systemic upset?*
  T – *timing, was the onset sudden or gradual? And has it changed?*
  A – *associate, is it associated with any other symptoms?*

Record the findings of each element of the physical assessment, which should provide the following evidence regarding the patient.

- *Respiratory rate, character and work of breathing*
- *Heart rate, character, volume and rhythm*
- *Blood pressure (BP)*
- *Electrocardiogram (ECG), including 12 lead ECG where available and if qualified*
- *Blood glucose levels*
- *GCS neurological status*
- *Pupils*
- *Peak expiratory flow (PEF) (best of 3 readings)*
- *Temperature*
- *Oxygen saturations (SpO$_2$)*
- *Pain score*
- *Signs and symptoms of each system obtained during the secondary survey.*

The use of the following **SAMPLE** framework may assist the paramedic/clinician (Bledsoe and Benner 2006, p197):

> S – Signs and symptoms
> A – Allergies
> M – Medications
> P – Past medical history
> L – Last meal
> E – Events leading up to the incident.

IMPRESSIONS (OVERALL OF THE PATIENT/ SITUATION) (IMP)

- What is your overall impression of the patient and the situation? Remember someone who is undressed and/or unwashed without their hair being groomed halfway through the day may be like this due to the effects of their illness/condition.
- If the scene is the patient's home what is the condition of their surroundings?
- All of this information is useful to handover, if the patient is being conveyed. Any information you have about the patient's home surroundings is lost once you leave the patient, if you do not mention any concerns/observations. If not provided as part of your patient handover then this may mean that the patient is discharged without appropriate support or investigation.
- Is their accommodation safe for them to return to?

OTHER CONSIDERATIONS

During each chapter the following considerations will be discussed where appropriate/applicable to either the system and/or the patient's age/gender/ religion:

Communication problems – How the paramedic/clinician deals with the problem of communicating with someone whose first language is not English, patients who may be deaf or have a learning disability.

Destination/receiving specialist units/non-conveyance – How does the paramedic/ clinician decide on the destination if the patient needs to be transported? What specialist units are available 24/7 for primary angioplasty? Are there specialist stroke, burns or trauma units available? What implications are there for the patient and paramedic/clinician if their decision is not to convey the patient?

Social/family/carer/guardian – What social implications are there when patients are transported for care, either for the patient or the family/carer/guardian? If a full-time carer was taken ill and required hospitalisation, what problems would this cause the attending paramedic/clinician?

Ethical and legal – What are the ethical and legal dilemmas of obtaining consent in every emergency situation? What happens when a patient does not have capacity to provide consent?

2 Respiratory assessment

Matthew Lane and James Rouse

In the out-of-hospital environment patients often present with a wide range of acute and chronic respiratory emergencies. For safe practice the paramedic/clinician should rely on effective and thorough assessment skills in order to provide timely intervention to sick patients. The aim of this chapter is to provide an overview of the clinical skills required for an effective respiratory system assessment to be conducted in the pre-hospital environment. It shall identify areas of key importance and discuss the equipment available to aid in the assessment process.

SCENE ASSESSMENT

Information provided by the caller on the mobile data terminal (MDT) can alert you to the patient's condition and provide clues as to the likely respiratory assessments and treatments the patient may require. Specifically respiratory emergencies could include asthma, dyspnoea and trauma to the respiratory system.

Use the time whilst en route to the scene to prepare yourself. Ask yourself:

- How am I going to approach the scene?
- What equipment will I need to perform a respiratory assessment?
- What primary survey Airway and Breathing problems are time critical?

Equipment required for respiratory assessment:

- Stethoscope
- Peak flow meter
- If available and trained consider assessing the following: SpO_2, $EtCO_2$

Global overview

This is the paramedic/clinician's immediate impression of the patient's condition from the scene that presents them and should not take more than a few seconds.

Efficacy of this skill will improve with both experience and clinical knowledge and can perhaps begin to explain how experienced paramedic/clinicians can simply tell when somebody is unwell. An abundance of information from both the environment and patient can be obtained prior to verbal questioning or physical assessment and should not be overlooked by the paramedic/clinician, as it will support them in their preferential diagnosis.

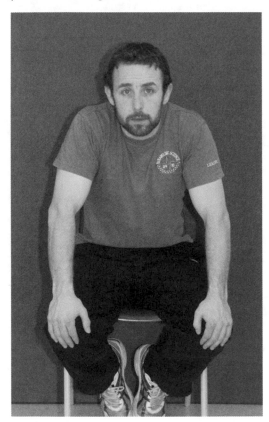

Figure 2.1 Tripod position

Look for signs of respiratory distress in the patient(s):

- Unable to complete a sentence
- Sitting forward in the tripod position (see Figure 2.1)
- Use of accessory muscles
- Intercostal recessions
- Flared nostrils/pursed lips
- Wheezing
- Stridor
- Cyanosis
- Reduced level of consciousness

Consider, where appropriate, information within the environment:

- Immediate surroundings – industrial (chemicals), agricultural, fire calls, water and/or explosive/flammable products
- Home oxygen
- Cigarettes
- Medication – inhalers
- Smells – gases, damp.

PRIMARY SURVEY

The primary survey is fundamental in the successful and timely assessment of the respiratory system. Any patient that fails an element of the primary survey should be treated as time critical and treated en-route to hospital. Remember do not move onto the next element of the primary survey until the element you are dealing with is rectified.

DANGER

- The majority of patients we see with respiratory disorders present with an exacerbation of a chronic respiratory illness. Environmental factors are rarely the cause of respiratory distress but should always be considered.
- Environmental risks that may affect the respiratory system can occur from toxic agents e.g. smoke/gas/carbon monoxide.

Possible actions to be taken:

- Remove patients into an open space and fresh air
- Request fire brigade/police assistance
- Request Hazardous Area Response Team (HART) if available

RESPONSE

- Initial response using the AVPU scale: A – Alert, V – Verbal, P – Pain or U – Unresponsive
- If there are multiple patients and none are responding to you, initiate STEP 1, 2, and 3 and move away from scene. (*An approach used to collapsed casualties by emergency service personnel*).
    - *Step 1* – One Collapsed Patient – Approach using normal procedures – (*CBRN contamination unlikely*)
    - *Step 2* – Two Collapsed Patients – Approach with caution – (*CBRN contamination possible*)
    - *Step 3* – Three or More Collapsed Patients – DO NOT approach the scene – (*CBRN contamination likely*)
    - If Possible: Withdraw, Contain and Report. Do Not compromise your safety or that of your colleagues or the public (JRCALC 2006, Ref. 2).

Possible actions to be taken:

- Major incident – provide a METHANE report

AIRWAY

- Is the airway patent? Is the patient able to maintain their own airway?
- Correct any airway deficits immediately by stepwise airway management.

■ Are there any abnormal sounds? If so, the airway may be obstructed.

    ▨ Gurgling: fluid in the airway and there is need for suction

    ▨ Snoring: soft tissue problem due to the tongue occluding the airway

    ▨ Stridor: upper airway problem (*partial obstruction of the larynx or trachea*)

    ▨ Wheezing: lower airway problem (below the vocal cords) (Bickley and Szilagyi 2007).

Possible actions to be taken:

(Consider cervical spine)

■ Head tilt, chin lift/jaw thrust

■ Recovery position

■ Suction

■ Oral/nasopharyngeal airway adjuncts

■ Supraglottic airway device

■ Endotracheal intubation

■ Needle cricothyroidotomy

BREATHING

■ Look, listen and feel for breath sounds for no more than 10 seconds to see if the patient is breathing (Resuscitation Council (UK) 2005).

    ▨ If the patient is apnoeic commence immediate ventilation using the bag-valve-mask (BVM) and supplemental oxygen before commencing the next part of the assessment.

    ▨ A patient with a respiratory rate of <10 or >29 breaths per minute may potentially require ventilatory support, as both rates are indicative of inadequate minute volumes and respiratory failure (*carpopedal spasm of the patient's hands may be due to hyperventilation*).

■ Feel for and ascertain if the trachea is central (*tracheal deviation is a late sign of a tension pneumothorax*).

■ When appropriate expose the patient's chest and look for chest rise and fall, ascertain the use of accessory muscles and any chest trauma (*sucking chest wounds, or flail segments, if so manage appropriately*).

■ Auscultate the chest for breath sounds over the apex, axilla and bases of both lungs (*ascertain if there are any abnormal sounds*).

■ Feel the patient's chest for equal expansion, crepitus and tenderness.

- If possible measure the patient's oxygen saturation (SpO_2).
  - Oxygen should be prescribed to achieve a saturation of 94%–98% for most acutely ill patients or 88%–92% for those with chronic obstructive pulmonary disease (COPD) (BTS 2008).

Possible actions to be taken:

- Look, Listen and Feel for breath sounds for no more than 10 seconds (*note abnormal sounds*)
- Seal sucking chest wounds, stabilise flail segments, decompress tension pneumothoraces accordingly (*see Trauma Assessment: Chapter 7*)
- Ensure the patient is not hypoxic
- Administer oxygen appropriately to patient's illness/injury

---

CIRCULATION

Circulatory problems such as pulmonary oedema and anaemia may impede gas exchange and therefore have a resultant effect on the respiratory system (Moore 2007). Basic circulatory checks within the primary survey are therefore vital in providing an insight to underlying respiratory problems.

- Palpate and assess the patient's radial pulse and ascertain if it is tachycardic or bradycardic (*unexplained tachycardia and hypotension are strongly suggestive of a developing tension pneumothorax*).
- Assess the colour of the skin, is it pallored? (*indicating poor tissue perfusion*), or is it cyanosed? (*indicative of hypoxaemia*). Also assess the skin temperature as moist clammy skin (*suggests decreased perfusion*), and finally assess the patient's capillary refill, as a delayed refill >2 seconds (*suggests poor perfusion*). All of these findings are indicative of respiratory problems being demonstrated in the circulatory system.
- Remember the pleural space of the lungs can hold up to 3 litres of blood and therefore can represent a significant source of blood loss (Salomone and Pons 2007).

Possible actions to be taken:

- Ascertain if there is internal haemorrhage (*haemothorax, acute thoracic aortic dissection. If branch arteries are affected the patient can present with the absence of pulses and unequal blood pressure in their arms*)
- Arrest external haemorrhage
- Manage shock accordingly (*see Trauma Assessment: Chapter 7*)

DISABILITY

Underlying respiratory problems such as hypoxia may result in cerebral deficit and loss of consciousness and can be identified in the disability assessment of the primary survey.

- AVPU scoring is an adequate measure of a patient's disability within the primary survey.
- The Glasgow Coma Scale (GCS) requires accurate recording and may not be an appropriate measure in the immediately life threatening situations.
- Assess the patient's pupils for both size and reaction. Check to see if the pupils are equal, round, react to light and accommodate. The use of the following framework will assist the paramedic/clinician: Pupils Equal and Round; React to Light and Accommodation (PERRLA).

Possible actions to be taken:

- Document AVPU score
- Document size and equality and accommodation of pupils
- If available monitor and record blood glucose levels

EXPOSE/EXAMINE/EVALUATE

- Exposure of a patient in the emergency setting is of vital importance in order to make an accurate assessment of their presenting condition. However a pragmatic approach needs to be taken in order to ensure the patient's dignity is maintained and unnecessary hypothermia is avoided.

Possible actions to be taken:

- Fully expose and examine the patient
- Remember patient dignity and possible hypothermia
- Evaluate – transfer immediately or move onto secondary survey

SECONDARY SURVEY

History

History taking is an important skill for paramedic/clinicians to master in order to provide timely interventions and treatment. Below are a series of questions that you should be asking your patient in order to gather an accurate history:

Presenting complaint

- Have you got any difficulty in breathing (DIB)?
- If the patient has a chronic respiratory condition (COPD etc.) ask them if the DIB is normal for them.
- Are there any associated signs or symptoms?
- Are these new or old?

The use of the following framework will assist the paramedic/clinician:

    S – Signs and symptoms
    A – Allergies
    M – Medications
    P – Past medical history
    L – Last meal
    E – Events leading up to the incident

History of presenting complaint

- When did the DIB start?
- What were you doing when it started?
- Have you experienced previous episodes of this before?
- If so, when?
- Do you have a cough?
- The paramedic/clinician should consider that a cough can be a relatively non-specific symptom, which can occur due to irritation of the air passages from the pharynx to the lungs. The character of the cough may however give these clues:
  - Loud brassy cough – suggests pressure on trachea e.g. tumour
  - Hollow 'bovine' cough – suggests recurrent laryngeal nerve palsy
  - Barking (croup) cough – suggests acute epiglottitis
  - Chronic cough – suggests pertussis, TB, foreign body, asthma (e.g. nocturnal)
  - Dry, chronic cough – suggests either acid irritation of the lungs, oesophageal reflux, or due to the side effects of ACE inhibitors.
- DO NOT ignore the change in chronic coughs as it may indicate a new problem such as infection. Remember to ascertain if the cough:
  - Is productive? If so,
  - What colour is the phlegm?
  - Yellow/green sputum may suggest infection, possible bronchiectasis or pneumonia.
  - Pink frothy sputum may suggest pulmonary oedema.
  - Haemoptysis (blood in sputum) may suggest malignancy, TB, infection or trauma.
  - Clear sputum (probably saliva) (Longmore *et al.* 2004, p49)

- Have you taken any of your prescribed medicine?
- If so when?
- Has it relieved the symptoms?
- Do you have any pain?
- Is it worse on inspiration? Remember that:
  - Pleuritic pain is exacerbated by inspiration, whereas:
  - Musculo-skeletal pain, such as a fractured rib is exacerbated by pressure on the affected area (Longmore *et al.* 2004, p92).

See Box 2.1 for an outline of the pain framework.

Box 2.1 Pain framework

The framework (**OPQRSTA**) will assist the paramedic/clinician in assessing pain:

Onset – Time of day? Is there a regular pattern?
Provokes – What makes it better? What makes it worse? Is there pain on inspiration? Does the pain get worse on deep inspiration?
Quality – Describe the pain in your own words. Is it a sharp/dull/burning pain?
Radiates – Does the pain move anywhere else in your body?
Severity – Can you score the pain out of ten?
Time – Was the onset sudden or gradual? And has it changed?
Associate – Are there any associated symptoms?

Past medical history

- Do you have a history of a chronic respiratory illness? If so what is the condition?
- Do you suffer with asthma, emphysema or bronchitis?
- Have you ever been hospitalised with the condition/s?
- Have you spent time in intensive care with this condition/s?
- Have you ever had a pulmonary embolism?
- Have you ever had any surgery?
- If so, what for?
- Do you have any other medical conditions?

Drug/medication history

- Do you take any prescribed medications?
- If so, what are they? The paramedic/clinician should note the type and dosage of each drug, the time of day the drug is administered and whether the patient is compliant with their medication. In

addition the paramedic/clinician should take time to check if the drug is in date.

- Do you have a history of allergies?
- If you have an allergy can you describe the symptoms you presented with?
- Have you purchased any over the counter medications?
- Have you taken any analgesics?
- If so, what time did you take the medicines?
- Are you undergoing any courses of complementary therapy?
- Do you take any recreational drugs?
- If so, what did you take and when?

Social/family medical history

- Do you smoke?
- If so, how many cigarettes do you smoke a day?
- How long have you been smoking?
- Have you been in contact with any external agents that could cause respiratory agitation? For example: industrial chemicals, building site materials such as cement or asbestos, farming chemicals or prolonged exposure to a damp environment.
- Do you have a family history of asthma or any other respiratory illness?
- Is there a family history of any other medical conditions? For example: ischaemic heart disease or cancer.

REVIEW OF SYSTEMS RELATED TO THE RESPIRATORY SYSTEM

Cardiovascular

- Do you experience shortness of breath (SOB) on exercise?
- Are you experiencing any chest pain or palpitations?
- Do you have any DIB when lying flat? *Orthopnoea* is the sensation of breathlessness in the recumbent position, relieved by sitting or standing.
- Have you been using more pillows to help you sleep at night?
- *Paroxysmal nocturnal dyspnoea* (PND) is a sensation of shortness of breath that awakens the patient, often after 1 or 2 hours of sleep, and is usually relieved in the upright position. It is often seen in patients with left ventricular failure (LVF).
- Is there any pitting oedema of the peripheries?
- Do you suffer with anaemia?

Neurological

■ Have you experienced any dizziness recently?
■ Have you experienced any fits, faints or funny turns recently?
■ Have you experienced a headache, lethargy or SOB?
■ Is there a history of any head trauma recently?
■ Was there any loss of consciousness (LOC)?
■ Have you vomited?

Musculoskeletal

■ Do you have any muscular pain surrounding your chest?
■ Does this pain get worse on inspiration, palpation or coughing?
■ Have you experienced any recent trauma to the chest?

VITAL SIGNS

Vital signs are essential to all patient assessments. They should be used in conjunction with the information found within the history taking and physical examination process to differentiate between time critical and non-time critical patients.

The paramedic/clinician must remember continual reassessment of the vital signs is an essential part of patient assessment.

Respiratory rate

The respiratory rate is notoriously poorly recorded by paramedic/clinicians even though it is the most sensitive physiological indicator if there is deterioration in a patient's condition (Hodgetts and Turner 2006).

The following will help accurate measurement:

■ Record the rate, depth and rhythm over one minute. Do not tell the patient you are recording their respiratory rate as they may alter their breathing rate as a result. The paramedic/clinician could record the respiratory rate immediately after taking a pulse rate without the patient's knowledge. A patient with a respiratory rate of <10 or >29 breaths per minute may potentially require ventilatory support, as both rates are indicative of inadequate minute volumes and respiratory failure.
■ Other methods for obtaining an accurate respiratory rate from the patient are observing oxygen mask misting, abdominal breathing or chest rise where appropriate.

Pulse oximetry

Pulse oximetry provides a measurement of the arterial blood saturation of oxygen (Greaves and Porter 1999). The paramedic/clinician should recognise recording of a waveform is required alongside a percentage figure for a reliable reading.

- Advantages of pulse oximetry are:
    - Simple, quick and non-invasive measurement.
- Limitations of pulse oximetry are:
    - Inaccurate measurements when exposed to movement, bright light, metallic nail varnish or cold environments.

The paramedic/clinician should be aware that haemoglobin has a greater affinity to carbon monoxide compared to oxygen. This may result in a dangerously false pulse oximetry reading, as the pulse oximetry sensor cannot differentiate between oxyhaemoglobin and carboxyhaemoglobin (Moyle 2002).

Peak expiratory flow rate

Peak expiratory flow (PEF) provides a measure of adequacy of the ventilation within the lungs in the form of the forced expiratory volume (FEV). The paramedic/ clinician should recognise that the patient may not be able to perform the task due to the severity of their dyspnoea. This is an essential assessment tool for any asthmatic patient.

- A peak flow meter with a disposable mouthpiece is required. Be careful to warn the patient not to obstruct the movement of the measurement gauge.
- PEF should be recorded as the best of three forced expiratory volumes. This should be compared to the patient's estimated value from a peak expiratory flow chart or known normal value (JRCALC 2006, Ref. 1).
- Readings should be taken both pre and post treatment so a comparison can be made on the effectiveness of the treatment provided.

Special attention should be given to asthmatic patients with peak flows of 33%–50% (acute severe asthma) or <33% (life threatening asthma) (BTS 2009a).

Capnometry ($ETCO_2$)

$ETCO_2$ is a non-invasive measurement of carbon dioxide at the end of expiration and provides an accurate insight into the ventilation and circulation of a patient. Normal physiological range is 35mmHg–45mmHg (Kupnic and Skok 2007).

■ Provides confirmation of endotracheal tube placement. During cardiopulmonary resuscitation $ETCO_2$ will give the paramedic/clinician an indication of success of resuscitation and early recognition of return of spontaneous circulation (ROSC).

Pulse rate

The pulse rate may provide valuable information as to whether a presenting respiratory dysfunction is related to a cardiac cause. Record the rate, quality and rhythm over one minute.

■ Normal range = 60–100 bpm
■ Bradycardic <60 bpm
■ Absoute bradycardia <40bpm
■ Tachycardia >100bpm (Resuscitation Council (UK) ALS 2011).

Blood pressure

Blood pressure is a primary vital sign and gives an important indication of the patient's cardiovascular status.

■ Normal range = 120/80 mmHg–140/90 mmHg
■ Hypertensive >140/90 mmHg
■ Hypotensive <systolic 90 mmHg (Bickley and Szilagyi 2007).

Electrocardiogram (ECG)

When appropriate it is important to obtain a 12 lead ECG to exclude any underlying respiratory/cardiovascular causes of respiratory dysfunction.

■ Sinus arrhythmia can occur in a patient presenting with a normal respiratory rate, rhythm and depth.
■ A patient presenting with a respiratory illness and tachypnoea may produce large amounts of artefact on the ECG making it impossible to read accurately.
■ Paramedic/clinicians should be aware that changes in ECG features associated with pulmonary artery obstruction can occur and may cause acute right ventricular dilation. This can produce an S wave in lead I, a Q wave in lead II, and T wave inversion in lead III, producing the well-known S1, Q3, T3 pattern. The S1, Q3, T3 pattern is seen in approximately 12% of patients presenting with a massive pulmonary embolus (Morris *et al.* 2003, p47).
■ Approximately 75% of patients with COPD have ECG abnormalities. P – pulmonale is often seen, along with poor R wave progression; there

may also be low amplitude of QRS complexes as hyperinflated lungs are poor electrical conductors (Morris *et al.* 2003, p46).

Capillary bed refill (CBR)

A CBR assessment can be recorded peripherally or centrally, although cold temperatures and dirt may hinder peripheral recording.

- For peripheral CBR assessment use the fingernail beds.
- For central CBR assessment use the sternum or forehead.
- Pressure should be applied for 5 seconds and capillary refill should return in less than 2 seconds.
- >2 seconds suggests poor tissue perfusion.

Glasgow Coma Score (GCS)

The GCS evaluates three areas of behaviour: eye opening, verbal response and motor response to give a cumulative score out of 15. Due to the complexity of GCS and the time required to measure it effectively the AVPU scale may be a more appropriate measurement in the immediate out-of-hospital environment.

Blood glucose level (BGL)

Recording the patient's glucose level gives the paramedic/clinician an indication of the systemic blood sugar levels in mmols/l.

- Normal range for non-diabetic patient 3.0–5.6mmols/l (JRCALC 2006 Ref. 4).
- A patient that is hyperglycaemic may present with Kussmaul's breathing, which is a deep sighing respiratory pattern and is associated with diabetic ketoacidosis.

Temperature

The paramedic/clinician should be aware that extremes of temperature can affect the patient's respiratory rate, rhythm and depth. You should:

- Record using a tympanic thermometer
- Hypothermia <35°C
- Severe hypothermia <30°C and may cause bradypnoea
- Hyperthermia >40°C and may cause tachypnoea/hyperventilation syndrome (Greaves and Porter 1999)
- Monitor the temperature for a possible underlying chest infection.

PHYSICAL ASSESSMENT

As the paramedic/clinician enters the room it is appropriate practice to introduce yourself and your colleagues and ask for the patient's name. This helps to foster the trust of the patient and will provide a good environment for gaining the consent required to perform the respiratory assessment.

Creating a suitable environment

Patients value their privacy and dignity and paramedic/clinicians should promote and protect their modesty at all times. This could be facilitated in an office environment by asking colleagues to leave the room or utilising the private setting of the ambulance (DH 2001a).

Consent

The Health Professions Council (HPC) states that a paramedic/clinician must ensure that they gain informed consent for any treatment they carry out. This must be documented accurately and passed onto other members of the health care team. In emergencies it may not be possible to gain consent, so the paramedic/clinician must act in the patient's best interest (HPC 2008).

RESPIRATORY ASSESSMENT – *INSPECTION, PALPATION, PERCUSSION, AUSCULTATON (IPPA)*

Inspection

Appropriately expose the patient's chest whilst maintaining their privacy and dignity at all times. The paramedic/clinician should inspect the whole chest including the posterior, anterior and axilla surfaces for:

- Respiratory rate, depth and rhythm (note abnormal, Kussmaul's, Cheyne-Stokes)
- Normal chest shape and equal chest rise
- Paradoxical breathing (Longmore *et al.* 2004, p48)
- Accessory muscle use – sternocleidomastoid, scalene muscles
- Chest wall markings – wounds, bruising, bleeding, swelling
- Scars – with credible history
- Implantable devices – pacemaker, implantable cardioverter-defibrillator (ICD)

- Medication patches – GTN, nicotine, analgesia
- Rashes – hives indicative of allergy or petechial haemorrhage indicative of meningococcal septicaemia.

Palpation

The paramedic/clinician is required to use both their hands and fingers to palpate the anterior, posterior and axilla chest walls. Palpation should start above each clavicle and systematically progress down the anterior chest wall followed by the posterior chest wall then axilla. The paramedic/clinician should note any of the following findings:

- Tenderness – bruising, muscle damage
- Crepitus – fractures
- Surgical emphysema – popping under the skin caused by trapped air.

Equal and bilateral air entry of the lungs can be palpated through visualising respiratory expansion. The paramedic/clinician can enhance this movement by appropriately placing their hands on the posterior chest wall with their thumbs meeting over the spine. Equal and symmetrical hand movement, associated with normal inspiration, can be seen when thumbs separate on inspiration and return to original position on expiration. A lack of symmetry could indicate problems on either or both sides of the thorax.

Tactile fremitus is the palpable vibration created by the spoken word and indicates areas of consolidation within the lungs (Bickley and Szilagyi 2007a). The paramedic/clinician should use the ulnar edge of their hands and systematically move over the anterior and posterior aspects of the chest wall asking the patient to repeat '99' at each point. Areas of consolidation, from pneumonia for example, produce increased fremitus whereas conditions where there is reduced air entry, such as emphysema, produce decreased fremitus.

Percussion

The paramedic/clinician should recognise that percussion is best performed in a quiet and calm environment in order to hear the resonance of the lungs. This environment is hard to create in the pre-hospital setting and therefore its application may be limited.

Percussion should start above the clavicles and systematically progress down the chest wall at 3 to 4 cm intervals (Rees 2003). The left side of the chest wall should be compared to the right side of the chest wall at each percussion point. The middle finger of one hand is placed on the chest wall with the remaining fingers spread. The middle finger of the opposing hand should be used to strike the planted finger on the chest wall. See Table 2.1.

Table 2.1 Percussion notes and their meaning (Rathe 2000)	
Flat or Dull	Pleural effusion or lobar pneumonia
Normal	Haemothorax
	Healthy lung or bronchitis
Hyper-resonance	Emphysema or pneumothorax

Auscultation (see Figures 2.2, 2.3, 2.4)

Prior to completing the assessment the paramedic/clinician should ensure that the earpiece of the stethoscope is pointing forward into the external ear. In addition they should check that the diaphragm is engaged and used for the auscultation process (Bickley and Szilagyy 2007).

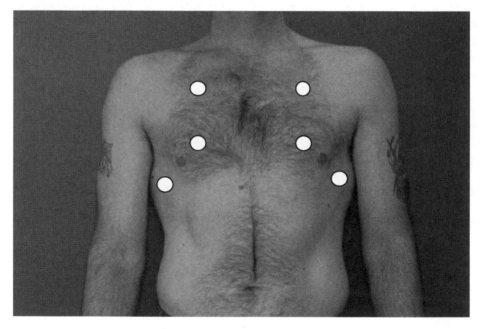

Figure 2.2 Auscultation areas of anterior chest wall

Anterior chest: Auscultate at least 6 areas on the anterior chest in order to listen to all lobes. Compare the left side of the lung to the right side moving systematically down the anterior wall.

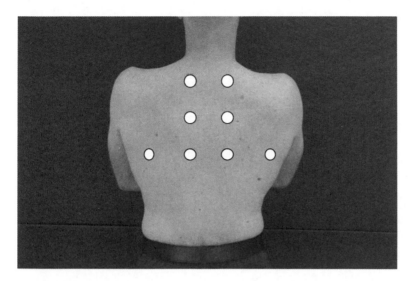

Figure 2.3   Auscultation areas of posterior chest wall

Posterior chest: Auscultate at least 8 areas on the posterior chest in order to listen to all lobes. To enhance auscultation ask the patient to cross their arms, which will remove the scapula from the auscultation field. Compare the left side of the lung to the right side moving systematically down the posterior wall.

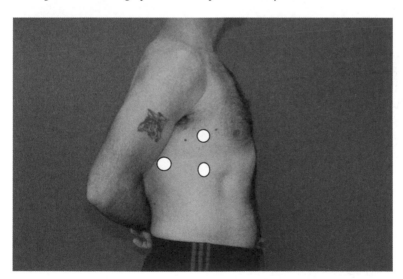

Figure 2.4   Auscultation areas of axillary region

Axilla: Auscultate at least three areas on each axilla in order to listen to all lobes. Move systematically over each axilla separately.

Sounds found on auscultation:

- Expiratory wheeze – sound created by air passing through narrowed airways on expiration (asthma, COPD)
- Inspiratory wheeze – high pitched sound heard on inspiration (foreign body obstruction)
- Fine crackles – sound created at the end of expiration by the reopening of the small airways or air passing through intra-alveolar fluid. This is normally heard in the basal lung fields (pulmonary oedema) (Adam and Osbourne 2005)
- Coarse crackles – sound created on both inspiration and expiration due to fluid or sputum in the larger airways (pneumonia)
- Pleural rub – creaking sound heard on deep inspiration and expiration (pleurisy)
- Absent breath sounds – could indicate a severe life threatening condition (tension pneumothorax, life threatening asthma).

COMMON RESPIRATORY CONDITIONS

Asthma

Asthma is a common and chronic inflammatory condition of the airways.

Epidemiology

5.4 million people in the UK currently suffer with asthma which equates to 1 person in every 5 households (Asthma UK 2009).

Pathophysiology

Asthma is often triggered by an inhaled irritant that causes the muscles of the airway walls to constrict. In addition it is often characterised by an increased inflammation of the lining of the airways, which causes swelling. The narrowing of the airways is occasionally exacerbated by the production of excessive sticky mucus.

Signs and symptoms

An asthmatic patient presents with a variable airway obstruction and more than one of the following symptoms:

- Wheeze
- Breathlessness
- Tight chest
- Cough
- Moderate exacerbation of asthma

- Increasing symptoms
- PEF >50%–75% best or predicted
- No features of acute severe asthma.

Acute severe asthma

- PEF 33%–50% best or predicted
- Respiratory rate ≥ 25/min
- SpO$_2$ ≥ 92%
- Heart rate ≥ 110/min
- Inability to complete a sentence in one breath.

Life threatening asthma

- PEF < 33% best or predicted
- SpO$_2$ < 92%
- Altered consciousness level
- Exhaustion
- Arrhythmia
- Hypotension
- Cyanosis
- Silent chest
- Poor respiratory effort (BTS 2011).

Patient specific questions

- Is there a family history of asthma?
- How regularly do you have asthma attacks?
- Have you ever been admitted into intensive care due to your asthma?

Possible actions to be taken:

- Auscultate all lung fields to confirm an expiratory wheeze and to exclude evidence of a pneumothorax
- Provide supplementary oxygen to maintain saturations of 94%–98% (BTS 2008)
- Regular PEFR measurement and reassessment
- Administer drug therapy for asthma as per current JRCALC guidelines
- Pre-alert to hospital depending on the severity of the attack

Chronic obstructive pulmonary disease (COPD)

COPD is the preferred term for patients suffering with airway obstruction associated with emphysema and bronchitis, although remodelling of airways in chronic asthma can lead to the disease too. It is a chronic progressive disease process which is not fully reversible and is predominantly caused by smoking.

Epidemiology

An estimated 3 million people are affected by COPD in the UK of which 2 million remain undiagnosed. It accounts for approximately 30,000 deaths within the UK of which 90% occur in the over 65 year old age group. By the year 2020 COPD is set to become the third leading cause of death worldwide surpassed only by heart disease and stroke (NICE 2004a).

Pathophysiology

Emphysema is characterised by the destruction of alveolar walls and reduction in elasticity of the lungs, which reduces the effective surface area for gas exchange. As a result large spaces remain filled with air during expiration. Smoking is thought to reduce the effectiveness of the body's defence mechanism against this process allowing sustained alveolar destruction to occur.

Bronchitis is characterised by excessive secretion of bronchial mucus and a productive cough for at least 3 months a year for 2 successive years (NICE 2004a). Chronic mucus production affects both large and small airways as a result of an increased number and size of mucous glands and goblet cells. This process causes a narrowing of the airways increasing airway resistance.

Signs and symptoms of exacerbation of COPD (NICE 2004a)

- Dyspnoea
- Tachypnoea
- Increased sputum production
- Increased wheeze on auscultation
- Chest tightness
- Reduced exercise tolerance
- Fatigue
- Acute confusion
- Cyanosis
- Tachycardia
- SpO_2 – markedly reduced. (The paramedic/clinician should be aware of hypoxic drive and the possible effect of oxygen on these patients.) (BTS 2008).

Patient specific questions

- Does your difficulty in breathing increase with exercise?
- How far can you walk without stopping on a normal day? How does this compare to today?
- Do you have a productive cough? What colour is the sputum?
- What is your normal SpO_2 level?
- Do you use home oxygen? How many litres are you on and for how long in the day?
- Have you been admitted to intensive care with the condition before? If so, when?

Possible actions to be taken:

- Early respiratory assessment including SpO_2 reading
- Provide supplementary oxygen for a target saturation of 88%–92% (BTS 2008)
- Administer drug therapy for COPD as per current JRCALC guidelines
- Pre-alert to hospital depending on the severity of the attack

Pulmonary embolism (PE)

A pulmonary embolism is caused by the obstruction of the pulmonary artery or one of its branches by an embolus, usually a blood clot from a deep vein thrombosis (DVT). Emboli can also be caused by air and amniotic fluid in the gravid female. Paramedic/clinicians should be aware that acute changes in a patient's respiratory condition, such as a pulmonary embolism (PE), might be seen within the ECG.

Epidemiology

In the UK, a pulmonary embolism (PE) following deep vein thrombosis (DVT) causes between 25,000 and 32,000 deaths each year in the hospitalised patient. It is the immediate cause of death in 10% of all patients who die in hospital. This figure exceeds the combined total of deaths from breast cancer, AIDS and traffic accidents (House of Commons Health Committee 2005).

Pathophysiology

A PE is a thrombus, commonly formed in the lower limb or pelvic veins, which becomes dislodged and is carried in the blood to the lungs where it occludes the pulmonary artery or one of its branches. An acute massive pulmonary embolism often kills immediately.

Signs and symptoms

- Dyspnoea
- Tachypnoea
- Acute onset of pleuritic chest pain
- Confusion/apprehension
- Tachycardia
- Cough
- Haemoptysis
- Leg pain/clinical deep vein thrombosis (DVT) (JRCALC 2006, Ref. 5).

Patient specific questions

Does the patient present with any of the following pre-disposing risk factors?

- Recent surgery
- Prolonged period of recent immobility
- Pregnancy and recent childbirth
- Malignancy
- Recent myocardial infarction (MI)
- Oral contraceptive pill
- Age >40 years old
- Family history of DVT/PE (NICE 2007a).

Possible actions to be taken:

- Provide supplementary oxygen to maintain saturations of 94%–98% (BTS 2008)
- Thorough history taking with high index of suspicion
- Be prepared for a cardiorespiratory arrest
- Pre-alert to hospital depending on the severity of the attack

Anaphylaxis

Anaphylaxis is a severe, life threatening systemic hypersensitivity reaction.

Epidemiology

1 in 1333 patients in the English population has experienced anaphylaxis at one point in their lives. There are approximately 20 anaphylaxis deaths per year, although this figure is believed to be an underestimate due to a lack of clinical recognition (Resuscitation Council (UK) 2008).

Pathophysiology

Anaphylaxis is a form of shock that affects both the respiratory and circulatory system. An initial exposure to an allergen stimulates the production of antibodies, such as immunoglobulin E (IgE), which attach to mast cells. Secondary exposure to the same allergen triggers IgE that stimulate the mast cells, causing them to degranulate and produce large quantities of histamine. The subsequent release of histamine causes vasodilation, increased permeability of the blood vessels and constriction of the smooth muscle in the airways.

Signs and symptoms

Anaphylaxis is likely when all of the following three criteria are met:

- Sudden onset and rapid progression of symptoms
- Life threatening airway and/or breathing and/or circulation problems
- Skin and/or mucosal changes (Resuscitation Council (UK) 2008).

Sudden onset of symptoms

- Airway swelling
- Dyspnoea/dysphagia
- Stridor/hoarse voice
- Shortness of breath
- Tachypnoea
- Lethargy and confusion
- Cyanosis
- Respiratory arrest
- Signs of shock – pale/clammy
- Tachycardia
- Hypotension
- Decreasing levels of consciousness
- ECG changes (ischaemia and arrhythmias)
- Cardiac arrest
- Sense of 'impending doom'
- Urticaria (hives)
- Pruritus (itching) (Resuscitation Council (UK) 2008).

Patient specific questions

- Have you experienced an anaphylactic reaction before?
- If so, when?
- Describe the symptoms you experienced?
- Do you have an Epipen?
- Have you used it today?

■ Do you know what triggered this reaction?
■ Have you been admitted to an intensive therapy unit (ITU) with this condition?

Possible actions to be taken:

■ Early adrenaline therapy if indicated, as per current JRCALC guidelines
■ Provide supplementary oxygen to maintain saturations of 94%–98% (BTS 2008)
■ Administer drug therapy for anaphylaxis as per current JRCALC guidelines
■ If time critical pre-alert the hospital with information of the attack

---

Pneumonia

Pneumonia is an infection causing the inflammation and oedema of the alveoli and small airways of the lungs.

Epidemiology
The incidence of community-acquired pneumonia (CAP) varies with age and is commonly found in the elderly or very young. Between 22% and 42% of adults with CAP are hospitalised (BTS 2009).

Pathophysiology
Pneumonia can result in consolidation throughout the lungs or to an isolated lobe within the lung. Consolidation, also known as exudate, is a solid mass containing a mixture of white blood cells, red blood cells and fibrin, which are leaked through capillary walls as a result of inflammation. Pneumonia reduces the viable surface area for external respiration, resulting in less oxygen reaching the pulmonary circulation.

Signs and symptoms
■ Dyspnoea
■ Tachypnoea
■ Productive cough
■ Reduced breath sounds
■ Tachycardia
■ Pyrexia (JRCALC 2006, Ref. 3)

Patient specific questions
- Have you had a recent chest infection?
- Do you suffer with recurrent chest infections?
- Are you a smoker?

Possible actions to be taken:

- Provide supplementary oxygen to maintain saturations of 94%–98% (BTS 2008)
- If possible collect sputum sample for culture analysis at hospital
- Beware of sepsis in the critically ill patient
- If time critical pre-alert the hospital

Pulmonary oedema

Pulmonary oedema is an accumulation of fluid in the lungs which inhibits gas exchange across the alveoli and capillary membranes.

Epidemiology
Pulmonary oedema presenting to the UK ambulance service is predominantly caused by acute heart failure (JRCALC 2006, Ref. 6). The condition is associated with significant morbidity levels within the pre-hospital arena, with an in-hospital short-term mortality figure varying between 20% and 30% and a five-year mortality figure nearing 50% (Hubble *et al.* 2006).

Pathophysiology
Pulmonary oedema is caused by left ventricular failure (LVF) as a result of the myocardium becoming damaged. This damage results in the left ventricle becoming an ineffective pump creating an accumulation of blood in the left atrium. Over time this results in the back-up and accumulation of blood in the pulmonary veins, increasing the pressure at the pulmonary capillaries, leading to pulmonary oedema.

Signs and symptoms
- Dyspnoea
- Pink stained frothy white sputum
- Orthopnoea
- Anxiousness/restlessness
- Associated with angina (JRCALC 2006, Ref. 6).

Patient specific questions
- Have you been waking at night with shortness of breath?
- Have you been sleeping with more pillows recently?

- Have you noticed any swelling in your legs recently?
- Do you suffer with heart failure? Have you had a previous MI, angina attack, angioplasty or coronary artery bypass?

Possible actions to be taken:

- Provide supplementary oxygen to maintain saturations of 94%–98% (BTS 2008)
- Upright patient positioning
- Consider early sublingual glyceryl trinitrate (GTN) as per current JRCALC guidelines
- Consider continuous positive airway pressure (CPAP) therapy if equipment and training allow
- If time critical pre-alert the hospital

Hyperventilation syndrome

Hyperventilation syndrome is an anxiety disorder defined by a tachypnoea exceeding normal physiological requirements. The cause may be related to a stressful event, pain, excitement or an idiopathic reason.

Epidemiology
There is limited statistical data as to the occurrence of hyperventilation syndrome. Experience has shown that this syndrome can occur at any age after infancy but the onset is usually between the ages of 15 and 55 years affecting a greater proportion of females.

Pathophysiology
The underlying mechanism of how some patients develop hyperventilation is unknown, however once initiated it can become a vicious cycle. During episodes of tachypnoea the patient expires excessive carbon dioxide (CO_2) resulting in hypocapnia. This leads to respiratory alkalosis causing the common symptoms of tetany, paraesthesia and carpopedal spasms. The experience of these symptoms exacerbates the patient's anxiety which fuels further hyperventilation.

Signs and symptoms
- Acute anxiety
- Tachypnoea
- Tetany
- Paraesthesia (mouth, lips and fingers)
- Carpopedal spasms

- Palpitations
- Dizziness.

Patient specific questions
- Do you suffer with anxiety attacks?
- What has happened to cause your anxiety today?

Possible actions to be taken:

- Take a thorough history and examination of patient to eliminate life threatening causes of hyperventilation (i.e. PE, asthma, hypovolaemia, myocardial infarction)
- Maintain a calm and sympathetic approach to the patient's condition
- Provide an explanation as to the symptoms the patient is experiencing and reduce their respiration through effective coaching

---

INJURIES TO THE RESPIRATORY SYSTEM

Chest trauma

Chest trauma is a major contributor to mortality in the pre-hospital environment and can involve injuries such as flail segments, massive haemothoraces, open pnuemothoraces and tension pneumothoraces (Lee *et al.* 2007).

Epidemiology
Thoracic injuries account for 25% of all deaths in trauma. The primary cause of death is due to hypoxia caused by ventilatory failure or secondary to hypovolaemia from a massive haemothorax (JRCALC 2006, Ref. 7).

Flail segment

A flail segment occurs when two or more adjacent ribs are broken in two or more places. A paradoxical movement of the lungs occurs due to the free floating flail segment that moves independently of the remainder of the ribs. The flail segment moves in with inhalation and out with exhalation, opposing the normal movement of ribs in respiration, causing inadequate ventilation.

Signs and symptoms
- Significant blunt trauma to the chest
- Paradoxical breathing
- Reduced chest expansion on affected side

- Pain
- Dyspnoea.

Possible actions to be taken:

- 15 l/min O_2 for trauma patients (BTS 2008)
- Appropriate positioning of patient and stabilisation/splinting of the flail segment
- Analgesia as per current JRCALC guidelines
- Pre-alert to the nearest trauma centre

Tension pneumothorax

A tension pneumothorax occurs when an opening is created within the pleural lining of the lung. If a one-way valve is created air will enter the pleural space on inhalation but will not leave on exhalation. This creates an increased intra-pleural pressure leading to the collapse of the lung. As the tension pneumothorax increases in size the pressure pushes the contents of the mediastinum to the opposite side of the body obstructing blood flow of the heart reducing cardiac output. In addition the tension may compress the diaphragm and opposing lung. Without immediate interventions this condition will lead to cardiac arrest.

Signs and symptoms
- Blunt or penetrating trauma to the chest
- Dyspnoea
- Reduced air entry on injured side
- Reduced SpO_2
- Surgical emphysema.

Possible actions to be taken:

- 15 l/min O_2 for trauma patients (BTS 2008)
- Needle decompression as per current JRCALC guidelines
- Constant reassessment of presenting condition
- Pre-alert to the nearest trauma centre

Open pneumothorax

An open pneumothorax is caused by a penetrating injury to the chest wall causing air to enter the pleural space. The negative pressure created in the thoracic cavity can draw air through the hole in the chest wall. This may present as a 'sucking chest wound'.

Signs and symptoms
- Penetrating trauma to the chest
- Dyspnoea
- Sucking chest wound
- Reduced air entry on affected side
- Surgical emphysema.

Possible actions to be taken:

- 15 l/min O_2 for trauma patients (BTS 2008)
- Three sided dressing applied to the wound with opening on inferior side
- Constant reassessment with high suspicion of tension pneumothorax
- Pre-alert to the nearest trauma centre

Haemothorax

A haemothorax occurs when blood enters the pleural space within the lungs. The pleural space of the lungs can hold up to 3 litres of blood and therefore can represent a significant source of blood loss (Salomone and Pons 2007).

Signs and symptoms
- Mechanism of injury – blunt or penetrating trauma to the chest
- Dyspnoea
- Reduced chest expansion on side of injury
- Reduced air entry on side of injury
- Signs of hypovolaemic shock.

Possible actions to be taken:

- 15 l/min O_2 for trauma patients (BTS 2008)
- IV access and intravenous fluids en route as per current JRCALC guidelines
- Pre-alert to the nearest trauma centre

MECHANICAL FACTORS THAT AFFECT THE RESPIRATORY SYSTEM

The paramedic/clinician should be aware that the following mechanical factors might have an influence over the efficacy of undertaking a respiratory assessment and could impact on the normal and therefore distort a paramedic/clinician's assessment of the respiratory system:

- *Pregnancy* – A gravid female may not be able to fully expand her lungs due to the splinting of the diaphragm by the in-situ foetus.
- *Obesity* – These patients may have an increased weight on their chest and therefore will require a greater mechanical effort to breath normally. In addition their increased abdominal mass will impede on lung expansion.
- *Abdominal distension* – this could be due to either: *fluid* from ascites, impacted *faeces, fat, foetus* and *flatus.*

CHAPTER KEY POINTS

- In your initial assessment of the respiratory system the **DR ABCDE** framework should be utilised to identify life threatening conditions and the time critical patient, convey to the appropriate treatment/ management unit.
- If the patient does not have a time critical condition a thorough secondary survey should be performed.
- The paramedic/clinician should endeavour to maintain a professional approach to all patients and treat them with the dignity and respect that they deserve.

3 Cardiovascular assessment

Graham Harris and Mark Whitbread

The cardiovascular system (CVS) is in essence the '*transport*' system of the body comprising the pump (heart), a control centre and miles of various blood vessels: the heart being the central component. It is connected to all the other body systems; supplying oxygen and nutrients and removing waste products, to help maintain homeostasis.

The aim of this chapter is to provide the paramedic/clinician with a systematic approach to the assessment of the cardiovascular system to enable them to identify cardiac conditions, whether they are of a non-serious, serious or life threatening nature.

SCENE ASSESSMENT

Information received regarding the incident may provide the paramedic/clinician with potential expectations prior to arriving at the scene. A call given as: 'Male, 55 years of age, Collapsed? Heart Attack?' indicates a potential medical emergency, whereas a call given as: 'Male, 55 years of age, massive blood loss' indicates a potential trauma emergency (*see Trauma Assessment: Chapter 7* for cardiothoracic injuries).
Initial questions to ask are:

- Is the patient in a collapsed condition? If so,
- Is this because the patient has suffered a cardiac arrest, or due to shock?

A cardiovascular assessment commences as you approach the patient, these observations may provide evidence of cardiovascular compromise:

- Do they appear to be in obvious distress?
- Do they have obvious dyspnoea?
- Do they appear ill or time critical?
- Are they holding their chest?
- Do they look pale?
- Are they diaphoretic?

- Are they cyanosed?
- Are they sitting upright with legs dependent?

PRIMARY SURVEY

The patient may present and appear well to the paramedic/clinician, however, remember that as with other systems, deterioration of the cardiovascular system (CVS) can be both rapid and potentially fatal.

DANGER

- Ensure the safety of yourself, your colleague(s), the patient, relatives/bystanders.
- Patients with existing cardiac conditions may have an implanted cardioverter defibrillator (ICD) fitted, or be administered glyceryl trinitrate (GTN) via patches; the latter may present a potential safety issue.
- External defibrillators may be utilised in cardiac resuscitation and the paramedic/clinician has a responsibility to ensure the safety of all persons present prior to delivering shocks as part of advanced cardiac life support (Resuscitation Council (UK) ALS 2011).

RESPONSE

- Assess the patient's response using the AVPU scale and record appropriately.
- Remember that alterations in the patient's level of consciousness (LOC) may be cardiac in origin; a patient's cerebral hypoxia may be due to inability of the heart to pump effectively.
- Remember that brain malfunction (LOC) may be the first symptom of hypoxia (BTS 2008, pvi13).

AIRWAY

- Ascertain if the patient has a patent airway, and is able to maintain it.
- A patient who has collapsed and may have had a heart attack may also have vomited.
- The mouth and/or oropharynx may require immediate management.

> ## Possible actions to be taken:
>
> ■ Ensure airway is patent and secure before proceeding to next element

BREATHING

■ Ascertain the patient's oxygen saturation levels (SpO_2) as oxygen desaturation occurs in over 50% of cardiac patients (Buist *et al.* 2004, p137).

■ Does the patient have shortness of breath, '*dyspnoea*'?

■ Is the dyspnoea exacerbated by exertion?

■ Does the dyspnoea wake them up? (paroxysmal nocturnal dyspnoea (PND))

■ Is the dyspnoea due to an existing cardiac condition such as left ventricular failure (LVF) or mitral stenosis? If so,

■ Is the LVF associated with '*orthopnoea*'? Ask the patient about changes to their sleep patterns; how many pillows they sleep with?

■ Does the patient have a dry, chronic cough? This could be an imminent sign of PND.

■ Ask the patient if they are prescribed ACE inhibitors, beta blockers or amiodarone? Coughing may occur as a side-effect of the drugs (Longmore *et al.* 2004, p48).

> ## Possible actions to be taken:
>
> ■ Ensure that the patient is not hypoxic, administer O_2 if required to overcome any hypoxia (Resuscitation Council (UK) 2009)
> ■ Manage breathing problems and associated hypoxia effectively before moving to the next element

CIRCULATION

Is the patient complaining of central chest pain? Ascertain if cardiac in origin, obtain electrocardiogram (ECG) trace and manage accordingly (Ballinger and Patchett 2008, p441).

Patients presenting with a ruptured abdominal aortic aneurysm (AAA) may present with signs and symptoms of hypovolaemic shock.

If the patient presents with chest trauma or shock, manage accordingly (Salomone and Pons 2007). (*See Trauma Assessment*: Chapter 7.)

- Assess the patient's radial pulse to ascertain the *rate* and *rhythm*.
- Assess the patient's brachial or carotid pulses to ascertain the *character* and *volume*.
- Is the rate tachycardic (>100 beats per minute)?
- If so, identify the cause and manage accordingly, if appropriately qualified (Olshanky 2010).
- Is the rate bradycardic (<60 beats per minute)? If so, ask the patient if they take any of the following medications:
  - calcium channel blockers, such as diltiazem, amlodipine, nifedipine
  - alpha-(α) or beta-(β) adrenergic blockers such as atenolol
  - glycosides, such as digoxin, as these can all contribute to bradycardia (Palatnik and Kates 2002).
- Check the *rhythm* of the pulse; an irregularly irregular pulse may occur in either atrial fibrillation (AF) or multiple ectopics. However a regular irregular pulse can occur in a second degree (2°) heart block.

The patient's blood pressure (BP) can provide the paramedic/clinician with important information concerning the assessment of their CVS. Remember that hypotension (<90mmHg) is a significant clinical observation of the patient's cardiac output (Manza 2002, p123).

Ascertain if they have a radial pulse.

Possible actions to be taken:

- Administer O_2 and gain IV access (Resuscitation Council UK. ALS (2011), pp17–18)
- Obtain an ECG trace and manage accordingly
- Control external haemorrhage (*see Trauma Assessment: Chapter 7*)
- Manage shock accordingly (*see Trauma Assessment: Chapter 7*)

DISABILITY

- Assess the patient's level of consciousness (LOC), record the AVPU level (*see Neurological Assessment*: Chapter 5) (Jevon 2008, p26–7). Consider the younger patient who presents with a transient loss of consciousness may have an undiagnosed cardiac arrhythmia (DH 2005b)
- Assess the patient's blood glucose levels (Badriraju *et al.* 2006, p1573).
- Assess the patient's pupils for size and reaction (PERRLA).

Possible actions to be taken:

- Assess and document (LOC)
- Assess and document blood glucose levels
- Assess and document size and equality of pupils

EXPOSE/ENVIRONMENT/EVALUATE

Expose and examine the patient, look for scars over sternum (cardiac surgery), check for pacemakers and or an ICD (normally found just below the patient's left clavicle, or if the patient has GTN patches on their thoracic wall. Remember: consider the environment and maintain dignity, as far as possible. Consider consent, especially in emergency situations (DH 2009, p5).

Evaluate the findings from the primary survey. If any time critical problems have been identified within any of the elements, then transport and transfer immediately to an appropriate treatment centre, if not, then remain on scene and conduct a secondary survey (Terkelsen and Lassen 2008).

Actions to be taken:

- Expose patient and examine
- Remember consent and patient dignity
- Evaluate – transfer to the appropriate treatment centre (*primary angioplasty*), or move onto the secondary survey?

SECONDARY SURVEY

The focused history and assessment conducted as part of this survey can assist the paramedic/clinician to establish illnesses and problems that may not have been identified within the primary survey. These may be due to either new or pre-existing cardiac conditions. The paramedic/clinician should remember that patients presenting with cardiac conditions can and will be from across the lifespan. However, the types of cardiac conditions that patients typically present with are likely to be from either one or more of the following:

- Angina
- Atrial fibrillation (AF) (commonest arrhythmia)
- Ischaemic heart disease (IHD)

- Heart attack – acute myocardial infarction (AMI)
- Heart failure – right ventricular failure (RVF), left ventricular failure (LVF), and congestive cardiac failure (CCF)
- Cardiac arrythmias
- Congenital heart disease
- Inherited cardiac conditions (ICC)
- Valvular heart disease.

HISTORY

Presenting complaint (PC)

Asking the patient to explain what the problem is and to explain their symptoms will assist the paramedic/clinician. The most common symptoms that patients with cardiac conditions present with are:

- chest pain
- dyspnoea
- palpitations
- dizziness and syncope
- oedema
- transient loss of consciousness (Swanton 2003; Longmore *et al.* 2004; Bickley and Szilagyi 2007; Ballinger and Patchett 2008).

Patients may present with one or more symptoms simultaneously, or in certain cases be asymptomatic. The symptoms may be related to specific cardiac conditions. Acute central chest pain is a common presenting symptom of cardiovascular disease. The site, character and related symptoms can assist in identifying the cause. It can be associated with *stable angina* which starts in the retrosternal region and may or may not radiate to the jaw, teeth or arms. Patients complain of either tightness or heaviness which is associated with exercise and is normally relieved by rest. (ECG recordings of angina patients often show ST segment depression, and either flattening of or inversion of the 'T' wave.) However, patients with *unstable angina* may have similar symptoms but explain that the pain occurred at rest, potentially more serious as it may progress to a myocardial infarction (MI). Patients who have other forms of chest pain such as *pericardial pain* often present with sharp pain, either retrosternal or epigastric. It is exacerbated by movement and respiration, but relieved by sitting forward. (ECG recordings in patients with pericarditis may show saddle-shaped ST elevation (Longmore *et al.* 2004, p124).)

Aortic pain due to acute thoracic aortic dissection presents as a sudden severe tearing retrosternal pain which radiates to the back; the degree of the radiation will depend on the blood vessels involved. If branch arteries are affected the patient can present with neurological signs, the absence of pulses and unequal blood pressure in their arms (Ballinger and Patchett 2008, p483). *Non-cardiac pain* can be oesophageal (reflux oesophagitis); the patient complains that the pain occurs when they bend or lie down, or occurs only at night.

Patients with cardiac conditions commonly present with dyspnoea; the commonest cardiac cause of exertion dyspnoea is left ventricular heart failure. Dyspnoea can also occur at rest; patients present with breathlessness when they lie flat (orthopnoea). Alternatively the patient may present or complain of waking suddenly at night because of paroxysmal nocturnal dyspnoea (PND) due to pulmonary oedema caused by the accumulation of fluid in the lungs. (An imminent sign of PND is a dry nocturnal cough.) However, in acute pulmonary oedema the patient may cough up pink frothy sputum streaked with haemoptysis (Swanton 2003, p3).

Palpitations are an awareness of the heartbeat. There are times, such as during exercise, or if when anxious, that we become aware of our normal heartbeat. However, if the patient presents with palpitations in other circumstances they may indicate a cardiac arrhythmia, notably ectopic beats or a paroxysmal tachycardia. Assessment: ask the patient to tap out the rate and regularity of the palpitations. Irregular fast palpitations are likely to be atrial fibrillation, whereas slow palpitations are likely to be due to beta-blocker drugs (Longmore *et al.* 2004, p78). Ascertain from the patient when the symptom occurs, and if it is associated with other symptoms, such as dyspnoea or syncope, which may indicate haemodynamic compromise.

Patients presenting with *dizziness* or *syncope* (faint), may classically explain that they had one of their 'funny turns'. Cardiac causes of syncope can be due to either a ventricular tachycardia (VT) or complete heart block, both of which are unable to maintain cardiac output in the acute setting. Ask the patient or eye-witness what they were doing when the syncope occurred? It can occur in men at night after micturition, whereas effort syncope occurs with exercise in patients with aortic stenosis and hypertrophic obstructive cardiomyopathy (HOCM) (Ballinger and Patchett 2008, p697).

Patients with deep vein thrombosis (DVT) or right heart failure may present with *oedema* caused by increased venous pressure. Dependent oedema appears predominantly in the feet and ankles when sitting; however in patients who are bedridden the oedema will transfer and occur in the sacrum (Bickley and Szilagyi 2007, p146).

History of presenting complaint (HPC)

The following questions can assist the paramedic/clinician in obtaining the appropriate history surrounding the presenting complaint:

- What were you doing before the problem started?
- When did the symptom(s) start?
- What was the first thing that you noticed?
- Have you ever had this problem before?

Utilise either the OPQRSTA or the SOCRATES framework to structure your pain assessment questions; the SOCRATES framework is described below:

- Site – Is it retrosternal? Acute central chest pain is normally cardiac in origin.
- Onset – Did it commence gradually (heart attack, MI) or suddenly (aortic dissection)?
- Character – Do they explain it as a tightness, heaviness or crushing?
- Radiation – To the jaw or arms (angina) or to the back (aortic dissection)
- Associations – Are they nauseous, or diaphoretic (myocardial infarction)?
- Timing – When did the pain commence, and its duration?
- Exacerbating/alleviating factors – Does the pain increase with movement? Or is it relieved by sitting forward (pericarditis)?
- Severity – How does the patient score the pain on a scale of 0–10? (Longmore *et al.* 2004, p34).

Past medical history (PMH)

When asking patients about their medical history the paramedic/clinician should utilise the appropriate terminology. If you ask them if they have hypertension they may answer *no*, but if you ask if they have any problems with their blood pressure their answer is *yes*. The purpose of this element is to ascertain the patient's past medical history, which can provide important information concerning their condition.

- Have you had this problem before? If so, when?
- Do you have angina?
- Have you ever had a heart attack?
- Do you have a problem with your heart?
- Can you tell me what this is?
- Do you have a problem with your blood?
- Can you tell me what this is?
- Do you have a problem with your blood pressure?
- Have you ever had an ECG recorded before? If yes, why?
- Have you ever had an ultrasound of your heart? If yes, why?
- Have you ever had a stroke?
- Do you have any other medical problems that you see your doctor about, or take tablets for? (Patients with diabetes have a risk of atherosclerosis,

increased if they smoke, have hypertension or hyperlipidaemia) (Ballinger and Patchett 2008, p663).

- Have you had rheumatic fever? (Patients may develop right heart failure/ mitral stenosis.)
- Have you ever been admitted to hospital or had any operations?
- If so, what was it for? Consider that cardiac operations/surgery may include:
  - heart transplant
  - coronary artery bypass grafting (CABG)
  - percutaneous transluminal coronary angioplasty (PTCA) (balloon dilation)
  - percutaneous coronary intervention (PCI) (stent)
  - valve replacement
  - pacemaker or implantable cardioverter defibrillator (ICD).

Drug/medication history (DMH)

Ask the patient general questions about any tablets or injections that they have to take or administer, remember to ask if they have purchased and or taken any *over the counter* (OTC) medicines, or if they are taking any herbal remedies.

- Is the patient currently prescribed or taking medications for any existing medical problem?
- If so, what for? Use the medications to confirm this by asking the patient what they take each medication for.
- Medications for cardiac conditions may include: beta-blockers, cardiac glycosides, ACE inhibitors, angiotensin II receptor antagonists, diuretics, anti-coagulants, statins, calcium channel blockers, potassium channel blockers and nitrates.
- Have they been compliant with their medications?
- Ask patients who present with angina and prescribed GTN spray, if they have used it?
- If yes, has it relieved the pain? If not, ask if they have a headache. If not, check that the drug is in-date.
- Have they recently started a new or stopped a previous medication.

Social/family medical history (S/FMH)

Consider that patients who present with cardiac conditions may be from across the lifespan; a young person presenting with syncope during exercise requires a detailed assessment of the family history to ascertain if there are risk factors. Alternatively, the older person who presents with symptoms of heart failure may have had recurrent scarlet fever as a child.

- Remember to use probing as opposed to prying questions, such as who else is there at home?
- Depending upon the age of the patient, ascertain if they live alone or have relatives who visit, carers, nurses or other external agency input.
- Consider mobility, does the person use any walking aids?
- Are there stairs in the property? If so, can the patient climb them unaided?
- What can the patient not do for themselves because of the illness or symptoms, which normally they could?
- Depending on the presenting medical condition, ask if other members of the patient's family also suffer from the condition or illness.
- Congenital conditions; long QT syndrome and hypertrophic cardiomyopathy (HCM).
- Ask about the patient's parents and siblings; specifically their age, health and if known, cause of death?
- To identify if there is a significant family history of coronary heart disease (CHD), ask the patient about the health of their grandparents and any male siblings, if they smoked, had hypertension or hyperlipidaemia before their 60th birthday, and where applicable, ascertain the cause of death.
- Ascertain and identify if the patient has any of the following risk factors: family history of CHD, hypertension, diabetes mellitus, sedentary lifestyle, diet, recreational drugs, alcohol and smoking status.
- Regular use of cocaine increases coronary atherosclerosis and the risk of a myocardial infarction (MI) (Burnett 2010).
- Regarding alcohol and smoking, ascertain how much, how long, and if appropriate when ceased.
- Smoking is quantified in pack years (20 cigarettes smoked per day for 1 year = 1 pack year) (Longmore *et al.* 2004, p34).

EXAMINATION

Whilst this commenced with the primary survey, the examination itself comprises various components, some of which may be new to the paramedic/clinician. The component tests are simple to perform and to the experienced paramedic/clinician their results will be objective.

The following systematic format will assist the paramedic/clinician. Appearance, hands, pulses, blood pressure, praecordium, jugular venous pressure (JVP), auscultation (heart and lungs), oedema, abdomen and peripheral pulses.

Appearance

- Does the patient look ill?
- Are they pale, cold, clammy (*signs of shock and cardiovascular compromise*)?
- Check their eyelids for evidence of xanthelasma (*sharply demarcated yellowish collection of cholesterol underneath the skin, around the eyelids, common in people of Asian and Mediterranean origin, and associated with hyperlipidaemia*).
- Do they have corneal arcus (*greyish-white ring, or part of a ring*) opacity occurring in the periphery of the cornea due to a lipid infiltration of the corneal stroma?
- Does the patient have proptosis (*bulging eyes*)? Graves' disease (*associated with atrial fibrillation*)?
- Does the patient have a Malar flush (*redness around the cheeks and is indicative of mitral stenosis*)?

Possible actions to be taken:

- Assess the patient's appearance, including face
- Assess the eyelids and cornea for evidence of hyperlipidaemia
- Record findings appropriately

Hands

- Are the patients hands warm, and well perfused, or sweaty, or cold and moist?
- Veins that are dilated may be due to carbon dioxide (CO_2) retention.
- Are any rings on the patient's fingers tight because of oedema?
- Are there splinter haemorrhages under the patient's nail beds?
- Do they have Janeway lesions (*red macules*) on the palm of the hand?
- Osler's nodes (*tender lumps in the pulp of the fingertips*)?
- Are there nicotine stains?
- Does the patient have finger clubbing (see Figure 3.1) (*associated with endocarditis, atrial myxoma and cyanotic congenital heart disease*)?

Possible actions to be taken:

- Assess the patient's hands, including fingers and nails
- Assess for finger clubbing (ask the patient to place the fingernails of the same finger on opposite hands against each other, nail to nail,

---

a small kite/diamond shape is normally apparent between the nail
beds) (see Figure 3.1)
- If this window is obliterated, the test is positive and clubbing is present

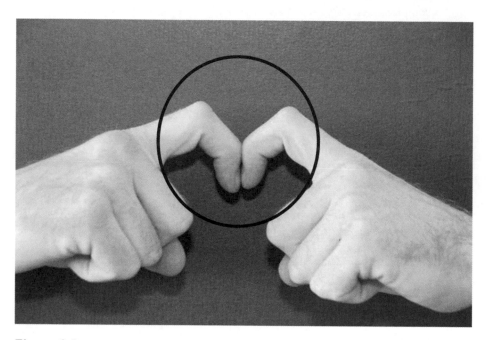

Figure 3.1   Finger clubbing assessment

Pulses

- Assess radial pulses for *rate* and *rhythm* and the carotid pulse for
  character and *volume*.
- Assess both radial pulses simultaneously and check that they are equal
  (*unequal pulses can indicate atherosclerosis or aortic dissection*).
- Is the pulse irregularly irregular (*indicative of atrial fibrillation (AF) or
  multiple ectopics*)?
- Is the pulse regularly irregular (*indicative of second degree heart block
  and ventricular bigeminy*)?
- Auscultate lightly and listen for carotid artery bruits (*indicative of
  artherosclerotic narrowing*) – (ask the patient to briefly hold their breath
  as you auscultate each artery in turn).

- A small volume pulse (*indicative of shock, aortic stenosis and pericardial effusion*).
- A jerky pulse (*indicative in hypertrophic obstructive cardiomyopathy HOCM*).
- Ascertain if *pulsus paradoxus* occurs when the patient inspires (systolic pressure reducing >10mmHg), this may be due to pericardial constriction or cardiac tamponade (Longmore *et al.* 2004, p42).
- A *collapsing pulse* can be felt radially. *Assessment* – Lift the patient's right arm up above the height of their shoulder, and let their radial pulse beat against the flat of your hand. If present, a slapping sensation caused by the collapsing pulse will be noted (Watson *et al.* 2006).

Possible actions to be taken:

- Palpate both radial pulses
- Ascertain if pulsus paradoxus occurs on inspiration
- Ascertain if a collapsing pulse can be palpated radially
- Auscultate both carotid pulses
- Note and record findings

Blood pressure

- Ask patients who have a history of hypertension if they know what their blood pressure reading is normally.
- The blood pressure may be either raised or lowered in patients presenting with unstable angina, myocardial infarction or a serious underlying arrhythmia.
- A narrow *pulse pressure* is indicative of aortic stenosis.
- A wide *pulse pressure* is indicative of aortic regurgitation.
- A fall in systolic pressure >10mmHg on inspiration indicates *pulsus paradoxus* and may be due to pericardial constriction or cardiac tamponade.
- Postural hypotension occurs with a fall of (systolic >15mmHg or diastolic >10mmHg) on standing, and may be due to hypovolaemia, idiopathic orthostatic hypotension or vasodilator and diuretic drugs.

Praecordium

- Inspect for scars (median stenotomy).
- Inspect for any deformity.
- Inspect for pulsations.
- Inspect for an ICD and or pacemaker (see Figure 3.2).
- Palpate the *apex beat*.
- An apex beat that is *tapping* (quick and light) indicates mitral stenosis.

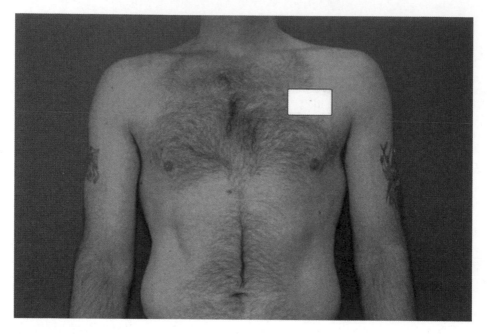

Figure 3.2   Position of implantable cardioverter defibrillator (ICD) or pacemaker

- An apex beat that is *thrusting* (diffuse and long) indicates aortic stenosis.
- An apex beat that is *heaving* (sharp and firm) indicates mitral or aortic regurgitation.

Assessment – Ask the patient to turn on their left side and hold their breath after exhalation.

The normal apex beat is found in the left 5th intercostal space, in the mid-clavicular line (see Figure 3.3). It is palpable but does not lift the finger off the chest wall (Swanton 2003, p9).

Jugular venous pressure (JVP)

As part of the assessment of the right side of the patient's heart the paramedic/ clinician will need to evaluate the JVP. The JVP of the internal jugular vein correlates with the pressure in the right atrium, and an elevation of the JVP may be indicative of right heart failure (RHF). There are two features requiring observation:

1   Visual assessment of the height-JVP.
2   The waveform of the pulse.

Whilst not every paramedic/clinician may be fortunate to have the expertise and ability to evaluate the waveform, you can, with practice, perfect the skill of assessing the height-JVP.

Assessment – Position the patient at 45° with their head turned slightly to the left. Locate and observe the right internal jugular vein, medial to the clavicular head of sternocleidomastoid; the vein passes behind the angle of the jaw in the direction of the earlobe (see Figure 3.3).

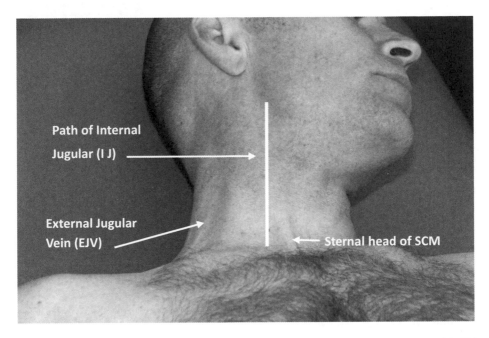

Figure 3.3   Landmarks required for jugular venous pressure measurement (JVP)

The JVP is the vertical height of the pulsation above the sternal angle. The pulsation reflects changes in pressure within the right atrium. The JVP is elevated if >4cm (see Figure 3.4).

- Raised JVP is indicative of right heart failure.
- Decreased JVP is indicative of hypovolaemia from GI bleeding or dehydration.
- Inspiratory filling of the neck veins (Kussmaul's sign) is indicative of constrictive pericarditis (Longmore *et al.* 2004, p42).

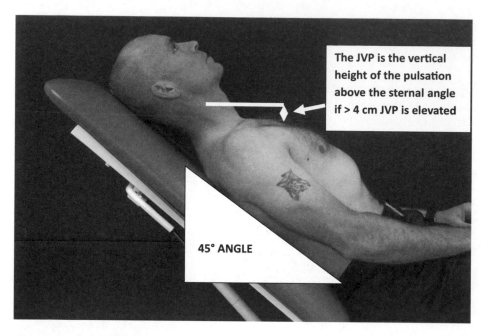

The JVP is the vertical height of the pulsation above the sternal angle if > 4 cm JVP is elevated

45° ANGLE

Figure 3.4 Position for measuring jugular venous pressure measurement (JVP)

Auscultation (heart and lungs)

Normal heart sounds are produced by the closing of the heart's valves, which cause changes to the flow of blood. The 1st heart sound (S_1) generates the 'lub' of the 'lub–dub' and is formed by the closure of the mitral (M_1) and tricuspid (T_1) valves at the start of ventricular systole. The 2nd heart sound (S_2) generates the 'dub' of the 'lub–dub' and is formed by the closure of the aortic (A_2) and pulmonary (P_2) valves at the start of ventricular diastole. The mitral (M_1) and aortic (A_2) are louder and occur before the tricuspid (T_1) and pulmonary (P_2) valves. Auscultation of these areas of the heart is obtained in the following positions (see Figure 3.5):

- Aortic (upper right 2nd intercostal space)
- Pulmonary (upper left 2nd intercostal space)
- Mitral (apex, in the left 5th intercostal space, in the mid-clavicular line)
- Tricuspid (left sternal edge for right ventricular area).

The 1st heart sound (S_1) 'lub' corresponds to the closure of the mitral (M_1) and tricuspid (T_1) valves. The sound may split on inspiration and is normal.

S_1 is accentuated or loud in: mitral stenosis (tapping apex beat), shortened PR interval and tachycardia.

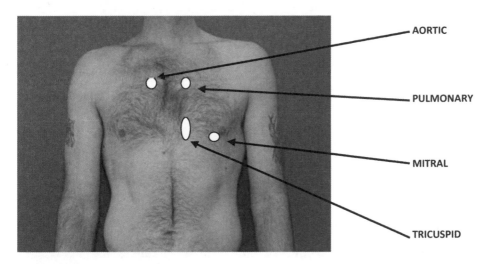

Figure 3.5 Auscultation positions

S$_1$ is diminished or soft in: mitral regurgitation, long PR interval (first degree heart block), heart block and diminished left ventricular contraction – infarction.

S$_1$ is variable in: third degree heart block, AF, nodal tachycardia and ventricular tachycardia (VT).

S$_1$ is widely split in: right and left bundle branch block (RBBB and LBBB).

The 2nd heart sound (S$_2$) 'dub' corresponds to the closure of the aortic (A$_2$) and pulmonary (P$_2$) valves. The most significant abnormality of A$_2$ is when it becomes diminished or softened due to aortic stenosis.

A$_2$ is accentuated or loud in: hypertension, tachycardia and transposition.

A$_2$ is widely split in: RBBB, hypertension, mitral regurgitation and deep inspiration.

A$_2$ is reversed split (*increased on expiration*) in: LBBB, aortic stenosis, and patent ductus arteriosus.

A single S$_2$ occurs in: severe aortic or pulmonary stenosis, hypertension, pulmonary atresia and Eisenmenger syndrome (*congenital ventricular septal defect*).

P$_2$ is accentuated or loud in: pulmonary hypertension, and P$_2$ is diminished or soft in: pulmonary stenosis (Swanton 2003, p10; Longmore *et al.* 2004, p44; Bickley and Szilagyi 2007, p160).

A 3rd heart sound (S_3) can occur just after the second heart sound (S_2). It is pathological in patients over 30 years of age, however:

- It can occur normally in fit young adults (athletes).
- Occurs abnormally in patients with heart failure.
- In patients with left heart failure – S_3 is best heard in the mitral area.
- In patients with right heart failure – S_3 is best heard in the tricuspid area.

A 4th heart sound (S_4) if produced occurs just before S_1 and is always abnormal. It signifies the atrial contraction against a stiffened ventricle which can be caused by aortic stenosis or hypertensive heart disease. It can also occur in heart failure.

Possible actions to be taken:

- Use the diaphragm of the stethoscope to auscultate for the high pitched sounds of S_1 'lub' and S_2 'dub'
- Auscultate and listen to all areas: M_1, T_1, and A_2, P_2
- Remember to listen on inspiration and on held expiration
- Listen at the apex, with the patient in the left lateral position, for low-pitched sounds of left sided S_3, S_4 and mitral stenosis, with the bell of the stethoscope
- Listen at the apex with the patient sitting up, leaning forward holding their breath after expiration for possible aortic regurgitation
- Lungs – Auscultate the base of the lungs and listen for evidence of cardiac failure crepitations and pleural effusion

---

Oedema

Oedema occurs due to the accumulation of excessive fluid in the interstitial tissue spaces and in patients with cardiac conditions should include both peripheral and pulmonary assessment.

- Bilateral oedema of the legs implies systemic disease, is dependent and the ankles and legs will be affected.
- In bed bound patients, the fluid moves to new areas and the sacrum will be affected.
- Patients with LVF can present with severe pulmonary oedema.

Abdomen

- Patients presenting with a ruptured abdominal aortic aneurysm (AAA) may present with signs and symptoms of hypovolaemic shock and intermittent or continuous abdominal pain that radiates to the back, iliac fossae or groins.

- A pulsatile mass may or may not be present.
- Ascites (*free fluid in the peritoneal cavity*) may occur in right heart failure.
- Check for bruits over the aorta and renal arteries (*indicative of artherosclerotic vascular disease*).

Peripheral pulses

- Palpate the patient's radial, brachial, carotid and dorsalis pedis pulses.
- Feel for radio-radial delay (*indicative of aortic arch thoracic aneurysm*).
- Auscultate for bruits over the carotid, aorta and renal arteries, particularly if there is inequality and or absence of the pulses (*this may be due to artherosclerosis in the older patient or vasculitis in the younger*).

Vital signs

Record the findings of each element of the assessment, which should, where appropriate, provide the following evidence regarding the patient:

- Respiratory rate, character and work of breathing
- Heart rate, character, volume and rhythm
- Blood pressure (BP)
- Electrocardiogram (where available a 12 lead ECG should be recorded when undertaking a cardiovascular system assessment, specifically when the patient presents with acute central chest pain)
- Blood glucose levels
- GCS neurological status
- Pupils
- Peak expiratory flow (PEF) (best of 3 readings)
- Temperature
- Oxygen saturations (SpO_2)
- Pain score
- Signs and symptoms of each system obtained during the secondary survey.

COMMON CARDIAC CONDITIONS

Angina

Angina pectoris is the name for the chest pain that arises from the heart due to myocardial ischaemia. The types of angina are *stable* (due to effort and relieved with rest and or medication), *unstable* (occurs at rest; has an increased risk of myocardial infarction), *decubitus* (caused by lying flat) and *Prinzmetal's* (caused by coronary artery spasm).

Signs and symptoms/presentations

- Central chest pain expressed as either tightness, heaviness or a crushing sensation.
- The pain may radiate to the neck, jaw, teeth and to either one or both arms.
- It can be exacerbated by cold weather, emotion (anger and excitement) and heavy meals.
- Diaphoresis, dyspnoea, nausea and faintness.
- ECG findings – ST segment depression, inverted or flattened 'T' waves.

Atrial fibrillation (AF)

Atrial fibrillation is a common arrhythmia which occurs in approximately 5%–10% of patients >65 years of age (Ballinger and Patchett 2007, p413), and is associated with an increased risk of thromboembolism.

Signs and symptoms/presentations

- Palpitations
- An irregularly irregular pulse
- Acute pulmonary oedema
- ECG findings – absent 'P' waves and irregular ventricular response (fine oscillation/fibrillation).

Ischaemic heart disease (IHD)

Ischaemia of the heart muscle arises from the imbalance between the supply and demand of oxygen to the myocardium. Atheroma of the coronary arteries coronary artery disease (CAD) is the leading cause of ischaemic heart disease due to obstruction of blood flow. It is the highest rated cause of death in the world (World Health Organization 2008, p2).

Signs and symptoms/presentations

- Patients with myocardial ischaemia caused by CAD can present with a variety of clinical presentations. These range from those presenting with stable angina, to the patient who may have an acute coronary syndrome (ACS) such as unstable angina and myocardial infarction.
- ECG findings – may include either ST segment depression, or ACS with or without ST elevation.

Acute myocardial infarction – heart attack

A myocardial infarction (MI) is caused by a rupture of an atherosclerotic plaque, resulting in thrombosis and occlusion of the coronary artery. Diagnosis is based upon presentation or assessment of two out of three of the following: (1) history (pain); (2) ECG changes; (3) cardiac markers (enzymes) rise. In the out-of-hospital arena, the paramedic/clinician is called to the first (acute central chest pain) and should be proficient in obtaining and interpreting the second (ECG changes).

Signs and symptoms/presentations
- Acute central chest pain >15 minutes duration.
- Patients may also present with no pain (silent MIs), this can occur in elderly, hypertensive or diabetic patients.
- Diaphoresis, dyspnoea, nausea, emesis, and appear pale and grey.
- ECG findings – ST elevation in two or more leads in the following views:
  - Inferior Infarct – In leads II, III, and AVF
  - Lateral Infarct – In leads I, II, and AVL
  - Anterior Infarct – In leads $V_2 - V_6$.
- Complications (cardiac arrest).

Possible actions to be taken:

- Undertake a cardiovascular assessment and obtain a 12 lead ECG recording
- If complicated establish cardiac arrest
- Manage in accordance with UK Resuscitation Council Guidelines (Resuscitation Council (UK) 2010, p60)

Heart failure (left ventricular failure – LVF, right ventricular failure – RVF and congestive cardiac failure – CCF)

Heart failure is the term used to describe the inability of the heart to pump effectively to meet the demands of the body, mainly due to inadequate cardiac output and blood pressure. It is a common condition with approximately 10% of people over 65 years of age developing the condition each year. The long-term prognosis is poor, as nearly 50% of patients die within 5 years of diagnosis (Ballinger and Patchett 2007, p423).

Signs and symptoms (LVF)
- Dyspnoea (associated with exertion)
- Tachycardia

- Tachypnoea
- Orthopnoea
- Dry nocturnal cough (associated with paroxysmal nocturnal dyspnoea)
- Coughing up pink frothy sputum streaked with haemoptysis (associated with acute pulmonary oedema)
- Wheeze
- Cold peripheries
- Muscle wasting and weight loss
- Basal lung crepitations
- Decreased systolic BP.

Signs and symptoms (RVF)
- Peripheral oedema (ankles and calves in ambulant patients)
- Sacral oedema (in bed bound patients)
- Abdominal distension (associated with ascites)
- Engorgement (puffiness) of the face
- Pulsation in the neck and face (associated with tricuspid regurgitation)
- Epistaxis
- Distended varicose veins
- Nausea
- Anorexia.

Signs and symptoms (CCF)
- Typically these present as a combination of RVF and LVF signs and symptoms.
- Consider that patients may also present with depression or the side effects of drug related treatment.
- Paramedic/clinicians should remember that the ECG itself is a poor indicator of heart size, however depending on the cause the ECG may show: ST depression – ischaemia, ST elevation – myocardial infarction, or left ventricular hypertrophy (LVH) – hypertension. There are various criteria in ascertaining LVH, the following are the Framingham criteria:
  - R AVL >11mm, R V4–6 >25mm
  - S V1–3 >25 mm, S V1 or V2 +
  - R V5 or V6 >35 mm, R I + S III >25 mm ((American Heart Association 1990) http://www.ecglibrary.com/lvhlah. 2011).

Cardiac arrhythmias

Some cardiac arrhythmias are common; these are often benign and intermittent. Occasionally, however, cardiac arrhythmias cause cardiac compromise. Depending on the arrhythmia, it may be classified as bradycardic or tachycardic in origin; remember that the patient may be asymptomatic.

Signs and symptoms

- Palpitations
- Chest pain
- Dyspnoea
- Collapse
- Hypotension
- Syncope
- Pulmonary oedema.

Possible actions to be taken:

- Obtain a 12 lead ECG recording and diagnose arrhythmia (bradycardia – tachycardia)
- Bradycardia – if <40 bpm or patient is symptomatic manage appropriately
- Tachycardia – ascertain from the ECG recording if it is broad complex (rate>100bpm and QRS complex >120ms) or narrow complex (rate>100bpm and QRS <120ms) and manage appropriately (Resuscitation Council (UK) ALS 2011)

Congenital heart disease

The diversity of congenital heart disease in adults is different from that of children due to adults being unlikely to have complex lesions. The commonest in order of occurrence are:

- Bicuspid aortic valve – In adulthood this is likely to develop aortic stenosis (AS) and/or aortic regurgitation (AR).
- Atrial septal defect (ASD) – A hole connecting the atria, the commonest of which (*ostium secondum*) occurs high in the septum. This type of ASD is often asymptomatic until adulthood. As the compliance of the ventricles diminishes with age the patient develops left to right shunting.

Signs and symptoms

- Dyspnoea
- Chest pain
- Haemoptysis
- Pulmonary hypertension
- Cyanosis.

Ventricular septal defect (VSD)

A hole connecting the ventricles which may be due to a congenital cause, it can also be acquired following a myocardial infarction. The signs are dependent on both the size and site; small holes tend to produce loud murmurs, whilst larger holes are linked with pulmonary hypertension.

Coarctation of the aorta

A congenital narrowing of the descending aorta, and more common in males. Signs include: radio-femoral delay, hypertension, weak femoral pulse and systolic murmurs.

Inherited cardiac conditions (ICCs)

ICCs are caused by mutations in the components of the heart's electrical and contractile system. Whilst it should be stressed that there are numerous conditions, there are in essence four main categories: arrhythmia syndromes, cardiomyopathies; inherited arteriopathies and muscular dystrophies (Burton *et al.* 2009).

Some examples from these categories include:

- *Long QT syndrome (LQTS)* – is characterised by a lengthening of the QT interval (measured from the beginning of the QRS to the end of the 'T' wave) on the ECG. This places the patient at risk of ventricular tachyarrhythmias; which may develop into syncope, cardiac arrest or sudden death.
- *Brugada syndrome* – is a disorder associated with one of a number of ECG patterns that are characterised by incomplete RBBB and ST elevations in the anterior precordial leads. Patients are likely to be young males who are otherwise healthy and may have normal CVS physical examination. Like LQTS they are prone to developing ventricular tachyarrhythmias and the associated problems of these (Dizon 2011).
- *Hypertrophic cardiomyopathy (HCM)* – is a disease affecting the myocardium and there are three main types. HCM also known as HOCM, dilated cardiomyopathy (DCM), and arrhythmogenic right ventricular cardiomyopathy (ARVC). In the UK the majority of sudden deaths in people <30 years of age are caused by inherited cardiomyopathies (British Heart Foundation 2009).

Valvular heart disease

Either through disease or age, the valves of the heart can and do become ineffectual and fail to close correctly and consequently leak (regurgitant) or they become narrow (stenotic) or both. The common consequences of this are acquired left ventricular valve problems: aortic or mitral stenosis, or aortic or mitral regurgitation.

Mitral stenosis – signs and symptoms
- Exertional dyspnoea
- Productive cough of blood tinged sputum and may be streaked with haemoptysis
- Malar flush on upper cheeks (dusky pink discoloration) occurs in severe stenosis
- Irregular pulse (as a result of atrial fibrillation)
- A loud 1st heart sound (S_1) is heard on auscultation at the apex.

Mitral regurgitation – signs and symptoms
- Pulmonary oedema (acute regurgitation)
- Exertional dyspnoea, fatigue and lethargy (chronic regurgitation)
- The 1st heart sound (S_1) is soft.

Aortic stenosis – signs and symptoms
- Patients usually have no symptoms until the valve is reduced to ⅓ of its size
- Angina
- Exertional syncope
- Congestive heart failure
- Carotid pulse may be slow rising (plateau pulse)
- ECG shows evidence of LVH. (If severe and demonstrating a LV strain pattern)
- ECG may show depressed ST segment and inversion of the 'T' wave in leads I, AVL, V5 and V6.

Aortic regurgitation – signs and symptoms
- Patients with chronic regurgitation remain asymptomatic and then develop:
- Dyspnoea and orthopnoea
- Fatigue (due to LVF)
- Collapsing pulse (with wide pulse pressure)
- ECG displays evidence of LVH.

OTHER CONSIDERATIONS

Ethnicity

Ethnicity is recognised as a risk factor for developing coronary heart disease (Astin and Atkin 2010, p2). A gene mutation that almost guarantees the development of heart disease is carried by 60 million people of Asian origin (BBC News 2009).

Communication

Patients whose first language is not English can and do when confronted with pain, and or stress, revert to their native language. By assessing a CVS emergency effectively the paramedic/clinician should consider this factor and manage accordingly.

Destination/receiving specialist units/non-conveyance

The Department of Health (DH) has stipulated that primary angioplasty is the preferred management of a heart attack and patients should be transferred by the paramedic to a 24/7 primary angioplasty unit. Where distances or local variations prevent this (i.e. some units not being open 24/7), then thrombolysis should be administered (if within local NHS Ambulance Service Trust guidelines) either by the paramedic or by the receiving emergency department (DH 2008, p21).

Social/family/carer/guardian

The worst case scenario when caring for a patient with a cardiac condition is that they may die. This will, understandably, have a disastrous effect on the family. In situations where the patient is transported for care, the paramedic/clinician should also consider the implications of their actions. Remember you may transport a patient whose relatives are with you, but they may also have to witness your resuscitation efforts, if the patient's condition deteriorates en route. Consider this possibility prior to agreeing to convey the relatives with the patient.

Ethical and legal

The paramedic/clinician may in certain situations need to consider the possibility of implementing and acting upon either Do Not Attempt Resuscitation (DNAR) directives or Living Wills in relation to the patient and the emergency cardiac situation, and or having to implement the Recognition of Life Extinct (ROLE) procedure.

CHAPTER KEY POINTS

- Identify time critical problems within the primary survey and manage appropriately.
- Undertake and interpret the 12 lead ECG.
- Undertake a complete secondary survey and history including the cardiovascular physical examination.
- Decide on the appropriate and opportune time to move the patient to hospital.

Abdominal and gastro-intestinal assessment

Chris Baker

The gastro-intestinal (GI) and urinary system organs are incorporated within the abdominal pelvic region, however the *Alimentary Canal* commences at the mouth and progresses down through the 'thoracic' cavity before it reaches the abdominal cavity. Due to the complex anatomy which varies between genders, assessment is often approached with concern by the paramedic/clinician. However, by following the format described, problems that may be of serious concern can be identified. This chapter aims to provide a structured systematic approach to the abdominal and GI assessment and will assist the paramedic/clinician in identifying abnormalities.

SCENE ASSESSMENT

As with any scene, paramedic/clinicians can gain a great deal of information from the initial assessment, whether it is an accident where the mechanism of injury (MOI) can highlight an index of suspicion of damage to the abdominal organs and systems. When approaching a patient who has been involved in a road traffic collision (RTC), consideration must be given to the MOI and the phases of the collision itself, specifically the deceleration forces on the vehicle/s, the patient, their organs and any subsequent collision and the manner in which these affect the body (Caroline 2008, Chapter 17, p14).

Alternatively, it could involve attending a patient with an illness, where positioning or movement of the patient may provide clues to the condition before the first question is asked. The patient may be either very still and deliberately ensuring minimal movement whilst experiencing pain, as in the case of peritonitis, or be unable to remain in one position, and writhing in agony as seen in uteric or biliary colic. Alternatively the paramedic/clinician may see or identify:

- Medications pertinent to conditions affecting the gastro-intestinal and urinary system.

- Receptacles containing vomit, it is important to note consistency and colour, for example may appear as dark ground coffee dregs (indicative of bleeding).
- There may be specific smells which could suggest gastro-intestinal or urinary upsets, such as a urinary tract infection (UTI), or diarrhoea.
- The patient may exhibit signs of long term alcohol abuse (alcohol abuse occurring within the home environment or outside), which can have serious effects on the liver, kidneys, and lining of the digestive tract.
- Evidence of smoking and its long-term use should prompt the paramedic/clinician to consider potential problems such as peptic ulcers, or cancers affecting the GI system including stomach, colon, pancreas or liver. Smoking can also affect the liver's ability to process toxins and remove them from the body which can also mean that higher doses of medication will be required in order to return a therapeutic effect (National Digestive Diseases Information Clearinghouse 2006).

Smokers are at a higher risk of developing:

- Crohn's disease
- Gallstones
- Gastritis (smokers >50 years of age)
- Increased pain in patients with irritable bowel syndrome (IBS).

PRIMARY SURVEY

The initial scene assessment may allow the paramedic/clinician the opportunity to begin making a decision on whether the patient is time critical or non-time critical. The clinical signs gained during the primary survey will assist in this diagnosis; however, the experienced paramedic/clinician will often know that a patient's condition is either serious or time critical from the moment they *set eyes* on them.

Even if the patient initially appears well, remember as with any time critical conditions, deterioration can be rapid. The paramedic/clinician should remember that patient assessment is a fluid process and ensure that they undertake the abdominal/GI primary survey properly to make certain that subtle signs will not be overlooked, and obtain the evidence to identify if the patient has a time critical condition or not.

DANGER

The matter of safety must be considered as with any scene or emergency. The appropriate personal protective equipment (PPE) must always be worn and the paramedic/clinician must consider any risks involved and other resources required.

Abdominal injuries and illnesses of the gastro-intestinal and urinary systems have an increased risk of body fluids whether they are of either a vomit or bloodborne origin. Consider the possible dangers during your initial assessment of the scene and consider if have minimised these dangers or taken necessary precautions, or decide if any further professional assistance may be required.

RESPONSE

As the paramedic/clinician introduces themselves to the patient they note the patient's ability to respond using verbal communication. Questions such as *what happened?* and *why have you called for us today?* offer the conscious patient the opportunity to introduce their presenting complaint. Remember that patients in severe pain may have difficulty communicating fluently. Consideration can once again be given to the position of the patient, and the unresponsive or unconscious patient who will require rapid intervention to protect their airway. At this stage an assessment utilising the AVPU scale will suffice.

AIRWAY

When attending a patient presenting with a problem of gastro-intestinal origin, the patency of the airway can be affected by the risk of aspiration of gastric contents. Remember that intermittent projectile vomiting in adults refers to periodic episodes of vomiting that are unusually violent or forceful. However, conditions such as bleeding oesophageal varices and ruptured peptic (gastric and duodenal) ulcers may also lead to the risk of blood, causing obstruction to the airway.

Possible actions to be taken:

- Consider causes of airway obstruction (vomit and/or blood)
- Suction as appropriate
- Position patient appropriately
- Consider 'C' spine techniques if appropriate

BREATHING

Pain pathologically increases the respiratory rate. Consider GI conditions that could increase or slow the respiratory rate such as hyperventilation or Kussmaul respirations (deep sighing respirations) classically seen in diabetic ketoacidosis (DKA) (Longmore *et al.* 2004, p74). Alternatively, is the patient presenting with hypoventilation due to vomiting and excessive loss of gastric hydrochloric acid (HCI)? (Yaseen and Thomas 2009).

- Remember that GI problems can and do present as chest pain. Heart attack pain sometimes feels like indigestion or heartburn, or patients present with nausea and vomiting.
- Can you smell hepatic foetor on their breath (indicates liver disease and smells like pear drops)?
- Consider the respiratory effort and ascertain if they are using accessory muscles or if they have diaphragmatic breathing.
- If the patient presents with a SpO_2 below 95%, then oxygen should be administered appropriately (BTS 2008).
- When listening to breath sounds consider the anatomical relationship between the thoracic and abdominal cavities (during respiration the external markings for the abdomen change and the organs move up and down within the cavities).
- Damage to the diaphragm may result in the contents of the abdominal cavity entering the thoracic cavity, such as a hiatus hernia (occurs when part of the stomach pushes up into the chest). Alternatively the patient may have an injury to the thoracic cavity which leaks through the damaged diaphragm and causes irritation/damage to the abdominal cavity contents.

Possible actions to be taken:

- Identify cause of dyspnoea (manage appropriately)
- If respiratory rate <10 or >29 breaths per minute assist ventilations
- Ensure the patient is not hypoxic and administer oxygen appropriately to patient's illness or injury

---

CIRCULATION

Having assessed the pulse and blood pressure including rate, regularity and efficiency, consider the conditions which could cause visible changes to the integumentary and/or circulatory system and are relative to the gastro-intestinal and genito-urinary systems. On approach the paramedic/clinician will have already made an initial assessment of the patient's colour; it must be remembered that some patients are naturally pale whilst others are naturally flushed. This can be verified by asking relatives and friends of the patient if this colour is normal for them. Alternatively, are they presenting with other visible signs of abdominal GI problems or complaining of specific related signs and symptoms:

- Does the patient present with hot, flushed skin suggestive of pyrexia and possible infection (Raftery and Lim 2004)?
- Do they appear jaundiced (icterus: yellowish discoloration of the skin associated with increased levels of bilirubin circulating, due to liver conditions and haemolytic anaemia) (Bickley 2003)?
- Are they presenting with haematemesis?
- Are they complaining of haematuria?
- Or complaining of melaena?
- Is the patient in a dehydrated state?

Haematemesis

Is often described as particles resembling coffee grounds in appearance. It must be remembered that this will be blood which has been partially digested by gastric juices after being in the stomach for some time. Fresh haematemesis (bright red blood) will be due to recent bleeding high in the gastrointestinal system, such as bleeding in the oesophagus or mouth, and care should be taken to consider the patient history and possibility of the blood originating within the respiratory system. Consider the causes of the bleed which include:

- Peptic ulcers
- Cancers of the digestive tract
- Blood thinning medications
- Oesophageal varices.

If the patient has had recent facial trauma, or suffered a nose bleed, is there the possibility that the particles resembling coffee grounds are due to blood swallowed after either of these events, rather than blood originating in the digestive system?

Haematuria

May be visible and occur in genitourinary trauma, but this is not always the case. The source of the bleeding may be suggested by a careful history; haematuria that occurs at the start of micturition is normally associated with urethral disease, whilst in haematuria that occurs at the end of micturition the prostrate or bladder base may be the source. However, if the bleeding is seen as an even discoloration throughout the urine, then the origin could be either in the bladder or above (Ballinger and Patchett 2008, p339).

Genito-urinary damage is likely to occur in patients with blunt or penetrating trauma to the back or flanks. Special attention should be paid to patients with bruises, contusions or tenderness around these areas, as damage may have occurred to the kidneys or ureters (Greaves *et al.* 2008, p267).

Damage to the bladder or urethra may lead to haematuria whilst other causes include glomerulonephritis (inflammation of the glomeruli within the nephron of the kidneys), which may be due to infection or long term use of non-steroidal anti-inflammatory drugs (NSAID). Cancer anywhere along the urinary tract, kidney and bladder stones, and use of medications that can thin the blood (*aspirin, clopidogrel*) are also causative factors.

Melaena

Bleeding from the lower part of the gastrointestinal tract, which is seen as dark tarry stools, whilst the term haematochezia may be used to describe red or maroon coloured stools due to fresh blood as would be associated with a bleeding rectal pile.

Dehydration

The physical signs of dehydration are usually only apparent with moderate to severe dehydration. The first physical symptom is thirst, and the patient has a dry and parched mouth. The tongue can be inspected to see if it is wet, and the eyes should be glistening. Skin turgor is lost with marked dehydration (Epstein *et al.* 2008). Skin turgor can be assessed by pinching the skin on the neck or the anterior chest wall, although many practitioners check the skin on the back of the hand as this is less intrusive for the patient. When pinched and released, hydrated skin should immediately spring back to its original location, whilst dehydrated skin returns slowly. This test is unreliable in those whose skin may be losing its elasticity as part of the natural process of ageing.

Possible actions to be taken:

- If haematemesis is present, ascertain if dark or fresh (manage airway as appropriate)
- If no external haemorrhage visible but signs and symptoms of shock present, consider internal haemorrhage and manage as appropriate (*see Trauma Assessment: Chapter 7*)
- Ascertain the colour and frequency of the haematuria (record findings)
- Ascertain the colour and frequency of the melaena (record findings)
- Assess skin turgor (lost in marked dehydration) (manage shock accordingly, see Chapter 7).

DISABILITY

Assess the patient's level of consciousness and record the appropriate element of the AVPU framework. Assess the pupils and ascertain if they are: Pupils Equal and Round; React to Light and Accommodation (PERRLA). Specifically assess the patient's blood glucose levels. Consider if the abdominal GI condition has affected their ability to undertake normal and well activities of daily living (ADLs) (*a normally fit person can become incapacitated due to severe diarrhoea or haematemesis*), consider the effects on an elderly person living alone or single parent with small children.

EXPOSE/EXAMINE/ENVIRONMENT

Expose and examine the patient, look for scars, visible pulsations (aneurysm), masses, distension, striae (stretch marks), hernia, bruising, and if trauma has occurred check for evidence of penetrating injury or eviscerated organs. Remember to consider consent, especially in emergency situations (DH 2009, p5).

Careful attention must be given to the sections of the abdomen and pelvis which could have been susceptible to damage, and the structures within these areas. The paramedic/clinician is reminded that the thorax and the abdomen contain the majority of the body's vital organs (Panté and Pollak 2010). Contemplating injuries to the abdomen will lead the paramedic/clinician to being armed with an index of suspicion as to potential findings upon examination. By dividing the abdomen into quadrants (see Figure 4.1) and then considering the organs of the GI and urinary systems located within them, the paramedic/clinician will be assisted in looking for specific signs and symptoms related to problems of the organs contained therein.

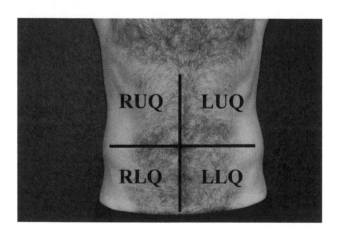

Figure 4.1 Abdominal quadrants

Possible actions to be taken:

- Remember patient dignity and obtain consent from the patient prior to exposing them for the examination
- Expose the abdomen and look for *scars, masses, distension, visible pulsations etc.*
- Evidence of trauma: ascertain if there are any penetrating injuries or eviscerated organs (*manage appropriately, see Trauma Assessment: Chapter 7*)
- Assess each quadrant and be aware of the potential damage which may have occurred to underlying organs
- Evaluate – transfer to the appropriate treatment centre (*if time critical*), or move on to the secondary survey

SECONDARY SURVEY

Abdominal examination should be undertaken in a structured format. It can be undertaken in a rapid and systematic manner when the patient presents with a life threatening condition, however there is little in the way of interventions which can be undertaken in the out-of-hospital arena. Undertaking a focused history and assessment of the abdomen, gastro-intestinal (GI) and genito-urinary (GU) systems will enable the paramedic/clinician to establish illnesses and problems that have not been identified within the primary survey. Due to the nature and complexity of both illnesses and injuries involving these systems the paramedic/clinician may find assessing and diagnosing them a daunting task. However, by using the following structured format and examination process the paramedic/clinician will be provided the opportunity of detecting signs and symptoms of underlying medical conditions to the systems and associated organs.

HISTORY

Presenting complaint

Ascertain the reason why the patient has requested the attendance of a paramedic/clinician, it may be trauma or illness related, but may be as vague as *a pain in my stomach*. It may be the patient presents with symptoms that the paramedic/clinician identifies, and from these, the paramedic/clinician may gain some insight into the questions they consider relevant asking to enable them to make a differential diagnosis and form an initial impression.

The presenting symptoms are and can be related to either the GI or GU problem. Patients with a GI history may present with the following symptoms:

- Abdominal pain
- Mouth ulcers, dysphagia, indigestion, dyspepsia
- Appetite or weight changes
- Nausea, emesis, haematemesis
- Changes to bowel habits: diarrhoea, constipation
- Bleeding per rectum (PR), melaena
- Pruritus, dark urine, pale stools.

However with a GU history, the patient may present with the following symptoms:

- Fever
- Loin pain, dysuria, haematuria
- Urethral or vaginal discharge
- Painful intercourse, dyspareunia
- Menses (discharge from the uterus during menstruation)
- Menarche (the first appearance of menstruation)
- Menopause (period when ovaries cease functioning and menstruation stops) (Longmore *et al.* 2004, p52).

History of presenting complaint

What is the history of the presenting complaint? The patient who complains of acute abdominal pain, which has increased since eating a meal a few hours ago, may have an entirely different diagnosis to the patient who complains of abdominal pain but has a two day history of vomiting and diarrhoea. If the patient presents with abdominal pain, the paramedic should utilise the OPQRSTA framework, to assist them in gaining a more thorough impression of the presenting complaint.

Onset – Ask if the pain developed slowly or rapidly, was it over the course of minutes, hours or days?

Provocation – Ask about what eases or makes it worse? Look at the positioning of the patient, and the amount they are moving to confirm this?

Quality – Ask them to describe the pain, do they explain it as a: vague, stabbing, sharp, dull, crushing, cramping, burning or colicky pain?

Radiation – Does the pain move anywhere?

Severity – Ask them to score the pain. Utilise your local pain score, normally that of 0 to 10, where 0 is no pain and 10 the worst the patient can imagine.

Timing – How long has the pain lasted? What was the patient doing when the pain began? Did the pain wake the patient, or follow a particular event? Is there any history of trauma that the pain may be related back to?

Associated symptoms – Has the pain been associated with bowel movements, urination, flatulence or vomiting? Did it build in a crescendo and then drop off?

The paramedic/clinician when clarifying the history of the presenting complaint should ask relevant questions to ascertain the appropriate information. The following questions may be appropriate for a patient who presents with abdominal pain and vomiting.

- Did the vomiting precede the pain?
- Did they feel nauseous before they vomited?
- Frequency – how many times have they vomited?
- What is the consistency and character – watery, bile, faecal, blood, coffee dreg particles?

The following questions may be appropriate for an elderly patient who is complaining of abdominal pain and constipation:

- When did you last open your bowels?
- Did you have any pain on passing stools?
- Has the patient or their relatives/carers noticed a change in the smell of their faeces, changes in colour? If so, how long have these changes been taking place over?
- Was there any blood present? If so, was it fresh blood, or black and tarry?
- Does the patient have an absolute constipation associated with 'colicky' pain?
- Is there an associated swelling of the abdomen?
- Has the patient recently changed their lifestyle? For patients who have given up smoking, this may be the cause of the constipation.

Colic is defined as severe pain resulting from periodic spasm in an abdominal organ and is often associated with the peristaltic wave moving through the digestive system (Brooker 2008).

Past medical history

Does the patient have a history of GI or GU problems? Do they still have their appendix? Has the patient had recent surgery, or previous operations?

Ask if the patient has any recurring or previous GI or GU illnesses, including ulcers (peptic or duodenal), gallbladder disease, inflammatory bowel disease, jaundice, hepatitis, urinary tract infections, renal colic, gout, analgesic use, hypertension or GI bleeding. Ask female patients about their last menstrual period (LMP) (Schilling McCann 2003). When considering GI bleeds the following guidance may be of benefit:

- Is there unexplained syncope? (*should raise suspicion of concealed GI bleed*)
- Does the visible bleed originate from the upper or lower GI tract?
- When did the bleeding begin?
- Is there a history of GI disease?
- Is there a history of aspirin or non-steroidal anti-inflammatory drug (NSAID) use?
- Does the patient take beta blockers or calcium-channel blockers (which can mask tachycardia in the shocked patient)?
- Does the patient take iron tablets or have they consumed beetroot/drinks containing red dye? (may alter the colour of stools)
- Is there a history of anti-coagulatory or anti-platelet therapy?
- Is there a history of liver disease/abdominal surgery or alcohol abuse?
- Did the haematemesis present after an increase in intra-abdominal pressure (from retching or coughing), or several episodes of non-bloody emesis?
- What is the character and quantity of blood loss?

If blood loss is not visible ask the patient or relatives to estimate colour/volume (PR blood loss is difficult to estimate). The blood acts as a laxative, but repeated blood/liquid stool, or just blood, is associated with more severe blood loss than maroon/black solid stool (JRCALC 2006a).

Drug/medication history

Some medications will cause issues with the GI system, such as antibiotics leading to diarrhoea, pain killers leading to constipation. Does the patient need to take medication for a problem with another body system which has a direct effect upon the gastro-intestinal or urinary system, such as frusemide, which would result in excessive urination, or antibiotics which could lead to thrush due to lowering of the defensive fauna contained within the urinary tracts? Ask if they have or currently use: steroids, non-steroidal anti-inflammatory drugs (NSAIDs), or *the pill*, if female. Also ask if they have recently had any dietary changes, especially as those who have changed to a high fibre diet may present with swollen abdomens and excessive flatulence.

Social/family medical history

Does the patient require care at home? Are they receiving this care, or are they a potentially *vulnerable adult*? Is there a family history which may be of relevance to the presenting complaint, such as a parent who suffers with Crohn's disease? (Schilling McCann 2003) The paramedic/clinician should consider that certain GI conditions may be hereditary and therefore the patient should be questioned regarding their family history of the following conditions:

- Colon cancer
- Polyps
- Irritable bowel syndrome
- Stomach ulcers
- Jaundice
- Diabetes
- Alcoholism
- Crohn's disease
- Ulcerative colitis – a superficial inflammatory condition affecting the colon. It always involves the rectum and spreads continuously for a variable distance. The history will reveal blood in diarrhoea, mucus and pus being passed rectally, loss of weight, anaemia and abdominal pain (Brooker 2008, p495).

Regarding the patient's social history, the paramedic/clinician should ascertain information about the following:

- Smoking
- Alcohol
- Overseas travel
- Tropical illnesses
- Occupational exposures
- Sexual orientation (Longmore *et al*. 2004, p52).

EXAMINATION

When considering the examination of the patient it remains important to consider the modesty of the patient, and the fact that certain patients may find some of the questions somewhat embarrassing. It is also important to note that in order to gain an accurate impression, the paramedic/clinician will need to ask some of the embarrassing questions in a skilful and tactful manner. The history will have led the paramedic/clinician to the site of any abdominal pain. Tell the patient to let you know if you cause them pain during the physical examination. Exposure of the abdomen in order to inspect, auscultate, palpate and percuss remains an important aspect, but consider gaining the trust of the patient, consent to the examination, and the location in which you choose to undertake the examination. When operating as a mixed sex crew, paramedic/clinicians may find it necessary to change roles for the benefit of the patient (depending on gender of the patient) and also as children and young adults may find it harder to answer questions related to digestive and urinary habit, sexual activity or menstrual cycle.

The examination of the abdomen should be undertaken with the patient lying flat, arms at their side, using inspection, auscultation, palpation and then percussion, as palpation of the abdomen prior to auscultation may have an effect upon the frequency and location of bowel sounds (Schilling McCann 2003).

Inspection

Does the abdomen appear symmetrical; is it a normal shape with no protrusions? Bulges may be due to distension of the bladder above the level of the symphysis pubis, if low in the abdomen, or be due to a hernia. The bulge or (mass) may be seen to be pulsatile, suggesting that the patient may have an abdominal aortic aneurysm, for this reason a bulge should not be overlooked. If the patient is conscious, they may well be aware of a hernia, and of the normal appearance of this protrusion. Ask the patient in these instances whether the hernia has changed shape or size. Patients may also be aware of aortic aneurysms, and of their normal size, possibly even prognosis. An aneurysm is usually painless, so be aware that pain may be an indicator of the imminent or actual rupture of the aorta. Also examine the abdomen for rashes, dilated veins showing near the surface due to venous obstruction, and the presence of jaundice due to liver conditions.

Striae, or stretch marks on the patient's abdomen, may be different colours for different reasons. If the patient has previously lost weight or had skin stretched due to pregnancy then these lines will be silver in colour. New striae can be pink or blue, and may be seen with weight gain, and in patients with darker skin these may be dark brown in colour. Cushing's syndrome is caused by an excess of cortisol production by the adrenal glands or by excessive use of cortisol or other similar steroid hormones (Caroline 2008, Chapter 29, p17). This condition causes thinning of the skin and easy bruising, and can lead to pink or purple striae on the abdomen. These may also be seen on the thighs, breasts and shoulders. These patients are likely to have previously presented with life threatening illnesses including asthma, rheumatoid arthritis and some allergies, which will have been ascertained during the gaining of the patient history.

The abdomen may be protruding, and the size and shape of the rest of the patient requires consideration when this is the case. In a person of average weight, the abdomen is normally non-protruding, becoming rounded as more weight is carried. When the abdomen is protruding or distended it may be due to patient obesity, or pregnancy. When considering swelling of the abdomen, the five 'F's should be considered as causes. These are:

- *Flatus* – or gas in the intestinal tract.
- *Faeces* – contained within the digestive system. This may be palpated when undertaking deep palpation in the lower left quadrant of the abdomen. This is quite normal prior to a bowel movement, and should be soft if palpated.
- *Foetus* – will involve questioning around the patient's sexual activity, contraception and menstrual cycle.
- *Fat* – may bring considerations as to patient's diet, but can make a thorough palpation of the abdomen difficult.
- *Fluid* – ascites, ovarian cyst (Cox 2010, p 102).

Ascites is simply free fluid in the abdominal cavity due to an underlying oedema, and when palpating the abdomen a palpable fluid wave may be observed (Brooker 2008). Ascites is most typically seen in patients who suffer from liver disease, but it can also be appreciated with underlying malignancy and, to a certain extent, with renal and cardiac insufficiency (Caroline 2008, Ch. 19 p13).

Other waves which may be witnessed when inspecting the abdomen include that of peristalsis (the involuntary movements of the muscles of the digestive tract as they move food through the digestive system), although these are normally slight and more prominent in individuals with low body fat. When easily visible, stronger rippling waves can be seen that may be an indicator of a bowel obstruction, and would be associated with absent bowel sounds beyond the point of the movement. These will often be associated with colicky pain.

Undertake 'The Cough Test' assessment – look at the patient's face and ask them to 'cough'. If this causes pain, flinching or they move their hands to protect the abdomen, all of which are positive signs then suspect peritonitis (Longmore *et al.* 2004, p52).

When inspecting the abdomen of trauma patients, the paramedic/clinician should consider certain bruising patterns which are worthy of note. These include both Cullen's sign and Grey Turner's sign. Cullen's sign is bruising around the umbilicus, whilst Grey Turner's sign is bruising along the flank, due to retroperitoneal bleeding. The latter is indicative of blunt force haemorrhage, aortic leaking, pancreatic or renal bleeding. Both of these signs should alert the paramedic/clinician to retroperitoneal haemorrhage. Seat belt marking and pattern bruising may be present in road traffic incidents and related trauma. Once again it is important for the paramedic/clinician to consider the organs which may be damaged.

Possible actions to be taken:

- Inspect the abdomen and ascertain evidence of either visible pulsations, scars, masses, hernia, peristalsis, striae or distension

- If distension is present identify the cause (five 'F's)
- Undertake the cough test
- In trauma patients look for Cullen's and Grey Turner's signs
- Manage conditions accordingly (*see Trauma Assessment: Chapter 7*)

Auscultation

This provides important information about the movement of fluid and gases within the abdominal cavity. Listening for bowel sounds can be a confusing subject for the paramedic/clinician, with various texts suggesting differing optimal time/s spent listening to the abdomen between ten seconds and seven minutes. The latter is unlikely to be of benefit in the emergency situation, and would certainly not be pertinent to consider in a patient with a potentially time critical condition. For each patient, a time versus benefit analysis will need to be made in order to decide how long each quadrant will be listened to, and what the paramedic/clinician can gain from such an examination. In addition to this issue, and as with any auscultation of a patient, the environment needs to be quiet enough to allow the sounds to be heard. Finally, regular practice is required in order to ensure that the paramedic/clinician has gained a baseline of normal abdominal sounds.

When a patient is complaining of pain in a specific quadrant of the abdomen best practice is to commence the auscultation in the quadrant immediately adjacent to the *pain* quadrant in a clockwise direction. For example, if the pain is experienced in the left upper quadrant then commence the assessment in the left lower quadrant (see Figure 4.2). This will ensure that this routine will be followed when undertaking percussion and palpation of the abdomen and the purpose of this will be discussed shortly.

- Use the diaphragm of the stethoscope and begin by placing it in the chosen quadrant nearest to the umbilicus.
- Good practice dictates that both the stethoscope head and the hands of the paramedic/clinician are warm enough to ensure patient comfort.
- When time is of the essence, divide the quadrant into a further four quadrants, and then place the stethoscope in the centre of each of these smaller quadrants for 15 seconds, beginning in the quadrant closest to the umbilicus and moving in a clockwise fashion. In the time critical patient, this assessment is of limited benefit (Schilling McCann 2003).
- When time is not of the essence, the stethoscope is placed in each of the four quadrants spending at least 2 minutes in each quadrant in order to allow enough time to hear sounds (although a period of up to 7 minutes may be required).

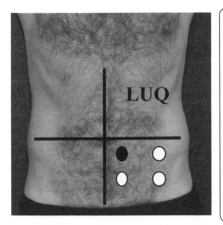

If the pain presents in left upper quadrant (LUQ):

- Commence auscultation in left lower quadrant (LLQ)
- Continue in a clockwise direction auscultating the 'pain' quadrant last
- If time is of the essence, divide each quadrant into four, commencing nearest to the umbilicus and continue in a clockwise direction

Figure 4.2 Auscultation of abdominal quadrants if the patient reports pain in their left upper quadrant (LUQ)

The majority of bowel sounds are normal. Normal bowel sounds are gurgling sounds (usually occurring 5 to 35 per minute) that can be heard with the diaphragm of a stethoscope. The paramedic/clinician needs to be able to identify abnormal sounds that will assist with the assessment of the patient's health. Abnormal sounds are described as absent, hypoactive or hyperactive.

- *Absent bowel sounds* – occurs when the paramedic/clinician is unable to hear any bowel sounds after listening to the abdomen, and indicates a lack of intestinal activity. It is also known as 'ileus' (where the intestinal muscle ceases movement and bowel contents remain in situ, presenting the same problems found with a bowel obstruction). Various medical conditions can lead to this but it is important to evaluate it further because gas, secretions, and intestinal contents can accumulate and rupture the bowel wall, although absent sounds often indicates constipation.
- *Hypoactive bowel sounds* – indicates a slowing of intestinal activity. This may be normal as occurs whilst sleeping or may suggest bowel obstruction, peritonitis, or generalised peritonitis, which is often secondary to a disease in the abdominal-pelvic organs. Some medications may affect bowel movements, for instance narcotics may slow movement through the digestive system, as will drugs designed to halt diarrhoea.

■ *Hyperactive sounds* – are described as an increase in intestinal activity (loud and high pitched). These are associated with progressive bowel obstruction, large amounts of fluid and gas accumulating in the bowel, and are an ominous sound which could suggest impending bowel paralysis. They are also associated with diarrhoea, hunger or after meals, so consider asking the patient about timing of their last meal.

Auscultate for hepatic bruits in patients with liver disease. Listen for bruits over the renal, iliac and femoral arteries as well as the aorta (Schilling McCann 2003, p197). Renal artery stenosis may be the cause of hypertension.

Auscultate for flow bruits over the femoral arteries, as patients with intermittent claudication may have arteries that have become narrowed due to atheroma (Cox 2010, p105).

Abdominal sounds should always be evaluated in conjunction with symptoms such as nausea, vomiting, the presence or absence of bowel movements or gas. When hypo- or hyperactive bowel sounds are present with abnormal symptoms, the paramedic/clinician must remember that continued evaluation is important.

Possible actions to be taken:

■ Identify the area of pain; commence auscultation in the next clockwise quadrant
■ Listen between 2 and 7 minutes, continue in a clockwise direction
■ If time is of the essence, sub-divide the quadrant into four and auscultate each area for 15 seconds
■ Identify and record any hypo/hyperactive or absent bowel sound activity
■ Auscultate for bruits over the renal, iliac and femoral arteries

---

Palpation

Palpation of the abdomen is undertaken using a light and deep palpation technique in each of the four quadrants. Initially palpate each quadrant lightly (1 to 2 cm depth). Light palpation involves placing your hand onto the patient's abdomen, and then flexing your fingers so that your finger tips push into their abdomen. The abdomen should be soft to the touch, and there should be no tenderness upon palpation. Then if appropriate increase the palpation depth (4 to 6 cm depth). When considering this action in an obese patient; the paramedic/clinician could apply one hand on top of the other to assist with this aspect of the examination.

Commence palpation in the appropriate quadrant, away from the site of pain. Whilst palpating observe the patient's face for signs of pain and establish if the palpation hurts them, due to either of the following:

- *Tenderness* – this can be superficial, deep or rebound
- *Rebound tenderness* – occurs from movement of inflamed viscera of peritonitis against parietal peritoneum. *Assessment* – To check for rebound tenderness (pain increased on release rather than on deep palpation), palpate (press) slowly on the tender area and then quickly release
- *Guarding* – reflex contraction of the abdominal muscles as you palpate
- *Rigidity* – sustained tension of abdominal muscles which become hard and inflexible (indicative of peritonitis).

Palpation should identify which organs are enlarged or tender, whether additional fluid is accumulating within the cavity, or if there are any masses, and whether these are solid or pulsatile. Locating pulsatile masses whilst palpating requires careful consideration as to the need for deep palpation. This could lead to damage to weak artery walls and a contained mass becoming an exsanguinating haemorrhage.

As has previously been stated, great care should be taken if a pulsatile mass is felt, and consideration should also be given to palpating a rigid abdomen. Palpating a rigid abdomen due to peritoneal inflammation could cause increased pain or, more importantly, rupture an inflamed abdominal organ.

Percussion

The purpose of percussion in the abdominal assessment is to discover the borders of the abdominal organs, their size, density and location and if they contain air or fluid. Hollow organs produce tympany, like the sound of a drum. Whilst solid organs produce dull sounds. Dullness may be due to faeces, fluid or a solid mass, it may also be due to a tumour. For instance, dullness over the ovaries could be due to a large ovarian cyst. Percussion is utilised to ascertain the size of the liver and spleen and to ascertain if there is air in the stomach or bowel.

To percuss the liver and estimate its size, start in the right mid-clavicular line and percuss below the umbilicus with tympany and percuss upward towards the liver, when it changes to dullness. Mark to indicate the liver border. Then in the same mid-clavicular line, percuss down from lung resonance to liver dullness. This indicates the lower border of the liver. Mark this and measure between the two lines. This is the height of the liver. When the spleen enlarges it does so anteriorly, downwards and medially. As it does so it replaces the tympany of the stomach and colon with dullness. Percuss in the lowest interspace in the left anterior axillary line for tympany. Ask the patient to take a deep breath and percuss on inspiration. The percussion note should remain tympanic, if it changes to dullness this suggests splenomegaly, and is known as a positive splenic percussion sign.

> **Possible actions to be taken:**
> - Palpate and percuss the four quadrants
> - Percuss and identify the size and borders of the liver and the spleen
> - Ascertain if there is air in the stomach or bowel
> - Percuss in several directions away from tympany or resonance to dullness to outline edges
> - In the LUQ a large dull area suggests splenomegaly (*enlarged spleen*)

REVIEW OF SYSTEMS AND VITAL SIGNS

When assessing a patient with inflammatory gastrointestinal conditions, the pulse and temperature are likely to be elevated. When the respiratory rate is also raised, the likelihood is that there is an additional infection of the chest, or that internal blood loss may be causing the signs of shock.

OTHER CONSIDERATIONS

Ethical and legal

The pre-hospital environment may not be the correct place to undertake an assessment of the genitalia, rectum and anus. This can create ethical and legal issues, as well as affecting professional practice. In the majority of instances there is usually no reason to undertake an examination of the genitalia unless the patient specifically complains of pain or discomfort in this area, or blood is noted in this area through clothing. Although a bleed in the genitalia can be extensive, gaining informed consent is an absolute necessity; with thorough documentation as to why it was undertaken and that consent had been gained from the patient (Caroline 2008, p28). If a persistent erection is seen through clothing in a male patient, damage to the spinal cord should be suspected, but questioning as to the use of sildenafil (Viagra) is also relevant. The patient may be embarrassed to admit to having used this drug, but it may prove to be an important part of the history taking and treatment plan.

Clothing associated with a sexual assault or rape victim must be handled as per local and national guidelines, in close liaison with (and taking advice of) the local police service. The patient may need to be taken to a specialist treatment centre, and consideration to having a paramedic/clinician of the same sex available to examine the patient if necessary is appropriate.

Rectal examinations may be seen in hospital assessments of trauma patients, but are rarely seen *out of hospital* unless there are doctors, such as GPs, or BASICS team attending the patient. For the majority of paramedics/clinicians, a rectal exam is seldom indicated, and the same guidance given for examination of the genitalia should be followed.

Destination/receiving specialist units/non-conveyance

The paramedic/clinician will be guided by local protocols as to the hospital destination of choice. In cases of trauma, it is often more relevant to convey the patient to a trauma centre, even though it may involve a longer travelling time, to ensure the best possible patient outcome. In cases of non-local conveyance, protocols must always be adhered to, with a thorough assessment having been undertaken.

The National Institute for Health and Clinical Excellence (NICE) offers specific guidance and is developing guidance in the following areas relevant to pre-hospital practice:

- Coeliac disease
- Constipation in children and young people
- Diarrhoea and vomiting in children under 5 years of age
- Dyspepsia
- Faecal incontinence
- Irritable bowel syndrome
- Neonatal jaundice
- Acute upper GI bleeding
- Colorectal cancer
- Crohn's disease (National Institute for Health and Clinical Excellence Guidance).

Professional

Although the Health Professions Council (HPC) has no specific guidance concerning abdominal pain and GI and GU assessment, the paramedic/clinician must ensure that consent is gained prior to any assessment. As has already been stated, consideration must also be given to the relevance of an examination of the genitalia and rectal area to avoid any accusations of professional misconduct.

Right Upper Quadrant
Acute cholecystitis
Duodenal ulcer
Hepatitis
Congestive heptomegaly
Pyelonephritis
Appendicitis
(R) Pneumonia

Epigastrium
Pancreatitis
Myocardial infarct
Peptic ulcer
Acute cholecystitis
Perforated oesophagus

Left Upper Quadrant
Ruptured spleen
Gastric ulcer
Aortic aneurysm
Perforated colon
Pyelonephritis
(L) Pneumonia

Right Lower Quadrant
Appendicitis
Salpingitis
Tubo-ovarian abscess
Ruptured ectopic pregnancy
Renal/ureteric stone
Strangulated hernia
Mesenteric adenitis
Meckel's diverticulitis
Crohn's disease
Perforated caecum
Psoas abscess

Umbilical
Intestinal obstruction
Acute pancreatitis
Early appendicitis
Mesentric thrombosis
Aortic aneurysm
Diverticulitis

Left Lower Quadrant
Sigmoid diverticulitis
Salpingitis
Tubo-ovarian abscess
Ruptured ectopic pregnancy
Strangulated hernia
Perforated colon
Crohn's disease
Ulcerative colitis
Renal/ureteric stone

Figure 4.3   Gastro-intestinal and genito-urinary conditions and area of presentation

COMMON ABDOMINAL CONDITIONS (SEE FIGURE 4.3)

Appendicitis

Inflammation of the vermiform appendix. The pain of appendicitis classically begins near the umbilicus, then shifts to the right lower quadrant (RLQ), and coughing increases it. Elderly patients report this pattern less frequently than younger ones.

Signs and symptoms
- Slight fever
- Nausea

- Vomiting
- Loss of appetite
- Constipation
- Diarrhoea
- Localised tenderness – (anywhere in the RLQ, or even in the right flank)
- Early voluntary guarding may be replaced by involuntary muscular rigidity
- Right-sided rectal tenderness.

Acute cholecystitis

Cholecystitis is inflammation of the gall bladder. Acute cholecystitis should be suspected whenever there is acute right upper quadrant (RUQ) or epigastric pain.

Signs and symptoms
- Pain in the RUQ
- The pain is usually constant and severe
- The pain may radiate to the right flank or right scapular region
- This pain may occur after eating greasy or fatty foods
- Fever
- Diarrhoea
- Nausea and/or vomiting.

Ectopic pregnancy

In ectopic pregnancy a fertilised egg is implanted somewhere outside the uterus, most commonly the fallopian tubes. The patient will generally exhibit some of the normal signs of pregnancy, including cessation of periods, enlarged and tender breasts, but without the ability to increase in size; as the embryo grows pain is felt by the patient as pressure is placed on the fallopian wall. Rupture of the fallopian tube will lead to shock and death if not recognised and treated urgently.

Signs and symptoms
- Pain in the pelvic region (typically severe, sharp and possibly stabbing)
- Pain may present in the shoulder and neck
- Spotting, and or abnormal bleeding, which may be lighter or heavier than a normal period, and more prolonged. This bleeding is often dark in colour and watery (similar to prune juice)
- Light-headedness, transient loss of consciousness, syncope
- Pain in the lower back
- Hypotension
- Experienced some early symptoms of pregnancy (missed or late period, enlarged and tender breasts).

Intestinal and bowel obstruction

Intestinal and bowel obstruction are common abdominal emergencies, often requiring surgery. Causes may be mechanical or due to compromised blood supply, and as has previously been mentioned the history is important when ascertaining the location and likelihood of intestinal obstruction.

Small bowel obstruction – signs and symptoms
- Central colicky pain
- Vomiting (*which may be food, bile or even possible faecal*)
- Abdominal distension (*unlikely to be tender on palpation*)
- History of abdominal surgery with associated scars.

Large bowel obstruction – signs and symptoms
- Central or lower abdominal colicky pain
- Constipation
- Abdominal distension (*tense and tympanic on percussion*)
- Absent bowel sounds
- Vomiting is more likely to be a late sign
- Changes in bowel habit and bleeding P R may suggest carcinoma.

Trauma

The abdomen may be affected by blunt or penetrating trauma, and there may be evisceration of the abdominal organs. When patients present with abdominal evisceration there may be little pain. Care should be taken to not applying dressings which may adhere to the abdominal contents, but covering the wound with a non-adherent dressing will assist in preventing the site becoming infected, or paralysed due to a cold external environment.

When objects are impaled in the abdomen the object should not be removed, as it may be preventing a severe bleed by remaining in situ. Although this may prove challenging, the impaled object should remain in place, and secured in the most stable manner possible.

When assessing the G I system in such instances, consider the likelihood of damage of organs obstructing the route the object will have taken. Assess for signs of shock, and also consider whether the object may have caused damage to other systems, for instance penetrating the diaphragm (*see Respiratory Assessment: Chapter 2 and Trauma Assessment: Chapter 7*) or vascular damage. (For more details on cardiovascular assessment see Chapters 3 and 7.)

CHAPTER KEY POINTS

■ Decide whether the patient is time critical or non-time critical.
■ Examine using inspect, auscultate, palpate and percussion (IAPP) in order to adhere to a logical, systematic methodology.
■ Utilise the OPQRSTA framework when assessing pain.
■ A thorough knowledge of the anatomy of the GI and GU structures, their location and function, aids accurate diagnosis and treatment.
■ Undertake a thorough secondary survey and gain a complete patient history, as soon as time allows.
■ Consider the necessity for an assessment of the rectum and genitalia, and the legal and ethical issues around undertaking such an assessment, especially in children.
■ In trauma patients consider the mechanism of injury.
■ Is the patient vulnerable, and are further steps required to be taken?

5 Neurological assessment

Jaqualine Lindridge

The neurological system is a control and communication system which connects with each of the other body systems. Due to its complex anatomy, assessment is often approached with trepidation by the paramedic/clinician, but although the examination itself appears complicated, its component tests are simple to perform and their results objective.

This chapter aims to provide a systematic approach to assessment of the neurological system and assist the paramedic/clinician in identifying neurological abnormalities.

SCENE ASSESSMENT

As you approach the scene try to gain an overview of events:

- Evidence of trauma?
- Overturned furniture consistent with a fall or collapse?
- Mobility aids?

Observation of the patient's position is vital; after all it is the neurological system which coordinates the body's movements as well as consciousness.

- Where is the patient located?
- Are they sitting or standing?
- Observe the general muscle tone of the patient:
    - Are they able to sit upright?
    - Are they leaning to one side?
    - Is there any obvious muscle flaccidity to the face or limbs?
    - Is this bilateral or unilateral?
- Are they moving, or still?
- Are their movements purposeful?
- Is the patient suffering a seizure?

PRIMARY SURVEY

Even if at first the patient appears well, deterioration can be rapid. If not properly assessed and reviewed, subtle signs will be overlooked; this is particularly true of the neurological system.

DANGER

Initially assess for actual danger/s that may have caused the patients neurological status.

If unconscious – are there contaminated needles/syringes, electrical cables/applicances, or was it caused by CO poisoning from an old faulty gas heater? Will these affect the paramedic/clinician, their colleague/s, patient and/or bystanders? It is essential that the paramedic/clinician remain alert for potential dangers; for example the patient's symptoms may be the result of a deliberate release of a neurological agent, such as Sarin. The paramedic/clinician must consider their own safety, especially where multiple casualties present with clusters of neurological signs and symptoms and withdraw to prevent or limit their own exposure to any dangers present. (Consider Step 1, 2, 3; see Chapter 2.)

Patients who are fitting may need protection. Nearby furniture should be moved away from the patient's body to prevent injury during the seizure, and if possible place padding around the head to prevent injury from a hard floor.

RESPONSE

Assess the patient's level of response using the AVPU scale; if their level of consciousness is reduced further evaluation will take place during the secondary survey.

AIRWAY

Assess the airway for patency and consider the patient's ability to maintain and protect their own airway. In the unresponsive patient always consider the possibility of injury to the cervical spine. Any insult to the cervical vertebrae has the potential to cause spinal cord injury (SCI), which at this anatomical level may paralyse some of the respiratory muscles.

In the unconscious patient the tongue will become flaccid and fall posteriorly into the oropharynx, thus occluding the airway. This can be corrected by manual airway manoeuvres ('C' spine appropriate) used in conjunction with patient positioning and airway adjuncts. It is important to remember that the unconscious patient is also at risk of aspiration, even if manual airway manoeuvres are used effectively (Wardrope and Mackenzie 2004, p217).

It cannot be assumed that the conscious patient will be able to protect their own airway; the paramedic/clinician must be alert to the possibility that the patient may need assistance in clearing secretions, blood or vomitus, particularly in patients whose neurological complaint may inhibit the gag reflex, such as a stroke.

If present, seizures can also inhibit airway management. Many patients who suffer seizures will exhibit trismus (*inability to open mouth fully*). In such cases, consideration should be given to the use of nasopharyngeal adjuncts.

Possible actions to be taken:

- Open and maintain airway
- Consider 'C' spine
- Consider appropriate stepwise airway management (*see Respiratory Assessment: Chapter 2*)

BREATHING

Disruption to the respiratory centre of the brainstem can disturb the rate and regularity of breathing and damage to the peripheral nervous system may cause dysfunction of the respiratory muscles. The phrenic nerve originates from the spinal cord at the level of C3–C5 and innervates the diaphragm; if the cord is damaged above this level, the impulses needed to initiate diaphragmatic contraction are blocked and respiratory arrest will result (Tortora and Derrickson 2007) hence the popular saying '*C3, 4 and 5 keep the diaphragm alive*'. Conditions such as stroke or intracerebral haemorrhage can affect the respiratory centre causing respiratory depression or arrest, whereas conditions which result in muscle weakness, such as Guillain-Barré syndrome, inhibit the action of the respiratory muscles (Gray and Gavin 2005, p400). Assess for the presence of breathing and evaluate the rate, depth and pattern of breathing and evaluate the need to assist ventilations.

Possible actions to be taken:

- If patient is not responding: look, listen and feel for breathing for 10 seconds
- Consider the need to ventilate

- Ensure that the patient is not hypoxic
- Manage breathing/hypoxia effectively before moving to the next element

CIRCULATION

The neurological system is essential for autonomic control of blood pressure and disruption can be caused by septic shock secondary to neurological infections, such as meningococcal meningitis as well as injuries causing neurogenic shock. High cord injuries can produce bradycardia and hypotension as sympathetic tone is lost and vagal activity is unopposed. Although these responses are of delayed onset and therefore infrequently seen in the pre-hospital arena (Guly *et al.* 2007, p60), they are important causes of cardiovascular compromise in the trauma patient and should be considered in patients who present with signs of shock without evidence of hypovolaemia. Where neurogenic shock is suspected, avoid endotracheal intubation and suctioning unless essential to preserve the airway as these manoeuvres may produce unopposed vagal stimulation.

DISABILITY

Examine the patient to confirm the absence of seizure activity. Observe for jerky movements of the limbs and test the joints for tone. Briefly observe the patient's muscle tone and movement. Look for any flaccid limbs, these will need protection to prevent injury, also note if they are moving the limbs; this is particularly important in the trauma patient. Note any abnormal posturing, such as decerebrate (see Figure 5.1). In decerebrate rigidity there is an abnormal extensor response; note

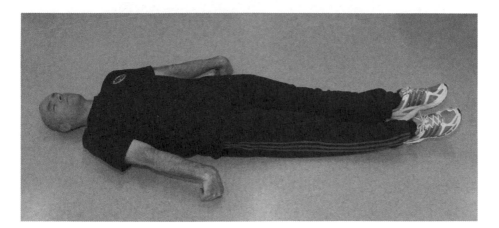

Figure 5.1   Decerebrate positioning – abnormal extensor response

the extension at the elbows with pronation and flexion at the wrists, or decorticate positions (see Figure 5.2). In decorticate rigidity there is an abnormal flexor response; note the flexion at elbows.

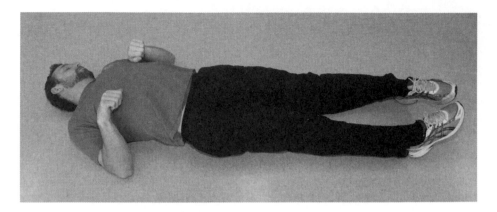

Figure 5.2 Decorticate positioning – abnormal flexor response

Alternatively the patient may demonstrate opisthotonus. In opisthotonus the back can be seen to characteristically arch in extreme hyper-extension and may result from brain injury, meningism or tetanus (see Figure 5.3).

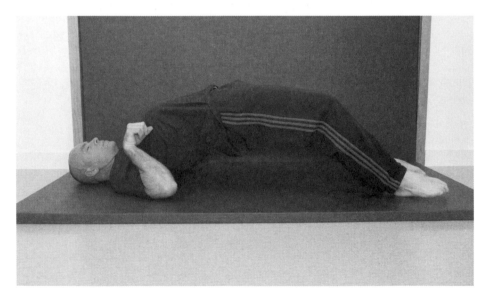

Figure 5.3 Opisthotonus positioning

Exclude the possibility of hypoglycaemia in any patient with a reduced level of consciousness. Hypoglycaemia can present with neurological signs, including hemiparesis, coma and seizures. Prolonged neuroglycopenia can cause neurological deficit and the importance of identifying hypoglycaemia cannot be over-emphasised. Keep In mind the common framework: **ABC 'DEFG'** – 'airway, breathing, circulation, *don't ever forget glucose'*. This is particularly important in paediatric patients (*see Child Assessment: Chapter 9*).

Test the pupils for light reaction. Using a suitable pen-torch, shine the light briefly into the patient's left pupil and observe the pupil's reaction to the light; it should briskly constrict when confronted with the light, and briskly dilate when the light is removed. Shine the light into the left eye a second time, this time observe the right eye; it should react in response to the light shone into the contralateral eye; this is known as the *consensual light reflex*. Repeat this procedure with the right eye. Whereas the assessment of '*accommodation*' occurs when the patient accommodates to a near object, they converge their eyes and constrict their pupils.

Pupils Equal and Round; React to Light and Accommodation (PERRLA).

Whilst bilaterally dilated pupils are suggestive of hypoxia or poisoning (benzodiazepines and tricyclic antidepressants (Gray and Gavin 2005, p441) unilaterally dilated and unresponsive pupils are suggestive of a significant cerebral event. If a lesion places pressure on the cranial nerves responsible for movements of the pupils then dilation may be seen; this is a significant sign and the paramedic/clinician should prepare for the possibility of deterioration.

Highly constricted ('pin-point') pupils are associated with certain types of poisoning. Classically, constricted pupils in poisoning are caused by opiates, such as codeine and heroin. Reactive, pin-point pupils are also associated with pontine stroke, usually of haemorrhagic aetiology (Kase *et al.* 2004, p366).

Also observe for any evidence of photophobia, suggestive of meningism and test for the presence of neck stiffness.

Consider the need to assess the patient's temperature. Serious neurological disorders can present with derangements of temperature. Derangements of temperature can cause neurological symptoms. In the paediatric patient seizures may be the result of fever; if the paramedic/clinician can confirm the presence of pyrexia at an early stage then the correct treatment modality can be initiated. Profoundly raised (hyperthermic) (*hyperthermia; core temperature >40°C*) or lowered (hypothermic) (*hypothermia; core temperature <35°C*) body temperatures can be life threatening and both will affect the neurological system in extremis. The combination of abnormal body temperature with abnormal neurology indicates a serious problem.

Possible actions to be taken:

- Assess and document (LOC)
- Assess and document blood glucose levels
- Assess and document size and equality of pupils (*consensual/ accommodating*)
- Undertake a Face, Arms, Speech Test (FAST) (DH 2007; NICE 2008a; JRCALC 2009a)
- Assess and record the temperature
- Pre-alert and transfer to a hyper-acute stroke unit.

EXPOSE/EXAMINE/ENVIRONMENT

Taking environmental and chaperone issues into account, expose the patient. Specifically expose the patient and examine for a rash. In meningococcal septicaemia look for a non-blanching petechial rash, the rash will develop rapidly from one or two small spots and is a late sign, but if the rash is obvious then the meningococcal septicaemia is at an advanced stage. Thoroughly examine the patient ensuring that the axillae are included, and in infants the nappy requires removal to examine the gluteal folds.

- Check for evidence of intravenous drug use and medical patches. In the case of the intravenous drug user, 'track-marks' may not be obvious, although often found in the antecubital fossa, the web spaces of fingers and toes are also used, amongst other sites.
- Look for medical alert tags; these will often reveal information about the patient's past medical history or supply a telephone number where this information can be obtained.

Possible actions to be taken:

- Check for evidence of intravenous drug use and medical patches
- Look for medical alert tags
- Examine and expose and assess as appropriate
- If the patient does not have a 'time critical' condition, then undertake an appropriate secondary survey

SECONDARY SURVEY

Having completed the primary survey, the paramedic/clinician should be aware of any immediately life threatening conditions. If the primary survey is 'positive' for such conditions, the paramedic/clinician must evaluate and treat simultaneously, but in the less time critical patient it is necessary to gain an understanding of their condition in greater detail. This begins by taking a history.

Presenting complaint

The presenting complaint need only be 2 or 3 words, examples from a neurological perspective include 'headache' or 'dizziness', with a brief descriptor of the patient.

History of presenting complaint

The history of the presenting complaint is a short story about how the patient has come to be unwell or injured, and how their problem is progressing. For example, for a patient presenting with dysarthria their documentation might read:

> **PC**: *80 ♀ C/O slurred speech.*
> **HPC**: *Sudden onset of slurred speech, at approximately 1445hrs, accompanied by weakness of the right arm and leg. Patient's husband states the left side of the patient's face appears 'droopy'. No change since onset.*

Here we have a brief story of what has happened to the patient. There are some key elements which are particularly important in the neurological history; the speed of onset should be noted, always observe if the onset is abrupt or insidious. Also note any improvements or deterioration; this information will assist in formulating differential diagnoses later.

Past medical history

The neurological system interacts with all of the other systems of the body so it is essential to note a complete history, not just the elements which are obviously neurological in origin. For example, the patient may report they suffer with the cardiovascular disorder Hughes syndrome. A patient with Hughes syndrome, otherwise known as *antiphospholipid syndrome or antiphospholipid antibody syndrome*, is a disorder of coagulation that causes blood clots (thrombosis) in both arteries and veins as well as pregnancy-related complications such as miscarriage, stillbirth, preterm delivery, or severe pre-eclampsia. The syndrome occurs due to the autoimmune production of antibodies against phospholipid (aPL) (a cell substance), and has an increased tendency to form emboli, so they are at an increased risk of ischaemic stroke; such information can be taken into consideration when evaluating any presenting neurological symptoms.

Drug/medication history

Enquire about the medications the patient is taking. Be sure to include *all* types of drugs, and not just those prescribed to the patient by other health care practitioners, including the use of illicit drugs. While it is recognised that this is a potentially awkward question, it must be addressed. Many neurological signs and symptoms can be caused by illicit drug use.

Always ask about allergies at an early stage; remember if the paramedic/clinician omits to gain this information and the patient loses consciousness then the opportunity to gain this vital piece of history is lost and the patient may be at risk from avoidable harm.

Social/family medical history

Enquire as to whether there is a familial history of neurological complaints; conditions such as stroke and migraine may have a familial link.

REVIEW OF SYSTEMS AND VITAL SIGNS

It is important to differentiate between signs and symptoms. Keep in mind that symptoms provide subjective data; symptoms are things which the patient *feels*, whereas signs present objective data; signs are something which the clinician can feel, see or hear. The purpose of the review of systems (ROS) is to 'interrogate' the patient's *symptoms*; it is an information gathering exercise designed to identify what symptoms the patient has or has not experienced.

If the patient is in pain, they usually will wish to discuss this first.

Pain

Onset
Ask if it came on suddenly or gradually. The speed of onset in neurological evaluation is vital in assessing the likely causes; a sudden onset of severe headache should raise the paramedic/clinician's suspicions of a serious pathology, such as sub-arachnoid haemorrhage.

Provocation/palliation
Provocation by sudden movements of the head, coughing or sneezing, may indicate raised intracranial pressure (Fuller 2004, p8). Palliation by rest or dimmed lights may be more suggestive of migraine.

Quality

Asking the patient what the pain is like will usually reward the clinician with a comment on its severity only. Ask the patient to describe what it *feels* like, only providing examples (i.e. sharp or dull) if necessary. The quality of pain in migraine will normally be consistent with previous episodes; a change in quality should raise suspicions.

Radiating

Where does the pain start and finish? Find out where the headache is located, is it unilateral or bilateral, does it radiate into any other portion of the head or neck (or vice versa!). Pain arising from an irritated nerve (radicular pain) will often radiate the length of that nerve, such as in sciatica, where the pain usually radiates along the tract of the sciatic nerve from the gluteal region to the foot.

Severity

Only the patient can decide how severe the pain is! If possible, the paramedic/clinician should use a validated pain scoring system to help understand how severe the pain is to the patient. A good paramedic/clinician never disregards a high pain score based on their own opinion of how much pain a patient is really suffering, and always investigates severe pain.

Timing

Try to gain an understanding of the relationship of the pain with other findings. What was happening when the pain started? What time of day do the headaches tend to occur? Is there a pattern forming which will aid diagnosis? Is this an apparent 'first and worst' headache, or is there a slower, more insidious crescendo?

Associated symptoms

Has the pain been associated with any other symptoms? If so, ask the patient to explain what these are.

Also enquire about other common symptoms:

- Dizziness. Distinguish from vertigo; if the patient is experiencing light-headedness, or feels as though they may faint, this is suggestive of dizziness. If however the patient reports a sensation of the room 'spinning' around them, this is more likely to be *vertigo.*
- Seizures, syncope, or any type of 'black out'. If syncope is present, ask about any patterns, e.g. during exercise, or if any prodromal symptoms were present.
- Sensory symptoms, such as pins and needles or loss of sensation.
- Motor symptoms, such as weakness or paralysis, and if there have been any involuntary movements, such as tremors or tics (Bickley and Szilagyi 2009).

After obtaining a through history the paramedic/clinician should approach the physical examination of the neurological system systematically and examine the following four areas: mental status, cranial nerves, motor system and sensory system.

Mental status

Evaluation of mental status comprises an assessment of level of consciousness, behaviour and appearance, speech and cognitive function.
Assess the patient's level of consciousness:

- Are they alert and responding readily?
- Do they need frequent stimulation to elicit a response (*stuporous*)?
- Are they *lethargic* and slow to respond with a tendency to drift off to sleep?
- Glasgow Coma Scale (GCS). Take the time to perform the test properly, and never attempt to guess the results! A score below 8/15 is indicative of unconsciousness (Gray and Gavin 2005, p441).

Observe the patient's general appearance and behaviour:

- Well kempt?
- Behaviour consistent with social or cultural norms?
- Flights of speech or ideas suggesting a psychiatric aetiology?

Listen to their speech:

- Word finding difficulties (dysphasia)?
- Is their speech slurred (dysarthria)?

Assess recall; the abbreviated mental test (AMT) (Hodgkinson 1972) is a useful tool, see Table 5.1.

Table 5.1	Mini mental status examination (<8/10 suggests confusion)
1	Age
2	Time to nearest hour
	Give patient a simple address to remember, e.g. 42 West Street
3	Year
4	Place
5	Date of Birth (exact)
6	Name of monarch/head of state
7	Count backwards from 20 (prompt to 18)
8	Start of WWI (? Age of Patient – Start of WWII)
9	Recognition of 2 people (e.g. relative, HCP)
10	Recalls address

Cranial nerves

Assessing the cranial nerves is not as difficult as it sounds; and some of the cranial nerves are already examined as part of the primary survey. A series of simple tests will confirm if the cranial nerves are intact.

Smell

The olfactory nerve (CN I) is not routinely tested in pre-hospital care.

Eyes and vision

The optic nerve (CN II).

- Visual acuity (VA) can be informally tested by reading newspaper text, starting with the headline and moving on to smaller fonts (formal examination requires a VA chart not usually appropriate to pre-hospital care).
- Visual fields are examined using a technique known as confrontation. The paramedic/clinician sits face-to-face with the patient, approximately 60cm (2ft) away. Both the paramedic/clinician and patient should cover corresponding eyes (e.g. if the patient covers the left eye, the paramedic/clinician should cover their right), the paramedic/clinician then 'confronts' the patient's vision by bringing their moving fingers into the peripheral vision of the patient in each quadrant bilaterally, comparing findings with their own vision.
- If trained, fundoscopy should be performed to assess for papilloedema.
- Observe the eyelids for ptosis (*the inability to elevate the eyelid*) and examine the pupils for consensual light reflex, and accommodation.
- Assess the extraocular movements. The oculomotor nerve (CN III), trochlear nerve (CN IV) and the abducens nerve (CN VI) are all involved in controlling the movements of the eyes and are examined together. Ensuring the patient's head remains still, ask the patient to follow your finger through the cardinal positions of gaze; left and right superior, left and right lateral and left and right inferior. This is done by drawing a wide, imaginary 'H' in front of the patient with your finger. Allow your finger to trace this shape, slowly hold each position of view briefly, watching for nystagmus (*an involuntary rapid movement of the eyeball*).

The face

The trigeminal nerve (CN V).

- Sensory assessment: apply light touch to the forehead, maxillae and mandible bilaterally.
- Motor assessment: with teeth clenched palpate the temporal and masseter muscle mass. The facial nerve (CN VII). Assess the motor

function of CN VII by assessing the symmetry of the following facial movements:

- Frown
- Tightly close the eyes and open them against (*gentle*) resistance
- Smile (*showing teeth*)
- Puff out the cheeks against resistance.

The ears

The vestibocochlear nerve (CN VIII) is responsible for hearing (cochlear division); it is also involved in balance and equilibrium (vestibular division).

- Stand behind the patient and rub your fingers together, or whisper quietly, asking the patient to repeat what you say (*cochlear division*).
- On the review of systems, complaint of balance disturbance, dizziness or vertigo may implicate the vestibular division of CN VIII.

The mouth

The glossopharyngeal (CN IX) and vagus (CN X) nerves are tested together.

- Open mouth and say 'aahh': the uvula should remain midline.

The hypoglossal nerve (CN XII) controls the tongue.

- When *stuck out* the tongue remains midline.
- Observe the patient's speech. If it appears abnormal, ask the patient to attempt a tongue twister, such as this commonly used phrase: 'round the rugged rock that ragged rascal ran'.

The shoulders

The accessory nerve (CN XI).

- Turning of the head against resistance.
- Shrug their shoulders.

Examination of the cranial nerves is now complete; although it may seem that there is much to do here, when practised the entire assessment will take only a minute.

Sensory assessment

Test the patient's sensory function by applying light touch to the skin, assessing for altered sensations bilaterally. Also assess joint position sense; both the cerebellum and the vestibular pathways need to be intact for this sensation to remain. Grasping the patient's hallux (*big toe*) at the sides, move the toe upwards and downwards, the patient (*with eyes closed*) should be able to identify what position the digit is in.

Motor assessment

Begin assessing the motor system by assessing the patient's muscle bulk and tone. Note any obvious atrophy. In their resting state, muscles should retain slight tension; this is known as resting tone. Assess tone by gently flexing and extending the elbow and knee joints, noting any increased or decreased resistance (Bickley and Szilogyi 2009).

Next, assess general muscle strength. This should be tested by asking the patient to move their limbs through their natural range of movement whilst the paramedic/clinician provides mild resistance. On the upper limbs: test flexion and extension at the elbow, wrist extension and grip. Also, assess for pronator drift. The patient should hold both of their arms straight out in front of themselves, palms uppermost. With their eyes closed, the patient should be able to maintain this position for at least 20 seconds; observe for any pronation of either arm, a downward drift may also be seen. This suggests a contra-lateral lesion in the corticospinal tract. On the lower limbs: test flexion and extension of the knee, against the paramedic/clinician's resistance. Also test dorsiflexion and plantar flexion at the ankle, by asking the patient to pull their foot towards the trunk against resistance and to push against the paramedic/clinician's hand (pointing their toes) respectively. This examination should reveal any power loss or loss of motor coordination. It does not represent a complete neurological assessment. If neurological involvement is suspected, the patient should be referred to a medical practitioner. Now assess the patient's coordination in four areas: observe gait, stance and examine the patient's ability to make point-to-point movements and rapidly alternating movements.

- Observe the patient's gait for ataxia. An ataxic gait refers to a gait which lacks coordination; this is often due to cerebellar disease. It is also seen in acute intoxication; however, this should never be the paramedic/clinician's initial assumption. Asking the patient to walk 'heel to toe' may reveal more discrete ataxias (Bickley and Szilagyi 2009).
- Perform the Romberg test. Ask the patient to stand with their feet together (ensuring their safety) and close their eyes for 20–30 seconds (Bickley and Szilagyi 2009). In cerebellar disease, the patient will be unable to maintain their stance with eyes open and closed. In a positive Romberg test, the patient stands well with their eyes open, but is unable to maintain their stance with eyes closed; this is due to a loss of joint position sense.
- Assess point-to-point coordination. The paramedic/clinician should hold their finger steady within easy reach of the patient and ask the patient to touch the end of this finger, followed by the patient's own nose. After a few repeats of this, ask the patient to close their eyes and continue. In the

absence of cerebellar disease, these movements should be smooth and accurate. If cerebellar damage has occurred, the patient's movements may appear clumsy and inaccurate; this will worsen when the patient closes their eyes and loses the compensation of vision. Also ask the patient to run their heel from the contra-lateral knee down to the ankle; failure to complete this test accurately suggests cerebellar disease, however inability to *find* the knee without looking is more suggestive of a loss of joint position sense.

■ Examine the patient's ability to perform rapidly alternating movements; the paramedic/clinician should demonstrate slapping the back of their own hand against their own thigh, followed by swiftly turning their hand over and slapping palm of their hand against their thigh. The patient should copy this movement and increase the speed of movement until they are performing the movements as rapidly as possible. If cerebellar disease is present the patient will be unable to perform these movements in a swift coordinated fashion and they will appear slow and clumsy (dysdiadochokinesis); it is important to note that the dominant hand may perform better in this task and this is quite normal (Bickley and Szilagyi 2009).

Once the clinician has completed the physical examination, the information can be added to that gleaned from the history and differential diagnoses considered. There are a number of common neurological complaints which the paramedic/clinician will see in practice, these are outlined below.

COMMON NEUROLOGICAL CONDITIONS

Stroke

Stroke can have an ischaemic or haemorrhagic aetiology; differentiation requires imaging and accurate diagnosis will take place in the hospital setting. Usually there is a sudden onset to the presentation and the patient's previous medical history may reveal risk factors for emboli, such as atrial fibrillation, valvular heart disease, hypertension or diabetes mellitus.

Headache is rare in stroke, if present is usually severe and consistent with a haemorrhagic cause. The stroke patient will more commonly present with one or more of the following symptoms:

■ Unilateral facial palsy (forehead sparing)
■ Hemiparesis or hemiplegia of the limbs (*usually* contralateral to the facial palsy)
■ Dysphasia/dysarthria.

If the patient remains ambulant, gait abnormalities may be observed due to hemiparesis of the lower limbs; an ataxic gait may suggest cerebellar involvement.

Vital signs
The respiration rate is usually normal; if the respiratory centre of the brainstem is affected, irregular bradypnoea may be seen. Hypertension is a common risk factor for stroke and can result in a full pulse. Haemorrhagic strokes can produce profoundly raised intracranial pressure; Cushing's Triad may also be seen, whereby bradycardia and hypertension are added to irregular respirations.

Assessment of the ECG results may reveal atrial fibrillation; this arrhythmia is often the cause of the embolus in ischaemic stroke. Although blood glucose is largely unaltered by stroke, hypoglycaemia must be excluded as a cause of sudden onset of neurological symptoms.

Usually the patient will present with an unaltered level of consciousness. Unconsciousness is unusual in stroke and should raise suspicions of a haemorrhagic cause.

Pupillary reaction is usually normal; ipsilateral dilatation of the pupils may be seen in severe cases. Bilaterally pinpoint pupils raise suspicions of pontine damage.

Transient ischaemic attack

The presentation of the transient ischaemic attack (TIA) patient is identical to that of an ischaemic stroke. TIA differs from stroke in that the neurological symptoms consistent with stroke syndrome completely resolve within 24 hrs of onset. Many TIAs resolve within a few minutes, and dependent on their risk stratification, may not need to be seen immediately in secondary care. However, the paramedic/clinician must be diligent in assessing these patients to ensure that no continuing symptoms are missed, and that the patient is safe to be referred to a less acute pathway; TIAs are often a precursor to a completed stroke and it is essential these patients are properly assessed and referred.

Possible actions to be taken:
- Exclude hypoglycaemia as a cause of sudden onset neurological symptoms
- Undertake a Face, Arms, Speech, Test (FAST) (Nor *et al.* 2004) (DH 2007; NICE 2008a; JRCALC 2009a)
- Pre-alert and transfer to a hyper-acute stroke unit

Sub-arachnoid haemorrhage

Sub-arachnoid haemorrhage (SAH) occurs when an aneurysm ruptures leaking blood into the arachnoid space below the arachnoid mater. SAH presents classically with sudden onset of first and worst occipital headache, often described as a thunderclap.

Additional *signs and symptoms* include:

- Nausea and vomiting
- Meningism
- Drowsiness
- Seizures
- Reduced level of consciousness or coma.

Vital signs

- If the brainstem is affected, irregular bradypnoea may be seen.
- Patients with SAH are prone to arrhythmias and may present with bradycardia, tachycardia or a normal pulse.
- ECG changes consistent with acute coronary syndromes may also be seen, including ST elevation, T wave inversion and a lengthened QT interval (Sommargren 2002).
- Hypertension is common, either as an existing risk factor, or as a result of raised intracranial pressure.
- The level of consciousness varies according to the severity of the haemorrhage; the patient may present with a GCS of 15/15 or may be moribund.
- Pupils may be normal; unilateral dilatation may progress to bilaterally fixed and dilated pupils as coma deepens.
- Temperature is usually normal in early presentation, though may rise over a period of days following the initial event.

Head injury

In practice, the paramedic/clinician will see both major and minor head injuries, resulting in both primary and secondary brain injuries. Primary brain injury results from the mechanism at the time of the injury. The paramedic/clinician can do little to reverse primary injuries; their focus is reducing the potential for secondary brain injury. Secondary brain injury is caused by a range of factors, many of which are preventable (Wyatt *et al.* 1999, p372). The paramedic/clinician should seek to ensure that any primary survey problems are identified and corrected, this will assist in preventing secondary brain injury as a result of hypoxia, hypovolaemia (*leading to inadequate cerebral perfusion*) and seizures. The brain injured patient is particularly sensitive to changes in pCO_2, and it is essential to ensure that when ventilating the patient, hypercapnia is avoided as this will raise intracranial pressure further (Wyatt *et al.* 1999, p372).

The patient may complain of headache, of varying severity, be alert for the possibility of contra-coup patterns of injury developing. When taking a history, the paramedic/clinician should specifically ask about symptoms suggestive of intracranial pathology:

- Nausea and vomiting
- Limb weakness or abnormal sensations
- Visual disturbances.

Record a set of vital signs at an early stage, paying particular attention to the patient's mental status.

- Glasgow Coma Score. The GCS should be re-assessed frequently, declines of a GCS score of two or more points may indicate an increased inter-cranial pressure (Salomone and Pons 2007, p216), whereas some types of brain injury (*in particular subdural and epidural haemorrhage*) (Clarke 2005, p1219) are associated with lucid intervals.
- Bradycardia and hypertension are associated with raised intracranial pressure. As the intracranial pressure rises as a result of haemorrhage or oedema, the blood pressure must rise also to 'overcome' this and achieve cerebral perfusion. Irregular bradypnoea and Cheyne-Stokes ventilation are associated with damage to the brainstem, possibly as a result of herniation.
- Blood glucose measurement is indicated in any patient with a reduced level of consciousness and should be corrected; in the head injured patient prolonged hypoglycaemia can contribute to secondary brain injury.
- Pupil examination may reveal unilateral dilation and loss of reaction to light; in the head injured patient this is a significant sign which may progress to bilaterally dilated pupils in herniation (Clarke 2005, p1219).

Assess for evidence of facial or skull fractures and look for signs of base of skull fracture:

- Periorbital ecchymosis (*purple discoloration*)
- Bruising to the mastoid process (*Battle's sign, late sign*)
- Otorrhoea
- Rhinorrhoea.

Where appropriate, assess the remaining cranial nerves, cerebellar function and the limbs for tone, power and sensation. Cranial nerve abnormalities may reflect primary or secondary injury as a result of compression of the affected nerves. Abnormalities in the limbs may reflect primary injury, or development of raised intracranial pressure; developing widespread paralysis may reflect herniation (Clarke 2005, p1219).

Meningitis

Meningitis is a condition which produces inflammation of the meninges. The patient will usually be pyrexic, with a history of malaise. Meningitis presents classically with meningism as a result of irritation to the meninges. Signs and symptoms of meningism include:

- Headache
- Photophobia
- Neck stiffness
- Kernig's sign (*with the patient supine, begin with the hip and knee in 90° of flexion, when the knee is extended pain is elicited in the neck*)
- Brudzinski's sign (*passive neck flexion produces an involuntary flexion of the hip*)
- Raised fontenelle in infants
- Severe cases, opisthotonus (*tetanic spasm causing hyperextension of the back*).

Signs of raised intracranial pressure may also be seen:

- Headache, often severe
- Reduced level of consciousness
- Irregular respirations/bradypnoea
- Bradycardia
- Hypertension.

If septicaemia complicates meningitis, classic findings can be a very late, potentially pre-terminal sign:

- Rash, classically a non-blanching, petechial rash
- Macular rash may be seen in the early stages.

As the patient deteriorates profound shock may occur and tachycardia, hypotension, seizures and coma may be seen.

- Pulse oximetry may be reduced, reflecting poor perfusion of the extremities in developing shock.

Patients with neurological signs on presentation have a 50%–90% mortality rate (Tidy 2008). It is essential to remember that the classic signs of neck stiffness and non-blanching rash are usually absent in the early stages. Where meningitis is suspected, particularly in a paediatric patient, look for the following signs (Thompson *et al.* 2006, p402):

- Cold hands and feet (despite fever)
- Abnormal skin colour
- Leg pain.

Possible actions to be taken:

- ■ Be alert!
- ■ Mcningitis Is a time critical emergency
- ■ Presentation may be deceptively mild

Seizures

Seizures are a common presentation in pre-hospital care, and are often associated with epilepsy. However, there are many causes of seizure activity beyond epilepsy and seizures can herald serious neurological pathology. The paramedic/clinician should also consider, and if possible reverse, the following causes:

- ■ Hypoxia
- ■ Hypoglycaemia
- ■ Electrolyte imbalance
- ■ Eclampsia
- ■ Intracranial pathology such as brain injury
- ■ Poisoning
- ■ Pyrexia
- ■ Psychogenic.

Although there are several classifications of seizure the tonic clonic seizure is the most common presentation to the paramedic/clinician and requires prompt identification and management. Prolonged tonic clonic seizures are associated with hypoxia and neuronal damage; seizures lasting longer than 30 minutes or multiple seizures with incomplete recovery over 30 minutes are classified as status epilepticus and represent a serious emergency (Reiser 2006, p441).

A tonic clonic seizure is associated with loss of consciousness, followed by a brief tonic phase. During this tonic phase the body's muscles contract firmly for a few seconds before the clonic phase begins. During the clonic phase, rhythmical and often violent muscular contractions occur throughout the musculoskeletal system, although due to the underdeveloped musculature of the paediatric patient, clonic activity can be more discrete in children. The length of the clonic phase is variable, and dependent on the pathology of the seizure. Often the patient will bite their tongue and become incontinent during the seizure, although a lack of these finding does not in itself preclude a seizure.

Vital signs
- ■ Effectiveness of ventilation be reduced although accurate assessment is extremely difficult in a patient exhibiting clonic activity.
- ■ Cyanosis is common.

- SpO_2 will be reduced.
- Hypoxia may lead to tachycardia.
- Blood glucose levels may be lowered; glycogen reserves may be depleted during prolonged seizure activity or represent the cause of the fit.
- Pupils are unresponsive during tonic clonic activity.

During a tonic clonic seizure, the patient will be unresponsive to stimuli; after cessation of the fit it is common for the patient to exhibit confusion and a reduced level of consciousness for some time; this is known as the post-ictal period. In all cases of seizure, once the patient has been stabilised, the paramedic/clinician should endeavour to discover the cause of the ictus, as well as examine the patient for injuries which may have been caused by a fall or accident during the tonic phase, or injuries caused by violent muscular contractions themselves.

Possible actions to be taken:

- Protect patient from injury
- Assess and manage hypoxia and hypoglycaemia accordingly
- Pre-alert and transfer to hospital as appropriate

Impressions

It will not always be possible, or appropriate to come to a diagnosis in pre-hospital care.

However, the paramedic/clinician should use their history and examination skills to produce an impression of the patient's conditions. Try to include the patient's circumstances in this impression; it should reflect more than a list of differential diagnoses. There are many conditions which can be managed at home, however the paramedic/clinician may feel that this is inappropriate and this should be recorded in the impression; for example the patient who presents with a minor head injury may have the added complication of living alone, which is a reason to admit to emergency department for observation.

OTHER CONSIDERATIONS

Communication

Many neurological disorders present with communication difficulties. Some patients will have difficulties making themselves understood and may also have cognitive difficulties affecting their ability to understand the paramedic/clinician. The paramedic/clinician should recognise this and tailor their communication accordingly, avoiding complex terms and seeking to communicate with the patient in the language they are most comfortable with at the time; for example some neurological patients may have been speaking fluent English as a second language for decades, but after a stroke may communicate better in their first language. The paramedic/clinician should also recognise the emotional impact that communication problems may have on the patient and approach communication with a patient and conscientious manner.

Social/family/carer/guardian

Consider the patient's social support needs; many neurological patients will need support when discharged and the paramedic/clinician should evaluate any obvious need for formal assessment and referral to social support agencies. In particular, conditions such as minor head injury and epilepsy, where early discharge from hospital, or even out-of-hospital care, are common, the availability of support at home can be a defining factor in the safety of such discharges, as can the structure of the home environment when considering discharge of the neurologically impaired patient.

Ethical and legal

Where consciousness is impaired, capacity issues immediately come to the fore. The paramedic/clinician should be careful to assess the patient who is thought to lack capacity in line with the Mental Capacity Act 2005 (Department of Health 2005) and ensure that they act in the best interests of the patient. In the case of the unconscious patient, the doctrine of necessity usually provides that paramedic/clinicians will act in the best interests of the patient, and effect any treatments deemed necessary by the paramedic/clinician to sustain life. This doctrine would only normally be overridden where a valid advance decision exists pertaining to life-sustaining care or where the patient has nominated a lasting power of attorney (personal welfare) under the Act, and their capabilities extend to making such decisions. Many patients with degenerative neurological conditions will make such advance plans; the paramedic/clinician has a responsibility to familiarise themselves with such points of law and adhere to them where appropriate.

Destination/receiving specialist units/non-conveyance

Conveyance to the emergency department is usually the default for the neurological patient. In some cases, patients presenting with minor neurological complaints, such as minor head injury or symptoms consistent with an ongoing problem (such as epilepsy) may not benefit from attendance at the emergency department. In such cases the paramedic/clinician must make a full assessment of the patient before making this decision. Paramedic/clinicians should feel the weight of responsibility in discharging patients from their care and ensure any decisions not to convey are safe and robustly made. If any doubt exists, seek assistance from a senior paramedic/clinician and consider referring the patient. Any decision not to convey a patient must reflect any national standards set, such as the National Institute for Health and Clinical Excellence (NICE) *Guidelines for Head Injury* (NICE 2007b). Many hospitals are now providing specialist services for some neurological conditions, such as head injury and stroke. Refer to local and national guidance for more information.

Professional

The neurological patient is often a vulnerable patient. The paramedic/clinician should in particular ensure that they meet their professional obligation to act in the best interests of service users. As previously discussed, the extent of the neurological evaluation included in this chapter does not reflect the complete assessment required by many neurological patients; the paramedic/clinician must therefore honour their professional obligation to ensure they do not exceed their scope of practice and make referrals where appropriate.

Facts and figures

After coronary heart disease, stroke is the second leading cause of death in the UK and accounts for approximately 53,000 deaths per year. Of this number, 9,500 are under the age of 75 years (Scarborough *et al.* 2009, p12). Thus, stroke is a common presentation to the paramedic/clinician and prompt recognition of stroke syndrome in the out-of-hospital environment contributes to reducing mortality and morbidity from this condition; remember time is brain. As a leading cause of mortality and morbidity, the paramedic/clinician should be alert to this potential diagnosis and act quickly to admit the patient.

CHAPTER KEY POINTS

- ■ When assessing the neurological patient; be systematic and thorough.
- ■ Ensure primary survey problems are identified, managed and reviewed.
- ■ Don't expect everything to be obvious – serious pathology can be subtle.
- ■ Ensure patients are referred appropriately.

6 Spinal injuries assessment

Nigel Ward

This chapter will discuss the considerations given by the paramedic/clinician when presented with a patient with possible spinal injuries. The National Service Framework for Long Term Conditions implemented 11 quality requirements, of these, number 3 advised that patients requiring hospital admission need to be assessed and treated in a timely way by paramedic/clinicians who have the appropriate neurological and resuscitation skills and facilities. These conditions occur as a result of injury or damage to the nervous system including the brain, spinal cord and/or their peripheral nerve connections (DH 2005a, p4 and 9).

SCENE ASSESSMENT

The existence of possible spinal injuries may be suspected by the paramedic/clinician even before a primary survey is possible. Initial information regarding mechanism of injury and the history of events is often available before arrival at the scene of an incident. In addition the scene presented on arrival, including both position and location of the patient can provide evidence of actual or potential spinal injuries.

Remember, spinal injuries are not only caused by road traffic collisions (RTCs). Damage to vertebrae and spinal cord can result from other trauma, such as sporting injuries, assaults, falls and accidents in public and working environments and in elderly patients may occur whilst performing normal daily activities (Snyder and Christmas 2003).

PRIMARY SURVEY

Particular attention should be paid to the methods of assessing and maintaining a patent airway in patients with suspected cervical spine injuries ('C' Spine), which the paramedic/clinician should understand that if they assess and therefore manage incorrectly have the potential to cause spinal cord injury (SCI).

DANGER

Danger considerations will vary greatly depending on the mechanism of injury and the location of any traumatic injury. On arrival at scene the paramedic/clinician should liaise with other emergency services present; if not already on scene and required then should request their attendance, via ambulance control. Full personal protective equipment should be worn.

When attending incidents on building and other industrial sites and railways the paramedic/clinician will be subject to, and must comply with, health and safety legislation specific to those sites (Health and Safety at Work Act 1974 part 1 section 7). It is worth noting that under CIMAH (Control of Industrial Major Accident Hazards) regulations, emergency planning on industrial sites is the responsibility of local Fire and Civil Defence Associations and that rendezvous points (RVPs) will be pre designated (Health and Safety Executive 1999).

When attending potential spinal injury incidents the paramedic/clinician should consider the cause(s) of the injury when assessing the risk of danger to self, colleagues and others at the scene. Possible sources of danger to the paramedic/clinician include (but are not limited to):

- Traffic and moving motor vehicles
- Fire and chemical hazards
- Falling objects from above
- Unstable or unsecured machinery or vehicles
- Unsafe walls and ceilings
- Assailants on scene
- Incidents that have occurred in water (diving).

Possible actions to be taken:

- Wear personal protective equipment (PPE)
- Request fire/police service assistance
- Request Hazardous Area Response Team (HART)
- Ensure the safety of others at the scene

RESPONSE

Ordinarily, the approach to a patient would include an assessment of their response to verbal commands and questions. A conscious patient would, naturally, turn their head and face a paramedic/clinician initiating contact verbally. For this reason a patient with suspected spinal injury should, whenever possible, be approached from the front. Ideally this assessment will be undertaken by two paramedic/clinicians, the first will make direct eye contact with the patient and tell the patient to '*look at me*', whilst the second will then undertake the appropriate stabilisation/neutral alignment of the 'C' spine. Bring the patient's neck into the neutral inline position. If there is any increased pain or neurological deficit or if there is resistance to movement this procedure should be ceased and the patient maintained in the position they are in (Trauma.org 2002). A brief explanation can now be given describing what assessment will follow.

Possible actions to be taken:

- Approach the patient from the front
- Explain your actions clearly and concisely
- Obtain and maintain neutral alignment
- Assess and record the patient's level of consciousness (AVPU)

AIRWAY

The airway should be assessed and, if not already patent, should be opened and assessed for patency. The paramedic/clinician has the responsibility of recognising the potential for spinal injury from the initial scene assessment and the need to employ the appropriate 'C' spine method of airway management (see Figure 6.1).

Studies have shown that between 3% and 25% of spinal injuries are exacerbated by excessive and unnecessary movement of the patient within the emergency department (Banit *et al.* 2000). This may be reduced if the paramedic/clinician instigates the correct handling of the patient at the onset of treatment before arrival at the emergency department.

Movement should be minimal as any pressure on the spinal cord from misaligned or fractured vertebrae may cause neurological damage. In order to avoid this, the initial airway management is manual but may be assisted later, by oropharyngeal airway (OP), endotracheal tube (ET) or laryngeal mask airway (LMA) if required (Salomone and Pons 2007, p95).

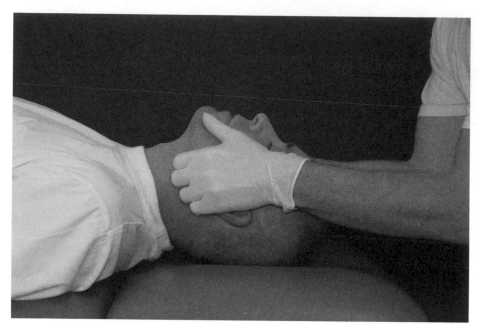

Figure 6.1   Jaw thrust manoeuvre

Possible actions to be taken:

■   Recognise the possibility of 'C' spinal injury, utilise jaw thrust manoeuvre
■   Stepwise airway management as appropriate (see Chapter 2)
■   Ensure airway is patent before proceeding to next element

BREATHING

When assessing the patient's breathing the first concern should be '*is the patient breathing?*'

Poor or inadequate breathing may, in itself, be as a result of spinal cord injury (SCI). Damage to the spinal cord above C5 will have a direct effect on the mechanism of respiration caused by weakness or paralysis of the diaphragm and usually require mechanical ventilation. Their vital capacity can be reduced to 10%–20% of normal with either weak or ineffective coughing (Greaves *et al.* 2009, p139).

Diaphragmatic paralysis causes the accessory respiratory muscles to take up some, or all, of the work of respiration by contracting more intensely. This can lead to muscle fatigue and possibly respiratory failure. The paramedic/clinician should look for a breathing pattern of paradoxical abdominal wall retraction which occurs during inspiration (Nader and Shahriar 2009). If the patient is apnoeic ventilate as appropriate (Resuscitation Council (UK) 2008).

- Inadequate ventilations (rate <12 per minute) should be assisted using bag valve mask (BVM) with additional oxygen therapy to maintain SpO_2 levels at 94%–98%.
- Normal ventilation rate (between 12 and 20 per minute) should be monitored and oxygen therapy considered in the case of the trauma patient.
- Fast ventilations (20 to 30 per minute) should also be monitored. The cause of increased respiration is increasing levels of carbon dioxide or reducing levels of oxygen in the blood. This should be addressed with oxygen therapy at high levels.
- Abnormally fast ventilations (above 30 per minute) may be a result of hypoxia and oxygen therapy at high levels should be commenced. It may be necessary for the paramedic/clinician to assist ventilation using BVM and to find and reverse the cause of increased respiration (Salomone and Pons 2007, p95–6).

NB. *The above breathing rates are based on an adult patient. Adjustments should be made when dealing with infants and children.*

Possible actions to be taken:

- Assess breathing rate and function
- Ventilate apnoeic patients or those who have weak or diaphragmatic breathing as appropriate
- Administer oxygen accordingly (BTS 2008, pvi4)
- Assist inadequate ventilations, too fast as well as too slow
- Manage and reverse the causes of hypoxia
- Transfer to appropriate trauma unit

CIRCULATION

- Control any obvious external haemorrhaging. Nearly 80% of patients with spinal injury have multiple injuries. Symptoms of shock should not be attributed to the spinal injury until all haemorrhaging has been excluded (Greaves *et al.* 2009, p141). (*See Trauma Assessment: Chapter 7.*)
- Assess the colour and general appearance of the skin. Vasoconstriction and poor peripheral circulation can provide an idea of the perfusion of

vital organs. A conscious patient who is clearly cerebrally perfused with warm normal skin implies that the patient is not in shock. However, the opposite can also be the case.

■ Assess blood pressure and if the patient is hypotensive (systolic <90 mmHg), implement correction management.

■ Injury at or above thoracic (T6) can lead to considerable loss of sympathetic autonomic control. This results in hypotension and bradycardia due to heightened vagal responses. (In effect the 'accelerator' is not functioning and only the 'brakes' work.) Peripheral vasodilation, hypotension and bradycardia caused by the disruption of sympathetic nervous control is termed 'neurogenic shock'. However, hypovolaemia must be excluded before you attribute the cause of the hypotension to 'neurogenic shock' (Greaves *et al.* 2009, p139).

Possible actions to be taken:

■ Control external haemorrhage
■ Monitor and record capillary bed refill and pulses
■ Assess appearance and temperature/colour of skin
■ If hypotensive, assess and exclude hypovolaemia as the cause
■ Treat shock due to hypovolaemia in order to prevent secondary injury from hypoperfusion. (*See Trauma Assessment: Chapter 7.*)

DISABILITY

Symptoms of spinal cord injury can vary depending on the location and severity of the injury. Full dissection will result in complete loss of function but in the case of a partial dissection some motor or sensory function may be retained. Injury to the neck will affect the arms, legs and torso, and thoracic (chest level) injuries will affect the legs. The spinal cord does not go beyond the first lumbar vertebra so injuries below this point are not spinal cord injury but may cause 'cauda equina syndrome' which is damage to the nerve roots in this region.

■ Assess neurological symptoms by asking the patient if they are experiencing any loss of feeling or movement. The paramedic/clinician should assess and observe the patient's breathing, numbness or sensory changes, increased muscle tone, pain and limb weakness, and in the unconscious patient assess for any loss of bowel control (Zieve and Hoch 2010).

■ Assess the patient's level of consciousness (AVPU).

- Assess the blood glucose levels.
- Assess the patient's pupils (PERRLA).
- Abnormal posturing may be observed and is a sign of serious damage to the central nervous system. The following may be seen:
  - Decerebrate posture – rigid extension of the arms and legs, downward pointing of the toes, and backward arching of the head (see Figure 6.2), or
  - Decorticate posture – rigidity, flexion of the arms, clenched fists, and extended legs (see Figure 6.3).

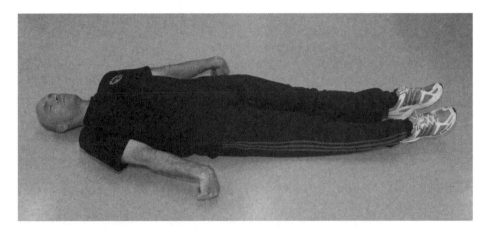

Figure 6.2   Decerebrate positioning – abnormal extensor response

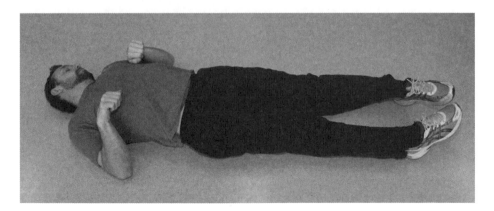

Figure 6.3   Decorticate positioning – abnormal extensor response

---

Possible actions to be taken:

- Assess and document LOC (AVPU)
- Assess and document blood glucose levels, and neurological symptoms
- Assess and document size and equality of pupils (PERRLA)
- Note abnormal postures (decerebrate/decorticate)

EXPOSE/ENVIRONMENT/EVALUATE

- Continued patient assessment requires the paramedic/clinician to expose and examine the injured patient by removing clothing or other materials covering the body. This should be performed with reference to previous findings to establish an evaluation of the patient's condition and ongoing prognosis.
- How much or how little to remove is a decision based on the environment and the ongoing findings. Remove as much as is necessary to ascertain either the presence or absence of injuries. Whilst patient modesty is a consideration it should not interfere with an examination. Consent must, however, be obtained (DH 2009, p9).
- Look for pre-existing injuries or injuries which might have caused subsequent trauma. For example an assault may have led to a fall from height in the patient's attempts to flee their assailant. A thorough examination after a relatively minor fall may lead to the discovery of a penetrating injury.
- Be aware of the patient's modesty and also the risk of hypothermia. Cover the patient with blankets during and after the examination and evaluation process (Salomone and Pons 2007, p99).
- Examine the patient with an open mind and be prepared to find the unexpected injury. If you don't look you won't find. (Complete a head to toe examination as part of the secondary survey.)

Possible actions to be taken:

- Expose, Examine, Evaluate
- Don't be blinkered, keep an open mind
- Consider dignity and hypothermia, blankets are an important part of patient assessment
- Transfer the patient to the appropriate trauma unit

SECONDARY SURVEY

Having completed a primary survey and documented the observations a secondary survey is initiated to ascertain if the patient requires spinal immobilisation. This involves a head-to-toe examination which includes every side of the patient, top, bottom, back, front and the left and right (Greaves *et al.* 2009, p141). This will enable the paramedic/clinician to gather more detailed information about the patient's condition and ascertain what happened to cause the injury. After undertaking this and evaluating the appropriate information the paramedic/clinician will be able to decide whether or not to proceed to immobilisation of the patient.

Presenting complaint

- What is the mechanism of injury? Is the patient in pain? Where is the pain? The presence of pain to the spinal region is a clear indicator of the possibility of spinal injury. However, the lack of pain to the spine should not rule out injury until it has been established that pain is not being masked by pain from another injury. Assess the pain using the OPQRSTA framework (Limmer and O'Keefe 2009, p436).
- Is the patient able to move their limbs individually?
- Does this cause further pain?
- Are there any abnormal sensations in the limbs or trunk?
- The nervous system is so complex and the range of symptoms associated with spinal cord injury or damage so varied that any unusual sensory or motor sensation should be taken seriously (Greaves *et al.* 2009, p141).

History of presenting complaint

The exact history of the injury is important when assessing the patient with a spinal injury and deciding whether or not to fully immobilise them. The paramedic/clinician should assess each patient with an open mind: there are some dangerous mechanisms of injury which require x-ray to exclude spinal injury in patients with head or neck pain. These are:

- Fall from height greater than five metres (or two to three times the patient's height)
- Fall down five stairs or more
- Impact to the head causing axial load to the spine, e.g. rugby scrum or diving into shallow water
- Motor vehicle collision with high speed impact, roll over or ejection of the passenger. Motor cycle and bicycle collision. Collision involving recreational vehicles (quad bikes etc.)

■ Impact from behind by bus, lorry or high speed vehicle or shunt into oncoming, moving traffic (Wardrobe *et al*. 2004).

Past medical history

The past medical history of the patient may have a bearing on their treatment and could provide valuable clues to the history of the presenting complaint in the confused or concussed patient. It can also lead the paramedic/clinician to suspect alternative events to those being described and expand the range of observations in their secondary survey.

■ What predisposing medical conditions does the patient have?
■ Diabetic patients may need a glucose challenge to correct hypoglycaemia. Indeed a hypoglycaemic episode may have been the cause of the initial trauma.
■ Cardiac patients who may initially have had some chest pain may be distracted from this fact by overriding pain from impact injuries. It is worth considering if an arrhythmia may have led to a loss of consciousness and, subsequently, to the resultant mechanism of injury.

Possible actions to be taken:

■ Undertake a full assessment and history
■ Immobilise the patient appropriately
■ Obtain information regarding the PMH and predisposing illnesses
■ Ascertain if the patient has diabetes
■ Be thorough in patient observations and only make exclusions with evidence
■ Transfer to an appropriate trauma unit

Drug/medication history

The patient may have taken/ingested alcohol or drugs that may reduce or mask the patient's perception of pain. Ascertain if the patient has other conditions they take medications for, or if they have any allergies to any drugs.

OTHER CONSIDERATIONS

Patient specific factors may indicate a higher level of risk of spinal injury. Elderly patients over 65 and those suffering from bone disorders such as osteoporosis, ankylosing spondylitis and rheumatoid arthritis are among these (Wardrobe *et al.* 2004).

An older patient who has fallen may be unable to distinguish between old and new neck pain. Elderly patients may also find it difficult to recall or describe a mechanism of injury, especially those with dementia. If there is any doubt the patient should be immobilised and transported to hospital. Some older people develop kyphosis, a spinal curvature, and it may be impossible to immobilise and apply a cervical collar. In such cases the head should not be forced into a neutral alignment. The patient should be made comfortable using blankets and other padding. Confusion may make spinal immobilisation distressing for patients and it may be appropriate to loosen belts and head blocks in order to minimise movement in the patient. Remember to reassure them. Spinal injury or SCI should not be excluded in an intoxicated patient with a significant mechanism of injury (Clubb 2007).

Communication

If communication barriers prevent reliable response to direct questioning and there is a significant mechanism of injury the patient should be treated for spinal injury until this can be excluded. Consider assistance from translator services if locally available.

Ethical and legal

In some cases of spinal trauma the police will be attempting to obtain statements from patients. The paramedic/clinician's first responsibility is to the patient and their priority is to assess and immobilise the patient. Police may travel with the patient as this provides a continuity of evidence should there be any criminal proceedings as the result of the injuries sustained.

Destination/receiving specialist units

A patient not in cardiac arrest should be conveyed to an appropriate trauma centre, depending on local guidelines, such as the new major trauma centres (Healthcare for London 2009).

Facts and figures

The Department of Health explains that two people in a population of 100,000 are likely to experience a traumatic spinal injury every year (D.H. 2005a, p10); however, the International Spinal Injuries and Rehabilitation Centre at the Royal Buckinghamshire Hospital estimate that there are 40,000 people in the UK alone that are paralysed through spinal cord injury (Spinal Injuries 2010).

CHAPTER KEY POINTS

■ When undertaking the assessment of a patient with suspected spinal injury, be systematic and thorough.

■ Ensure primary survey problems are identified, managed and reviewed.

■ Examine the patient with an open mind and be prepared to find the unexpected injury, remember that the range of symptoms associated with spinal cord damage is so varied that any unusual sensory or motor sensation should be taken seriously.

■ Ensure patients are referred to the appropriate trauma unit.

7 Trauma assessment

Graham Harris, David Kerr, Matthew Lane and James Rouse

Trauma is the acute physiological and structural change that occurs in a patient's body when an external source of energy dissipates faster than the body's ability to sustain and dissipate it (Caroline 2008). However *major trauma* is seen as trauma that may cause death or severe disability (Royal College of Surgeons of England (RCSE) 2009, p9).

In England alone there are approximately 20,000 incidents of *major trauma* which either result in death or permanent disabilities (National Audit Office (NAO) 2010). The commonest cause of death is due to road traffic collision (RTC). The NAO advises that there are around a further 28,000 cases which do not meet the precise definition of major trauma, but still require to be cared for in the same way.

The aim of this chapter is to provide the paramedic/clinician with a structured systematic approach to the assessment of the patient who has sustained trauma, resulting in multiple injuries which potentially could affect one or more systems.

SCENE ASSESSMENT

As you approach the scene take a 'global overview' in order to ascertain the mechanism of injury (MOI) and the potential cause of the trauma. Trauma may have occurred due to one or more of the following reasons:

- Mechanical   (moving vehicle, fall from height)
- Chemical   (acid burns or ingested agents)
- Thermal   (burns – wet or dry, frostbite)
- Electrical   (high voltage electrocution)
- Barometric   (sudden pressure changes – explosions)

When determining the cause of trauma and the MOI, first consider what form of energy was involved and its magnitude, as each variable produces differing patterns of injury and therefore dictates different management considerations. The energy transfer that the patient is subjected to will result in either or both of these types of trauma – blunt or penetrating:

- **Blunt trauma:** Where the tissues are not penetrated by an external object (bruising caused by a seat belt during sudden deceleration)
- **Penetrating trauma:** Where the tissues are penetrated by an external object (gunshot wound (GSW), stabbing or an impaled object).

PRIMARY SURVEY

The primary survey is modified for trauma to include **DR 'C' ABCDE**. This extra element covers major catastrophic haemorrhage which should be controlled during the primary survey phase and follows the evidenced based C-ABC algorithm (Hodgetts *et al.* 2006, p745–6).

The severity of the *trauma* and the resulting injuries will determine the possibility of the patient having sustained one or more life threatening injuries. As these have the potential to cause death or severe disability the paramedic/clinician should undertake the primary survey and implement as appropriate the following:

- Identify major trauma patients at the scene of the incident who are at risk of death or disability.
- Immediate interventions to allow safe transport.
- Rapid dispatch to a major trauma centre for surgical management and critical care (RCSE 2009, p10).

DANGER

- Ensure the safety of yourself, your colleague/s and the patient/s. Use your vehicle as protection at road traffic incidents.
- If not already on scene request assistance of other appropriate emergency services: Helicopter Emergency Medical Services (HEMS), Hazardous Area Response Team (HART), fire and rescue (entrapments, fires) and police (traffic or crime scenes).
- Ensure that personal protective equipment is worn as appropriate to the incident (high-visibility clothing, gloves, hats).

Possible actions to be taken:

- Ensure safety of self, colleague/s and patients
- Wear PPE as appropriate

- Request other emergency services (fire service/police) as appropriate
- Request specialist assistance (HEMS)/(HART) if available

RESPONSE

- Assess the patient's response using the AVPU scale and record appropriately.
- Remember that alterations in the patient's level of consciousness (LOC) may be due to an injury affecting their airway, breathing or circulation and resulting 'hypoxia'.
- The patient may be unable to respond due to obstruction of the airway.

Possible actions to be taken:

- Assess the patient's level of consciousness (AVPU)
- Record any period of unconsciousness (it may be part of the patient's lucid interval) (A lucid interval is the period of consciousness between two periods of unconsciousness.)

CATASTROPHIC HAEMORRHAGE

There will be incidents that paramedics attend where trauma has resulted in catastrophic haemorrhage. If this is not assessed and managed appropriately then the patient may die (Hodgetts *et al.* 2006; Thomas *et al.* 2010).

- Ensure the immediate control of obvious catastrophic bleeding.
- Utilise and apply appropriate tourniquet(s) or haemostatic dressing(s).

Possible actions to be taken:

- Control obvious catastrophic haemorrhage.
- Apply tourniquets or haemostatic dressings as appropriate.
- Ensure haemorrhage is controlled before proceeding to the next element.

AIRWAY

The paramedic/clinician should remember that patients with trauma have a higher risk of cervical 'C' spine injuries, and should therefore utilise the appropriate airway opening techniques. Remember that patients who do require resuscitation often have an obstructed airway (Resuscitation Council (UK) 2010, p69).

- If the patient is unresponsive, open the airway (with the appropriate 'C' spine manoeuvre).
- Airway obstruction may be due to oedema of the airway caused by burns, maxillo-facial injuries, or foreign bodies.
- Utilise stepwise airway management to secure a patent airway (airway manoeuvre – jaw thrust, suction, oral/nasal airway adjuncts, supraglottic airway devices, endotracheal intubation, needle cricothyroidotomy) (*see Respiratory Assessment: Chapter 2*).

Possible actions to be taken:

- Use 'C' spine airway manoeuvre if appropriate
- Utilise airway adjuncts (stepwise airway management, see Chapter 2) as appropriate
- Ensure airway is patent and secure before proceeding to next element

---

BREATHING

There are various life threatening injuries caused by trauma that affect the patient's breathing; the paramedic/clinician should ensure that they identify these as part of their assessment.

- Assess if the patient is breathing:
  - What is the rate?
  - Is it adequate?
  - Do they have any dyspnoea?
- Assess the SpO_2 levels and administer 15 l/min O_2, if appropriate (BTS 2008).
- Use the Look, Feel, Listen technique (Lee *et al.* 2007, p220–4).
- Auscultate and identify time critical respiratory conditions.

The following life threatening injuries may occur to the thoracic cavity of the trauma patient:

- Aortic dissection
- Tension pneumothorax
- Open pneumothorax
- Massive haemothorax/haemhorrage
- Flail segment
- Cardiac tamponade.

Aortic dissection

Aortic dissection is a condition that presents as a sudden severe tearing retrosternal pain which radiates to the back, the degree of the radiation will depend on the blood vessels involved. If branch arteries are affected the patient may present with either the absence of pulses and/or unequal blood pressure recording in each arm.

Signs and symptoms
■ Sudden severe tearing retrosternal pain (*may radiate to back*)
■ Absence of radial pulses and unequal blood pressure.

Tension pneumothorax

A tension pneumothorax occurs when an opening is created within the pleural lining of the lung. If a one-way valve is created air will enter the pleural space on inhalation but will not leave on exhalation. This creates an increased intra-pleural pressure leading to the collapse of the lung. As the tension pneumothorax increases in size, the pressure pushes the contents of the mediastinum to the opposite side of the body obstructing blood flow of the heart reducing cardiac output. In addition, the tension may compress the diaphragm and opposing lung. Without immediate interventions this condition will lead to respiratory arrest.

Signs and symptoms
■ Blunt or penetrating trauma to the chest
■ Dyspnoea/respiratory failure
■ Absent air sounds on injured side
■ Reduced SpO_2
■ Surgical emphysema.

Open pneumothorax

An open pneumothorax is caused by a penetrating injury to the chest wall causing air to enter the pleural space. The negative pressure created in the thoracic cavity can draw air through the hole in the chest wall. This may present as a *sucking chest wound*.

Signs and symptoms
■ Penetrating trauma to the chest
■ Dyspnoea
■ Sucking chest wound
■ Reduced air entry on affected side
■ Surgical emphysema.

Massive haemothorax/haemorrhage

A haemothorax occurs when blood enters the pleural space within the lungs. The pleural space of the lungs can hold up to 3 litres of blood and therefore can represent a significant source of blood loss (Salomone and Pons 2007). Massive haemorrhage classically presents with the various signs and symptoms of the *four stages* of shock. These signs and symptoms are often subtle and may not always be present.

Signs and symptoms
- Mechanism of injury – blunt or penetrating trauma to the chest
- Dyspnoea
- Reduced chest expansion on side of injury
- Reduced air entry on side of injury
- Signs of hypovolaemic shock.

Flail segment

A flail segment occurs when two or more adjacent ribs are broken in two or more places. A paradoxical movement of the lungs occurs due to the free floating flail segment that moves independently of the remainder of the ribs. The flail segment moves in with inhalation and out with exhalation, opposing the normal movement of ribs in respiration, causing inadequate ventilation.

Signs and symptoms
- Significant blunt trauma to the chest
- Paradoxical breathing
- Reduced chest expansion on affected side
- Pain
- Dyspnoea.

Cardiac tamponade

Cardiac tamponade occurs when there is bleeding into the pericardial cavity which can prevent effective contraction of the heart. A high index of suspicion should be held with any penetrating trauma within the *danger zone*. This zone is located between the nipple line and a horizontal line drawn perpendicular with the epigastrum.

Signs and symptoms
- Mechanism of injury (penetrating injury to the danger zone)
- Signs of cardiogenic/obstructive shock
- Beck's Triad – hypotension, distended neck veins, muffled heart sounds.

> ## Possible actions to be taken:
>
> - Ensure that breathing is adequate (respirations <10 or >29 breaths per minute require ventilatory support)
> - Seal sucking chest wounds, stabilise flail segments, decompress tension pneumothoraces accordingly
> - Administer oxygen appropriately to patient's injury(s)
> - Manage hypoxia appropriately
> - Transfer to appropriate trauma unit

CIRCULATION

Whilst the assessment of catastrophic haemorrhage is immediate, the patient who has sustained trauma may also have internal haemorrhage that is not so easily identifiable. It is imperative that paramedic/clinicians identify at the earliest opportunity patients who have hypovolaemic shock and deal appropriately. Remember these signs and symptoms are often subtle and may not always be present.

- Look to see if the patient has any form of haemorrhage, internal or external and manage accordingly.
- Assessment of the trauma patient's circulatory system includes palpating the radial pulse, or for penetrating torso injuries a central pulse.
- Assess peripheral if available, or alternatively assess central capillary refill taken over the sternum or forehead (*>2 seconds indicates poor perfusion*).
- Administer IV fluids appropriately (NICE 2004b; JRCALC 2006b).

> ## Possible actions to be taken:
>
> - Control external haemorrhage
> - Assess and manage shock accordingly
> - IV access and intravenous fluids en route
> - Pre-alert to the nearest trauma centre

DISABILITY

Remember that trauma patients may have sustained a head injury, or alternatively their injuries affecting the respiratory and circulatory systems may cause hypoxia, and result in altered levels of consciousness.

- Assess the patient's level of consciousness (AVPU).
- Ascertain if the patient has been unconscious – information from witnesses/bystanders (brain injuries are associated with lucid intervals) (Clarke 2005, p1219).
- Assess the patient's posture, note any decerebrate or decorticate positioning.
- Assess the patient's pupils for both size and reaction, dilation of pupils may be due to intracranial pressure (ICP) (PERRLA).
- Assess and note obvious deformities of limbs.

Possible actions to be taken:

- Assess the patient's LOC (AVPU)
- Record any periods of unconsciousness (it may be part of a lucid interval) (a lucid interval is the period of consciousness between two periods of unconsciousness)
- Assess the patient's pupils
- Assess and note posture and any obvious deformities

EXPOSE/EXAMINE/EVALUATE

In trauma situations it is imperative that injuries are identified and assessed, therefore it may be necessary to remove clothing to expose the injury(s).

- Expose fully and examine the patient's injury(s).
- Evaluate and determine the need to transfer to the nearest major trauma centre (Health Care for London, 2009).

Possible actions to be taken:

- Expose and examine injuries and evaluate the findings
- Identify and manage time critical conditions appropriately
- Pre-alert and transfer to the appropriate trauma unit

SECONDARY SURVEY

History

History taking is an important skill for paramedic/clinicians to master in order to provide timely interventions and treatment. In trauma it is vital to understand the mechanism of injury and the resultant possible major life threatening complications to the patient. Competent paramedic/clinicians should observe the scene and the patient to create a picture of events.

Remember to utilise witness observations as well as that of the patient.

Presenting complaint

- What has happened to cause these injuries?
- Do you have any pain? If so where?
- Have you moved from the scene? If so how?
- Do you remember the events fully?
- Did you lose consciousness?

The use of the following framework may assist the paramedic/clinician:

- S – Signs and symptoms
- A – Allergies
- M – Medications
- P – Past medical history
- L – Last meal
- E – Events leading up to the incident.

History of presenting complaint

A thorough understanding of the mechanism of injury is essential in identifying possible injuries the patient may have.

- Road traffic collisions (RTC):
  - Were they wearing a seatbelt?
  - Is there a 'bullseye' on the front windscreen? If so, is it inwards or outwards?
  - Is there any further damage to the vehicle?
  - Are there fatalities within the vehicle?
  - Was the patient ejected?
  - Has the vehicle overturned? (*All of these suggest a high transfer of energy*)
- Fall from height:
  - What was the distance of the fall?
  - What type of surface did the patient land on?
  - What part of the body took the impact of the fall?
- Penetrating injuries:
  - What was the instrument that caused the injury?
  - Where are the injuries on the body? (*This should highlight the possible injuries to underlying structures*)

- Burns:
  - What caused the burn?
  - When did the burn happen?
  - Where are the burns to the body?
  - Did the event happen in an enclosed space? (*This is indicative of inhalation injuries*)
  - Does the patient have any difficulty in breathing (DIB)?

Paramedic/clinicians should ensure they utilise a validated objective tool when assessing a patient's pain severity (Lord and Woollard 2011). Also ensure they utilise appropriate pain management to minimise the distress of the patients in trauma situations. The OPQRSTA framework will assist the paramedic/clinician in assessing pain:

- Onset: When did the injury(s) occur?
- Provokes: What makes the pain better? What makes it worse? Is there pain on inspiration or movement?
- Quality: Describe the pain in your own words. Is it a sharp/dull/burning pain?
- Radiates: Does the pain move anywhere else in your body?
- Severity: Can you score the pain out of ten?
- Time: Was the onset sudden or gradual? And has it changed?
- Associate: Are there any associated symptoms?

The following areas are important, but not essential, in patients with life threatening injuries. The paramedic/clinician must also remember that certain patient groups which include the elderly, the obese and pregnant women, are all at high risk in the trauma situation, therefore a thorough history is beneficial (National Confidential Enquiry into Patient Outcome and Death (NCEPOD) 2007).

Past medical history

- Have you had any recent operations?
- Do you suffer with clotting disorders?
- Do you have any chronic medical conditions?

Drug/medication history

- Do you take any anticoagulant medication?
- Do you take beta blockers?
- Have you taken recreational drugs or alcohol within the last 24 hours?

REVIEW OF SYSTEMS RELATED TO TRAUMA

In the out-of-hospital environment it is essential to review the following systems which may provide additional information on the condition of the patient. The paramedic/clinician should recognise that if they reach this point in history taking it is unlikely the patient's condition is life threatening.

Respiratory

- Can the patient talk in full sentences? (an inability could be indicative of an airway obstruction or breathing problem)
- Does your airway feel tight? (this may be indicative of inhalation burns)
- Do you have any difficulty in breathing?
- Do you have any pain on inspiration?

Circulation

In the trauma situation the paramedic/clinician will often rely on visual observation of external haemorrhage, and observation of cardiovascular vital signs rather than using questions to understand the circulatory system. See vital signs section below.

Neurological

- Was there any loss of consciousness (LOC)?
- Do you remember what happened?
- Do you have any neck or back pain?
- Can you move your arms and legs?
- Have you vomited?

Musculoskeletal

- Do you have any pain on movement?
- Prior to the traumatic injury did you suffer with any long-term musculoskeletal pain?

VITAL SIGNS

Vital signs are essential to every patient assessment. They should be used in conjunction with the information found within the history taking and physical examination process, to differentiate between patients with a time critical and non-time critical condition. The paramedic/clinician must remember continual reassessment of the vital signs is an essential part of patient assessment.

Respiratory rate

The paramedic should note the rate, depth and rhythm of respiration to provide a holistic view of the patient's respiratory function. Remember that patients with a respiratory rate of <10 or >29 breaths per minute will require ventilatory support, as both rates are indicative of inadequate minute volumes and respiratory failure.

Pulse oximetry

Pulse oximetry provides a measurement of the arterial blood saturation of oxygen, and the appropriate levels of oxygen should be administered accordingly (Greaves and Porter 1999). In the trauma situation the paramedic/clinician must be aware of the limiting factors in pulse oximetry, as inaccurate measurements can occur during exposure to movement, bright light, dirt or cold environments. Patients are more likely to be exposed to these environments in trauma situations.

Pulse rate

The pulse rate is a quick and non-invasive method of gaining an insight into the trauma patient's circulatory volume and function. The paramedic/clinician should initially assess the radial pulse, if palpable, ascertain if it is strong, weak or thready. A patient demonstrating tachycardia may be indicative of shock, whereas a patient with bradycardia may be demonstrating a pre-terminal sign (Salomone and Pons 2007).

Capillary bed refill (CBR)

The capillary refill can be taken both peripherally and centrally on the trauma patient. Paramedic/clinicians should be aware of limiting factors such as shock, which may contribute to a false reading. Undertaking a central capillary refill taken over the sternum or forehead may provide a more accurate indication of a patient's circulatory function.

- Pressure should be applied for 5 seconds and capillary refill should return in less than 2 seconds.
- >2 seconds suggests poor tissue perfusion.

Blood pressure

In the trauma situation changes in blood pressure are likely to occur due to a decrease in circulating blood volume caused by major blood vessel damage. The paramedic/clinician should be aware of the stages of shock and recognise that hypotension occurs in the latter stages of shock (Goldman and Ausiello 2008).

Capnometry – end tidal CO_2 ($ETCO_2$)

The paramedic/clinician should recognise the significance of using capnography when assessing the trauma patient. It is most often used in the intubated patient to confirm endotracheal tube or supraglottic airway placement. However, end tidal CO_2 with a normal wave form and constituent value is also indicative of an adequate circulatory volume. A poor wave form and a falling constituent value may be an early indicator of a falling circulatory volume due to continuous bleeding (Kupnik and Skok 2007).

Glasgow Coma Score (GCS)

Assess the patient's level of consciousness using the GCS. It is important to assess the GCS early in the trauma patient and to continue to reassess this as it may highlight underlying injuries, especially to the brain. This is a time expensive and subjective measurement assessment that the paramedic/clinician will become more effective at with time and experience.

- Record T if an endotracheal (ET) tube is inserted when scoring Best Verbal (Smith *et al.* 2008, p293).
- A GCS score of 3–8 indicates a severe head injury.
- A GCS score of 8 defines coma.
- A GCS score of 14–15 is mild.
- A GCS score of 15 is normal.

Pupillary assessment

The paramedic/clinician should continuously assess and reassess the pupils within the secondary survey as it may be indicative of rising intracranial pressure and an underlying brain injury. In trauma patients with head injury suspect brain injury if the patient's pupils are unequal in size. Assess accordingly (PERRLA):

- Right sided unilateral pupil dilation may be indicative of right sided brain injury
- Bilateral dilated pupils may be indicative of hypoxia or advanced signs of severe brain injury
- Irregular pupils can be indicative of direct trauma to the eye.

PHYSICAL ASSESSMENT

In the trauma situation the physical assessment of the patient is of the utmost importance in providing a thorough understanding of the patient's injuries. The paramedic/clinician must ensure all injuries are identified, documented and included in the patient handover.

CREATING A SUITABLE ENVIRONMENT

In trauma situations it is appropriate to fully expose the injured areas in order to make a thorough assessment. When the patient has multi-system trauma and is time critical the paramedic team may decide that all clothes should be removed from the patient; in these situations paramedic/clinicians should still give due consideration to the patient's privacy and dignity where possible (DH 2001a).

CONSENT

The Health Professions Council (HPC) states that paramedic/clinicians must ensure that they gain informed consent for any treatment they carry out. This must be documented accurately and passed onto other members of the health care team. In the trauma situation it may not always be possible to gain consent so the paramedic/ clinician must ensure that they act in the patient's best interest (HPC 2008).

EXAMINATION: 'TOP TO TOE' ASSESSMENT

In trauma situations the patient often has pain associated with their underlying injuries, therefore excellent communication skills are required from the paramedic/ clinician to build an effective rapport with the patient and gain their trust. Advise the patient what you are doing and ask questions appropriately as you progress through the assessment. The paramedic/clinician should assess the patient accordingly and use the senses of *touch, sight* and *hearing* to gather as much information about the condition of the patient as possible. Universal precautions in the form of gloves and protective eyewear should be worn when in contact with the patient due to the possibility of contact with body fluids.

The paramedic/clinician can adopt a 'toe to top' assessment when treating paediatric patients as this is a less threatening approach and will help to foster a relationship of trust with the patient.

Head

- Gently palpate and visually inspect the entirety of the head and face. Areas covered by hair are harder to assess visually therefore thorough palpation is necessary to identify underlying injuries.

- Any bruising, lacerations, abrasions, deformity and bleeding should be treated and documented. Palpate bones of the face and skull for crepitus, deviation, depression and abnormal mobility.
- Special attention should be given to the following findings:
  - 'Boggy masses' – possible fractured skull with underlying brain tissue injury
  - Cerebral spinal fluid (CSF) – a straw coloured oily liquid from the nose and ears suggests an underlying base of skull fracture
  - Periorbital ecchymosis and Battle signs – bilateral bruising around the orbits of the eyes and mastoid ecchymosis or bruising under the ears suggest a base of skull fracture although they may take several hours to become apparent (Salomone and Pons 2007).

Neck

The acronym 'TWELVE' is a useful aid in assessing trauma to the neck:

T – *Tracheal* deviation – is a late sign of a tension pneumothorax and not always seen.

W – *Wounds* – contusions, abrasions, penetrating injuries (entry and exit wounds), bleeding and lacerations need to be treated and documented. The paramedic/clinician should be aware of the underlying structures in relation to the wound and have a high index of suspicion to potential complications.

E – *Emphysema (surgical)* – identified on palpation as an air 'popping' sensation under the skin. This is often caused by a large transfer of energy, for example a fall from height, RTC or a penetrating chest injury.

L – *Laryngeal crepitus* – this is caused by direct trauma to the larynx and is associated with a hoarseness of voice. The paramedic/clinician should be aware this is a 'time critical' condition due to the potential deterioration of the airway.

V – *Venous distension* – this is indicative of obstructive shock, for example tension pneumothorax or cardiac tamponade.

E – *Exposure of the neck* (Hodgetts and Turner 2006).

A high index of suspicion of a 'C' cervical spinal injury needs to be observed when there is a mechanism of injury present. The C spine should be palpated centrally whilst maintaining in-line immobilisation of the neck. The following may be indicative of a C spine injury:

- Midline C spine tenderness
- 'Bony' deformity of the spinal processes

■ Neurological symptoms such as 'pins and needles'/numbness (paraesthesia), reduced power and movement of the limbs.

A C spine injury cannot be excluded if any of the following are present:

■ Intoxication with alcohol or drugs
■ Midline C spine tenderness
■ Neurological deficit
■ Distracting injuries
■ Reduced level of consciousness (Stiell *et al.* 2003).

Chest

The framework Inspection, Palpate, Percuss, Auscultate (IPPA) should be utilised by the paramedic/clinician (see Chapter 2).

Inspection
The paramedic should inspect the whole chest including the posterior, anterior and axilla surfaces for:

■ Symmetry of the thorax on inspiration/exhalation
■ Chest wall markings – contusions, abrasions, penetrating injuries (entry and exit wounds), bleeding and lacerations
■ Paradoxical breathing – a resultant injury of blunt trauma and indicative of a flail segment (Longmore *et al.* 2004, p48)
■ Penetrating objects that have remained in situ need to be left and secured to prevent excessive movement and increased damage to underlying structures.

Palpation
The paramedic/clinician should palpate the anterior, posterior and axilla chest walls of the trauma patient. In relation to the trauma patient the following findings should be noted:

■ Tenderness – bruising, contusions and fractures can be identified. The paramedic should have a high index of suspicion of possible underlying tissue injuries to the area of trauma
■ Crepitus – caused by rubbing of fractured bones
■ Surgical emphysema – 'popping' sensation under the skin.

Percussion
Whilst percussion has a limited role within the trauma environment due to excessive noise and chaos that is often associated with these scenarios, in the trauma patient percussion can be used to support the diagnosis of chest injuries:

■ Hyper-resonance – indicative of a pneumothorax
■ Hypo-resonance – indicative of a haemothorax or pulmonary contusions
(Salomone and Pons 2007).

Auscultation

The paramedic/clinician should perform auscultation on all trauma patients (initially within the primary survey). Due to the possibility of time critical injuries in trauma patients it is adequate to listen to the apex of the anterior chest, axilla and the bases of the posterior lungs. They should be aware of absent, reduced and added sounds in support of their diagnosis.

Sounds found on auscultation
■ Stridor – high pitched sound heard on inspiration (obstruction due to foreign body, oedema of airway due to burns)
■ Fine crackles/coarse crackles – pulmonary contusion, aspiration of bodily fluids
■ Reduced breath sounds – haemothorax
■ Absent or diminished breath sounds – tension pneumothorax.

Abdomen

The paramedic/clinician should focus on detecting concealed haemorrhage in the abdominal cavity as early deaths from trauma to this region typically result from massive blood loss (Salomone and Pons 2007). Consider a high index of suspicion in any patient who has sustained trauma to the abdomen due to the delicate and vascular nature of underlying organs. The paramedic/clinician should suspect an occult abdominal injury if there is trauma above and below this area (Hodgetts and Turner 2006).

The paramedic/clinician should focus on inspection and palpation of the abdominal region in assisting their diagnosis of injuries.

Inspection
The paramedic/clinician should expose and inspect the whole abdominal region including the anterior, flanks and posterior surfaces for:

■ Abdominal wall markings – contusions, abrasions, penetrating injuries (entry and exit wounds), bleeding and lacerations
■ Grey Turner's sign – bruising to the flanks
■ Cullen's sign – bruising around the umbilicus.

Both of these signs are indicative of retroperitoneal bleeding (Salomone and Pons 2007). Abdominal distension is a late sign that is associated with intra-abdominal bleeding and circulatory signs of shock. The peritoneal cavity can hold up to 1.5 litres of fluid before showing signs of distension, and the retroperitoneal cavity can hold 3 litres of fluid with no visible sign (Hodgetts and Turner 2006).

Palpation

The abdomen should be split into four quadrants for palpation, and the paramedic/clinician should palpate each quadrant for:

- Tenderness – a symptom experienced due to pain on palpation
- Guarding – tensing of abdominal muscles on palpation
- Rigidity – involuntary spasm of abdominal muscles.

The presence of any one of these signs is suggestive of intra-abdominal bleeding in the trauma patient (Hodgetts and Turner 2006).

Pelvis

The pelvis is a complete ring; a fracture in one part will often result in a subsequent fracture being present within the pelvic ring. It is possible to lose your total blood volume into the pelvic cavity, retroperitoneal space or a combination of both (JRCALC 2009b).

The paramedic/clinician should not manually compress the pelvis to confirm a fracture but instead hold a high level of suspicion if the pelvic injury is associated with the following findings:

- Relevant mechanism of injury
- Asymmetrical alignment of the pelvis on inspection
- Pelvic and/or lower back pain
- Injuries above and below the pelvis
- Lateral displacement of both legs classically seen in an 'open book fracture'
- Bleeding per rectum (PR), per vagina (PV) including instances of haematuria post-trauma.

Back

In the trauma situation patients who are identified with a potential CSI should be fully immobilised. The paramedic/clinician should not roll the patient to solely assess the back as the benefits of this are limited in the out-of-hospital field. However, if an opportunity arises to assess the patient's back, the paramedic/clinician should fully expose the area and inspect for:

- Contusions, abrasions, penetrating injuries (entry and exit wounds), bleeding and lacerations

- Paradoxical breathing – indicative of a posterior flail segment
- Vertebral bone deformity.

In addition, the following neurological signs and symptoms may be apparent in a patient with spinal injury:

- Paraesthesia
- Reduced power and movement of the limbs
- Priapism.

Extremities (legs and arms)

The paramedic/clinician should expose and assess the extremities, beginning with the legs. All injuries should be documented and treated. The following assessments of each individual limb should occur:

- Inspection – areas of deformity, contusions, swelling, lacerations and pallor
- Palpation – areas of tenderness and crepitus
- Motor, sensory, circulatory (MSC) (*of all limbs*)
- Motor – ask if the patient can move their limb
- Sensory – test for sensation in the extremity of the limb
- Circulatory – assess for the presence of distal pulses and capillary bed refill (CBR)
- Blood loss – fractured limbs can cause circulatory compromise due to blood loss.

The following table highlights potential blood loss in fractures of different bones:

The paramedic/clinician should be aware that an open fracture differs from a closed fracture, specifically concerning the potential blood loss which should be doubled with an open fracture.

Table 7.1 Potential blood loss in fractures of different bones

Bone fracture	Internal blood loss (ml)
Rib	125
Radius/ulna	250–500
Humerus	500–750
Tibia/fibula	500–1000
Femur	1000–2000

(Source: Salomone and Pons 2007)

Compartment syndrome

A limb threatening injury, caused by bleeding within a contained space. This prevents blood flow to the distal tissues causing ischaemia and necrosis. The following signs and symptoms are classed as the 'five P's' and may be associated with this condition:

- Pain
- Pulselessness
- Pallor
- Paraesthesia
- Paralysis (Greaves *et al.* 2004).

Penetrating trauma

Penetrating trauma creates a 'puncture' wound with potentially life threatening implications. Injuries can range from the subtle to the obvious, therefore a high index of suspicion and a thorough patient assessment is essential in reducing patient mortality. Common penetrating injuries include:

- Stab wounds (*not necessarily from a knife*)
- Bullet or gunshot wound (GSW) (*high and/or low velocity*)
- Impalement (*fencing, railings, wooden posts*).

The mechanism of injury will provide the paramedic/clinician with valuable information concerning any possible underlying trauma to the patient. A good knowledge of human anatomy is essential in determining underlying soft tissue injuries to major organs and blood vessels.

Stab wounds and impalement injuries are localised in nature and can have a predictable injury pattern. Bullet wounds can cause unpredictable injury patterns with widespread internal trauma.

Blunt trauma

Blunt trauma involves a combination of compression, shearing and rotational forces which can cause devastating underlying soft tissue injury to the major organs and blood vessels of the body. It is characterised by a high energy transfer over a large body area (Greaves *et al.* 2009). Experience has shown that road traffic collisions (RTC) are one of the most common instances in which patients may receive any of these forces (National Audit Office (NAO) 2010).

Epidemiology

Every year across England and Wales, 10,000 people die after injury. It is the leading cause of death among children and young adults of 44 years and under. In addition, there are many thousands who are left severely disabled for life. Already the commonest cause of loss of life under the age of 40, the burden of trauma is set to increase in the next 20 years. Taking a global view of 'life years lost' through premature death and disability, injury will be in second place by 2020 (Trauma Audit and Research Network (TARN) 2010).

Burns

Burn victims are a challenging category of patients to assess and treat due to the complexity of their injuries and associated pain. Burns can occur from thermal, chemical, electrical or flash insults and cause superficial, partial and full thickness injuries.

Elderly

When treating elderly people who have fallen, the paramedic/clinician should have a higher index of suspicion of injuries due to chronic conditions such as arthritis and osteoporosis, for example a fractured neck of femur (NOF). Common signs and symptoms of a fractured NOF are:

- Hip pain radiating into the groin – be aware the elderly patient may have a higher pain threshold (Salomone and Pons 2007)
- Shortening and lateral rotation of the injured extremity.

CHAPTER KEY POINTS

- The DR C ABCDE framework should be utilised to identify life threatening conditions affecting the trauma patient.
- If the patient has a time critical condition due to trauma, pre-alert to the nearest major trauma centre.
- If the patient does not have a time critical condition undertake a thorough secondary survey and record findings accordingly.
- The paramedic/clinician should constantly reassess the patient to identify changes in the patient's condition and the development of life threatening conditions.
- Definitive treatment occurs in hospital. Effective clinical interventions and history taking should occur in a timely manner in order to optimise the patient's chances of survival.

8 Musculoskeletal assessment

Kevin Dark

In the United Kingdom, 3.5 million patients attend hospital with isolated musculoskeletal conditions; the vast majority of these conditions are self-limiting (Wardrope and English 2003, p3). In addition, 70%–80% of patients subjected to multi-system trauma will also have secondary musculoskeletal injuries (MSI) that represent significant socioeconomic challenges for the National Health Service (Caroline 2008, p253). In 2010, the *Daily Telegraph* reported that during the winter months, hospitals in some of the worst affected areas reported a threefold increase in the number of patients arriving with injuries caused by slips, trips and falls due to ice and snow (Moore 2010).

Assessment of the musculoskeletal system requires the paramedic/clinician to have a clear understanding of normal anatomy and physiology and also to have a high index of suspicion with regard to:

- Life-threatening airway, breathing and circulation (ABC) conditions that may be masked by the presence of painful MSI
- Limb-threatening conditions (vascular occlusion, fractures, dislocation, septic arthritis, nerve damage, osteomyelitis/infection)
- Injury/illness physiology (strains, sprains, tendonitis, bursitis, osteoporosis, osteoarthritis, rheumatoid arthritis, gout and pathological fractures).

When the musculoskeletal system is compromised through disease or trauma, the connective tissue and associated structures elicit signs that the paramedic/clinician will see and symptoms that the patient may feel. Due to their protective nature, injuries to bones and joints may coexist with injury to soft tissues and some organs (rib cage – lungs). In practice, the paramedic/clinician must be able to differentiate between self-limiting conditions such as simple strains or sprains and more serious syndromes that will require onward referral to specialist units. Therefore in practice, musculoskeletal injuries present significant challenges in terms of pain management, immobilisation, moving and handling and transportation.

This chapter will examine the general assessment of musculoskeletal injuries. The primary and secondary surveys are used to guide the paramedic/clinician towards a more focused MSI assessment. This chapter is not intended to give detailed anatomy or physiology (see Box 8.1). Its purpose is to highlight some key assessment principles which will lead the paramedic/clinician to assess and refer the patient with MSIs effectively. In addition it will identify so called *'red flag'* conditions that present as a significant time critical emergency or which require immediate intervention or referral. These include haemodynamic and vascular compromise.

The musculoskeletal system consists of the bones, the joints they form and the muscle groups that facilitate movement. The skeletal system consists of 206 named bones. These bones are classified in terms of their function and grouped in terms of their position on either the long axis of the body (axial skeleton: skull, vertebral column, rib cage) or the appendicular skeleton (upper and lower limbs, shoulder bones and hip bones) that attach to the axial skeleton. The function of the skeletal system is to:

■ Provide support
■ Give protection to vital structures
■ Allow for body movement
■ Mineral storage
■ Blood cell formation (Marieb 2009, p135).

Box 8.1 Key physiological aspects of the musculoskeletal system

■ Muscle tissue works in conjunction with articulating joints of the skeletal system via tendons which attach muscles to the periosteum of the bone.
■ Ligaments in conjunction with muscular action provide stability to joint formations.
■ Cartilage forms a cushioning membrane in place of the periosteum when joints are formed between two bones.
■ Some joints have a bursa which allows for nutrition and protection of the joint capsule.
■ The contractibility, extensibility and elasticity of skeletal muscle allows for body movement, maintains posture, stabilises joints and generates and assists with thermostatic regulation. Skeletal muscle is encased in epimysium (there are usually many muscle fascicles that form a single muscle), and epimysium surrounds the total bundle of many fascicles, but does not allow for expansion beyond the normal limits of muscular contraction.
■ In general terms, every muscle is supplied by one nerve, an artery and a vein.
■ Muscular movement occurs through motor units consisting of somatic motor neurones.

- During increased muscular activity, a process called *recruitment* signals large muscle contractions as more neurones signal more muscle cells to contract. This is an all or nothing cascade.
- The voluntary and involuntary nervous control characteristics of skeletal muscle require a continuous supply of oxygen and essential nutrients which produce metabolic waste products that need to be removed to ensure efficient muscular activity.
- The energy required for musculoskeletal function can result in significant compromise in the patient suffering from multi system trauma. This is especially relevant in children where the paramedic/clinician needs to be aware of the effects of exhaustion.

SCENE ASSESSMENT

The paramedic/clinician must utilise all aspects of scene assessment to build a clinical picture of the potential injury patterns that may be appropriate to the patient's presenting signs and symptoms. The mechanism of injury (MOI), direct and indirect energy patterns, age, size and co-existing morbidity will have an impact on the likelihood of the presence of MSI and also the time it will take for the patient to recover functionality of the affected area. This includes sporting injuries. The injury shown in Figure 8.1 occurred during a match in February 2008: while playing

Figure 8.1   Assessment of a musculoskeletal injury scene

for Arsenal, Eduardo Da Silva received an appalling tackle by Birmingham City defender Martin Taylor. This resulted in Da Silva receiving a broken left fibula and a dislocation of his left ankle. Full recovery for this physically fit athlete from this musculoskeletal injury took a year (Elst, 2009).

PRIMARY SURVEY

The paramedic/clinician needs to be aware of the distracting nature of musculoskeletal injuries and the potential to miss fatal airway, breathing or circulatory conditions. Often MSI will have a clear history of trauma and may lead an inexperienced paramedic/clinician to move directly onto a secondary survey assessment; this should never be the case in practice.

The primary survey presents significant challenges for the paramedic/clinician. The patient may be in acute pain which may create barriers for the initial ABC assessment. For example, is the difficulty in breathing experienced by the patient due to their perception of pain or a pulmonary embolism from a fat embolus released from an associated fracture?

During the primary survey, the paramedic/clinician must exclude any ABC compromise before focusing on the musculoskeletal injury. Maxillo-facial (airway) and thoracic (breathing) injuries may potentially require immediate assessment and intervention. Catastrophic haemorrhage (circulation) should be controlled during the primary survey phase using the evidence based 'C' ABC algorithm (Hodgetts *et al.* 2006, p745–6). (*See Trauma Assessment: Chapter 7.*)

DANGER

The vast majority of musculoskeletal injuries will have a reliable history of recent trauma and an identifiable mechanism of injury (MOI). This can range from a simple mechanical fall in the home, to a sporting injury, or a multi-system trauma injury received during a road traffic collision. The MOI should be considered by the paramedic/clinician on approach to the incident and a risk assessment should be ongoing and reviewed as the incident develops. Patients with significant MSI will have specific implied needs as a result of their injury and existing co-morbidity. Patients need to be protected from the environment to ensure that the effects of weather, traffic movement, worried relatives, young children, pets, medical paraphernalia and large equipment items do not cause further injury and increase the level of risk and danger. The lack of mobility and the onset of conditions such as hypothermia should be a prime concern for the paramedic/clinician.

Possible actions to be taken:

- Assess the scene and ascertain actual and potential MSI
- Ensure personal protective equipment (PPE) in relation to the situation is worn
- Ensure that patients with reduced mobility due to a MSI are protected from further injury

RESPONSE

Patients with MSI may be in significant distress. The pain a patient experiences may present as aggressive behaviour as the injury dynamics affect the patient's ability to rationalise their condition. Pain relief should be instigated as soon as possible to reduce the risk of complications from serious injuries (Greaves *et al.* 2006, p217).

The majority of patients with MSI will be conscious and will respond to the paramedic/clinicians approach, or to verbal commands as higher centres in the brain are still functioning.

Eye contact and a response to verbal stimuli should be the parameter most consistent with this phase of assessment. A note of caution is suggested at this point with regard to 'lucid intervals' and the potential for patients to have concealed neurological compromise in head injuries (see Chapters 1, 5 and 7). Patients who are unable to respond spontaneously on approach or to verbal prompts should be considered compromised pending further assessment of primary function.

Possible actions to be taken:

- Record the patient's level of consciousness (LOC)
- Consider if pain is masking a more serious MSI (administer pain relief as appropriate)

AIRWAY

In any isolated musculoskeletal injury, the patient's airway as with any other condition needs to be evaluated and reviewed. Traumatic injury may present with unstable C spine conditions which may be masked by distracting MSI. The paramedic/clinician needs to consider inline stabilisation and airway adjuncts if they suspect C spine injury. Maxillofacial injuries and skull fractures may lead to significant airway compromise and reduced levels of consciousness (LOC). In addition, there is risk of nausea and vomiting as sympathetic fight or flight adrenal responses increase the risk of significant airway compromise. Outside of these specific instances, a patient with an isolated MSI should be in a position to maintain their own airway without the need for adjuncts. However, considerations need to be given to the occurrence of vasovagal episodes affecting cerebral perfusion states which may cause the patient to become unconscious. The adoption of positional support and the introduction of the step wise airway management are options available to the paramedic/clinician (see Chapter 2).

Possible actions to be taken:

(Consider cervical spine)

- Initiate positional support
- Recovery position
- Suction
- Airway adjuncts
- Advanced airway techniques (as appropriate, see Chapter 2)

BREATHING

Patients with an MSI which affects the mechanism of breathing may potentially have a time critical condition. The patient may be in significant pain and distress and this may have an effect on metabolic processes. An increase in respiratory rate or pattern of breathing should be expected in MSI as the patient copes with their injury. The paramedic/clinician should confirm that respiratory function is sufficient to sustain the patient. Watch for changes in respiratory effort. Supplemental oxygen should also be considered (JRCALC 2009c). Thoracic trauma needs to be identified early and pain management options considered. The following six deadly thoracic conditions can occur from an MSI: **aortic dissection, open pneumothorax, tension pneumothorax, massive haemothorax/haemorrhage, flail chest segment** and **cardiac tamponade**, and need to be identified early (see Chapter 7).

Possible actions to be taken:

- Ensure that breathing is adequate (respirations <10 or >29 breaths per minute requires ventilatory support)
- Seal sucking chest wounds, stabilise flail segments, decompress tension pneumothoraces accordingly
- Administer oxygen appropriately to patient's injury(s)

- Manage hypoxia appropriately
- Transfer to appropriate trauma unit.

CIRCULATION

Circulatory compromise is multi-layered when dealing with musculoskeletal injuries. During the primary survey, the paramedic/clinician will need to confirm the presence of a pulse which is perfusing in nature. Colour, temperature and aspects of symmetry need to be assessed. Later in the secondary survey process, the paramedic/clinician is concerned with the distal nature of pulses beyond the site of injury and in comparison with uninjured limbs. Capillary bed refill times can be assessed peripherally (nail-bed) and centrally (forehead or sternum).

The presence of long-bone fractures, pelvic injuries, thoracic compromise and abdominal trauma can lead to catastrophic blood loss. Circulatory compromise leading to de-compensated shock is a life threatening/life changing condition. Haemorrhage control (visible/concealed) and the prevention of exsanguinations from open and closed fractures should be managed appropriately as per current best practice.

Possible actions to be taken:

- Identify potential MSI injury (open and closed fractures)
- Estimate actual/potential blood loss; manage appropriately (see Chapter 7)
- Assess and palpate limb pulses
- Pre-alert to the nearest major trauma centre (if appropriate)

DISABILITY

The primary assessment of disability associated with MSI compromise should include both the neurological sensory function and motor function. Sensation and power should be recorded by the paramedic/clinician and the presence of asymmetrical findings noted. Check active, passive and resisted movements within the plane of a joint (see Table 8.1).

The mnemonic **SLIPDUCT**, Swelling, Loss of function, Irregularity, Pain, Deformity, Unnatural movement, Crepitus, Tenderness may assist the paramedic/clinician in identifying a fracture. Inspection and palpation to elicit the cardinal signs of MSI should be considered to identify if the patient has any Pain, Redness, Swelling,

Table 8.1 Passive, active and resisted movements

Movement type	Physical action
Passive	The limb is at rest. There is no muscular tension. The paramedic/clinician moves limb through the range of movements consistent with joint function. The *patient does not assist.*
Active	Patient initiates muscular movement through range of movement. The *paramedic/clinician does not assist.*
Resisted	The *paramedic/clinician should provide an opposing force* as the patient attempts to move limb/joint against this force.

Heat, and Loss of function. The paramedic/clinician should be aware of the *'red flag'* 5 P's of musculoskeletal injury assessment:

- Pain
- Paraesthesia
- Paralysis
- Pallor
- Pulse.

Assess the patient's pupils (PERRLA), particularly if the patient has a head or maxillo-facial injury. The palpation of a 'boggy' matter around the skull of a patient with a head injury should be *'red flagged'*, as should any disability finding with no history of trauma.

Possible actions to be taken:

- Record the patient's level of consciousness (LOC)
- Record any period of unconsciousness, it may be part of the patient's lucid interval (*A lucid interval is the period of consciousness between **Two** periods of unconsciousness*)
- Assess limb function (motor/sensory)
- Assess for cardinal signs of MSI
- Assess range of movement (ROM)
- Confirm trauma history (Hx) and 'red flag' non-traumatic cases with no clear history (Hx)

EXPOSE/EXAMINE/EVALUATE

The challenge for the paramedic/clinician is to ensure that they balance the environmental out-of-hospital constraints with the need to identify injuries sustained by the patient. Issues of consent, capacity, decency and culture/religion should be considered if the paramedic/clinician is to be holistic in their approach to patient care. The statement that 'you have not assessed the patient until you have reached the level of the skin', is as true today as it has ever been. When exposing the musculoskeletal injury; albeit an ankle injury or bilateral fractured femurs, consider how the environment (hypothermia) and dignity will impact on the patient. The use of a modesty blanket will aid in the retention of heat and allow for the systematic exposure/re-covering of the patient during assessment. In multi-system MSI trauma the methodology of 'skin to scoop' can be applied.

Evaluate the findings within the primary survey and if 'time critical' problems within any of the elements have been identified then manage appropriately and transfer immediately to an appropriate treatment centre, which with MSI patients may require the paramedic/clinician to transfer the patient to an appropriate trauma unit (see Chapter 7), alternatively if there are no time critical problems remain on scene and conduct a secondary survey.

Possible actions to be taken:

- ■ Expose, and examine injuries
- ■ Evaluate findings and if time critical manage conditions appropriately
- ■ Pre-alert and transfer to the appropriate trauma unit

SECONDARY SURVEY

Once the primary survey is completed, the paramedic/clinician should begin a secondary survey assessment. However, if during this process the patient's condition changes (possibly due to internal bleeding from closed fractures, and hypovolaemic shock developing), the paramedic/clinician should revert to primary assessment and evaluate the need to complete a secondary survey against the need for definitive care at an appropriate treatment centre. A secondary assessment carried out on scene needs to be justified by the paramedic/clinician and the need for concurrent secondary assessment and transport/referral ruled in or out.

HISTORY

A patient with an isolated musculoskeletal injury should have a reportable and clear history of trauma which is consistent with the reported symptoms. Any signs or symptoms that the paramedic/clinician may elicit from the patient history should also fall within the expected injury patterns. Reported incidence of MSI without a clear mechanism of injury should be *'red flagged'* and the patient further assessed in the emergency department of the appropriate hospital.

Presenting complaint

The musculoskeletal injury history should include an appropriate level of discussion regarding the reason why the paramedic/clinician has been asked to attend. Scene assessment and the MOI can and does provide additional information to the paramedic/clinician, whilst the use of open questions to establish the chief complaint is important as this directs the paramedic/clinician to ask link questions which bind the mechanism of injury to the condition. In addition it allows the paramedic/clinician to focus and prioritise a systems review which in turn will help with discovery of underlying morbidity, which may exacerbate the chief complaint. In the case of MSI, a clear history of an initiating trauma and a sudden change in activities of daily living (ADL) are the likely outcomes (Purcell 2003), alternatively the paramedic/clinician may suspect a non-accidental injury (NAI).

History of presenting complaint

The history of musculoskeletal injury is the key to identifying 'red flag' conditions that require further investigation. Information about the history of the presenting complaint linked to trauma will help identify key injury.

■ 'I heard a crack as I twisted my ankle' (may indicate bony or ligament injury).

Reports from the patient that the

■ 'Cold weather affects my joints' (may guide the paramedic/clinician towards a differential diagnosis and potential treatment methodology towards a chronic condition).

During this questioning process it is important that the paramedic/clinician allows the patient time to express in their terms what happened. A process of summary of the history, onset and mechanism of injury can be completed by the paramedic/clinician to confirm with the patient the events leading to injury, *'Let me just confirm that . . .?'*

Past medical history

The patient's past medical history is significant with regard to the chief complaint. Musculoskeletal injury or the reoccurrence of loss of function and or disability may be directly linked to a failure of a previous condition to heal appropriately. Misdiagnosis of the chief complaint is not uncommon with an MSI and the patient may need to be assessed several times by different clinical disciplines to establish the true nature of the injury. Ascertain if the patient has been diagnosed or treated for any of the following conditions: osteoporosis, arthritis, brittle bones, anaemia, metastial tumours, and systemic infections may all be related to the re-occurrence of MSI.

The paramedic/clinician will need to ask the patient about:

- Gout, arthritis, tuberculosis or cancer
- Recent blunt or penetrating trauma
- Surgery on muscles, joints or bones
- Assist devices such as frames or other mobility aids
- Changes in normal activities of daily living.

Drug/medication history

- Is the patient currently prescribed (*steroids, diuretics and statins*) medications for any pre-existing MSI conditions? If so, ascertain what for (osteoporosis, osteoarthritis, rheumatoid arthritis, brittle bone disease, back pain, fibromyalgia, neck pain or anaemia). Use the medications to confirm these by asking the patient why they take each medication.
- Ascertain if the patient is prescribed steroids, diuretics or statins, as these drugs are linked to osteoporosis, pathological fractures, and muscle cramping and generalised muscular pain.
- Is the patient compliant with their medications?
- Has the patient taken any analgesics for any pain they may be suffering? If so, what time did they take the medication?
- If an opiate based analgesic, ensure that these are recorded appropriately.
- Are they taking or undergoing any courses of complementary therapy medicines?
- If so, which therapy (acupuncture, diets, herbal medicine, homoeopathy, massage, or possibly supplements)?
- If conveying the patient to a treatment unit, best practice dictates that their medications should be taken with them. The paramedic/clinician should document fully any medications taken or prescribed and record the administration of any pharmacological interventions on scene. This is particularly relevant with regard to opiate based analgesics.

Social/family history

- Consider the activities of daily living (ADL), ascertain what they can or what they normally do for themselves. Has this changed? And if so, how will the MSI affect them?
- Depending upon the age of the patient, ascertain if they live alone or have relatives/carers or external agency input (social service input, meal deliveries etc.).
- Ask about hobbies and past-times that may be a cause of injury.
- Depending on the presenting medical condition, do other members of the patient's family also suffer from the condition/illness? Familial history is often a factor in patients presenting with many autoimmune conditions, for example, brittle bone disease, osteoporosis or arthritis.

REVIEW OF SYSTEMS

Regardless of the injury or illness, a general review of systems (ROS) provides the paramedic/clinician with a global picture of the patient's health. In addition a ROS may help establish a link to the presenting complaint. For example, a patient with diabetes can be at an increased risk of developing musculoskeletal injuries. Diabetes UK provides information about musculoskeletal conditions and diabetes, including:

- Dupuytren's contracture (the fingers can become permanently bent down)
- Carpal tunnel syndrome (occurs when the median nerve becomes pressed at the wrist)
- Tenosynovitis (inflammation of the tenosynovium, a sheath that covers tendons)
- Frozen shoulder (a stiffened glenohumeral joint that has lost significant range of motion (abduction and rotation))
- Limited joint mobility (a type of rheumatism that causes the joints to lose their normal flexibility, more common in the hands (diabetic cheiroarthropathy))
- Charcot joint (condition affecting one or more joints, due to peripheral nerve damage).

PHYSICAL ASSESSMENT

The physical assessment of the patient with an actual or suspected musculoskeletal injury is carried out after history taking and will include a top to toe survey (in children this can be conducted toe to head with a view to gaining the confidence and trust of the child) and baseline clinical observations. The review of symptoms added to the focused history will direct the paramedic/clinician to the sites of injury and facilitate the opportunity for comparison with uninjured structures of limbs.

The paramedic/clinician at this stage of assessment should be aware of the patient's normal activities of daily living (ADL). It is important for the paramedic/clinician to manage the expectations of the patient with regard to the effects of their condition. Sedentary workers may be able to function and still attend work, often with significant MSI. However the impact of an MSI on a trades person may significantly impair the patient's ability to secure an income during periods of injury.

Consent for examination of the patient should follow current guidelines consistent with current practice standards (HPC 2007, p11).

It is important that the paramedic/clinician consider the need for a chaperone when examining minors or members of the opposite sex. Documentation of consent should be recorded along with any capacity statements which may be needed in the case of refusal for examination, assessment or treatment.

Examination of musculoskeletal injuries should follow a systematic format to reduce the incidence of misdiagnosis or the oversight of an associated injury. The paramedic/clinician will need to negotiate with the patient to ensure that they are in the most relaxed position to carry out the physical assessment. This should include issues regarding modesty, temperature and 360 degree access to the patient where practical. Musculoskeletal injury should follow a stepwise approach and have clear goals in terms of identifying 'red flag' presentations and establishing treatment goals. A suggested format for examination is:

- Joint above
- Look
- Listen
- Feel
- Move
- Function
- Nerves/blood vessels (power/sensation/vascular compromise) (Wardrope and English 2003, p27–8).

The paramedic/clinician should recall the *'red flag'* 5 P's of musculoskeletal injury assessment:

- Pain
- Paraesthesia
- Paralysis
- Pallor
- Pulse.

And with any injury assessed the paramedic/clinician should also have a clear understanding of the general management principles to:

■ Reduce pain
■ Prevent further injury
■ Ensure neurovascular supply distal to injury
■ Reduce risk of fat embolism
■ Promote recovery (Gregory and Mursell 2010, p294).

Depending on the nature of the forces applied to cause an injury, associated proximal/distal injuries may be found away from the primary site. For this reason it is good practice to assess the limb/joint above the injury. By doing this the paramedic/clinician will limit the risk of missing an injury and also gain the patient's trust as they are likely to find no injury and this examination will not have caused any discomfort (Wardrobe and English 2003, Chapter 2, p16).

During this process the paramedic/clinician is looking for hierarchical injuries, the most serious having likely secondary complications. Complicated fractures may have the added challenge of circulatory compromise both in terms of flow and haemodynamic stability. Added to that, dislocation at the fracture site may be a consideration in terms of ligament injury as would a localised or systemic infection in the case of an open fracture. When the paramedic/clinician looks at the site of injury they are evaluating for a potential spectrum of damage directly related to the mechanism of injury. This may range from complicated fractures with systemic infections to simple self-limiting strains or sprains. Identification of a fracture is important as undiagnosed breaks, chips or cracks in the continuity of a bone can have serious socioeconomic consequences for the patient. As previously sited, the mnemonic SLIPDUCT helps the paramedic/clinician identify fractures or create the clinical climate for a high index of suspicion. Table 8.2 provides details of the component parts of this mnemonic and identifies the significance of each finding.

Table 8.2   Components of the SLIPDUCT mnemonic

Element of SLIPDUCT	Clinical findings on examination
Swelling	An inflammatory response at the site of the injury causes a vascular cascade as essential repair mechanisms are initiated. This may result in vascular compromise (*compartment syndrome*).

Table 8.2 Continued	
Loss of Function	Guarding, pain and the loss of muscular conformity cause the patient to partially or totally lose limb function. Loss of function may present as reduced ROM, absent mobility, reduced sensation or unequal muscular power.
Irregularity	Muscular contraction is unresisted by broken bones causing irregularity of the bone matrix which may be visualised or palpated.
Pain	Localised to the fracture site and backed up by a history of trauma. The patient may report hearing a crack or feeling the break at the point of impact.
Deformity	A reliable sign of a fracture. Shortening and/or rotation can also occur at the fracture site. This occurs when muscular contraction forces exceed the capacity for the fractured limb to resist the pressure. Often termed a displaced fracture, the ends of broken bones will have moved from their neutral position and may have overlapped in extreme shortening.
Unnatural movement	Paradoxical movement e.g. flail chest, produces opposing movements which can be life threatening.
Crepitus	Not always present in fractures but occurs as the broken ends of bones articulate at the fracture site. Crepitus should not be induced but should be documented if revealed on palpation or reports of 'grinding' are declared by the patient.
Tenderness	The sensation of pain reduces the patient's ability to move and is a primitive protective mechanism. Pain at, above or below the fracture site is common and will require appropriate pain management with splinting and analgesia.

Fractures that are undiagnosed and remain untreated will have a significant impact on the patient's health and limit the potential for the return of normal function. SLIPDUCT complements the joint above, look, listen, feel approach to MSI and is recommended. Differentiation between skeletal and muscular compromise can be difficult in the out-of-hospital setting as pain and swelling coexist for both injuries. Stiffness and/or weakness may provide the paramedic/clinician with evidence suggesting muscular injury but in the assessment cannot always exclude fracture.

Movement is used to assess the possible extent of MSI and loss of function (see Table 8.3). It is important as it gives the paramedic/clinician insight into the type and severity of injury:

Table 8.3 Movements to assess the extent of MSI and loss of function

Movement type	Description
Active range	Patient moves the limb. Muscles and ligaments are stretched. The joint is in motion.
Passive range	Practitioner moves the joint, ligaments are stretched, joint is moving, muscles inactive but are stretched at the limits of range.
Resisted movement	Muscles and tendons active against an opposing force. Joint is not moving.
Stress testing	Joints are stressed to look for signs of abnormal joint mobility. Pressure is directed towards and away from the midline (common in knee examination – lateral/medial flexion, draw test).
End of range feel	Sensation felt by the paramedic/clinician at the end of range of movement. Often described as 'empty' when there is little or no resistance or 'hard' when a ligament is structurally intact.
Capsular pattern	A pattern of restricted movement in synovial joints. Used to isolate joint injury.

(Source: Wardrope and English 2003, p17–23)

Joint injuries often present with characteristic limitations of movement. Active and passive range of movement (ROM) directly assesses joint function. Resisted movement and stressing of joints test for muscle, tendon or ligament injury. When a muscle or tendon is damaged the patient may feel pain on resisted movement. In addition, ligament tenderness may be experienced by the patient when stress is applied to an injured joint formation. The ROM should follow physiological patterns of movement consistent with joint function. The classification of joints is dependent on the presence or absence of a space between articulating bones (synovial cavity); and the type of connective tissue that binds bones together. A review of joint classification is shown in Table 8.4.

Directional terms are used to describe the range of movement (ROM) for each joint type. These are used in conjunction with the terms superior, inferior, lateral and posterior. Table 8.5 defines them.

In health, joints will be able to move in various planes depending on their structure and function. When assessing for movement it is important that movement is not forced. If in doubt, position patient appropriately and splint in position pending further in-hospital assessment.

Table 8.4 Joint classification

Joint type	Definition	Joint example	Normal ROM
Synovial	A freely moving joint which allows for several types of movement.	Elbow, knee	Extension, flexion, abduction, adduction, circumduction
Cartilaginous	Bones are held together with cartilage. There is no synovial cavity.	Pelvis, vertebral column	Little or no movement
Fibrous	Bones held together by collagen rich fibrous connective tissue. There is no synovial cavity.	Bones of the skull	No movement

Table 8.5 Range of movement (ROM)

Movement	Definition
Retraction	Moving backwards
Protraction	Moving forwards
Flexion	Decreasing the joint angle (bending)
Extension	Increasing the joint angle (straightening)
Circumduction	Movement in a circular pattern
Abduction	Movement towards the midline
Adduction	Movement away from the midline
Internal rotation	Turning towards the midline
External rotation	Turning away from the midline
Pronation	Turning downwards
Supination	Turning upwards
Eversion	Turning outwards
Inversion	Turning inwards

As a joint is taken through its ROM, crepitus or crepitations (crunching or popping sounds) may be felt and heard. These noises are produced by the rubbing together or grinding of bones and/or damaged cartilage. The combination of joint movement and palpation may elicit sounds of joint crepitus. Examples include temporomandibular (TMD) and scapulothoracic disorders and runner's knee (patella – cartilage rub). Whilst, on their own, audible crepitations or popping sounds are not diagnostic of MSI, they should be considered in general terms and linked to any abnormal pathology, injury or illness. It is worth noting that joint noise accompanied with joint pain and a reduction in ROM is often a sign of impending rheumatoid arthritis. Noises heard from joint manipulation on listening during assessment should be noted and consideration given to onward referral.

Assessment for musculoskeletal injury should be focused through history taking and will lead the paramedic/clinician to the injured area. However, in the case of non-specific or incomplete histories a structured head to toe process should commence.

HEAD TO TOE ASSESSMENT

Head, neck, jaw

Inspect the head, neck and jaw for signs of deformity, lack of symmetry, swelling and signs of trauma.

- Palpate for bony 'steps' in the cervical midline.
- Ask the patient to turn his head from side to side. Palpate for any lumps, tender areas, crepitus or resisted movement as you flex the neck forwards and extend the neck backwards.
- Check for ROM by asking the patient to touch his right ear to his right shoulder and then the same for the left. The patient should achieve a 40 degree range.
- Ask the patient to touch their chin to their chest and then look towards the ceiling.
- With the patient's shoulders parallel, they should be able to turn their head to the left and right to achieve alignment with the shoulders.
- Palpate for clicks and observe for abnormal jaw movement at the temporomandibular joint (TMJ). Document all findings.

Spinal column

Rule out the need for inline stabilisation, immobilisation or 'rapid takedown' from the mechanism of injury (MOI). Even if the patient is walking there may be occult injuries which will require immediate immobilisation. Consider the MOI and the potential arc of injuries e.g. axial loading.

- Observe the patient in a standing position. Check for scoliosis (uneven shoulder height and shoulder blade prominence) and kyphosis (abnormally rounded thoracic curve).
- Ask the patient to walk away from you, stop, turn around and walk back towards you. Check for symmetry of movement, symmetrical gait and pedal clearance as they step.

- Measure the distance from the nape of the patient's neck to their waist. Ask the patient to bend forward at the waist noting the increase in this measurement. An increase of less than 5 cm could indicate reduced spinal mobility.
- Palpation of the spinal processes should follow, noting any pain, swelling or deformity (Schilling McCann 2008, p352).

Shoulder (glenohumeral) joint

The shoulder is the most freely moving synovial joint (triaxial diarthrosis). The shoulder is a ball and socket joint. When the ball (humeral head) sits in the socket (glenoid cavity) the analogy is of a 'golf ball' sitting on shoulder. This is known as the glenohumeral joint. Damage to the joint occurs through either blunt trauma or indirect transmission of force (falling onto an outstretched arm). Traumatic displacements are often caused by concurrent abduction, extension and external rotation of the arm. The forces involved can either cause a subluxation (partial dislocation) or luxation (full dislocation) of the shoulder joint. Due to its extreme range of movement (ROM), the shoulder is the most commonly dislocated joint as a result of trauma (Bath and Lord 2010, p235). As the shoulder is weakest anteriorly and posteriorly, the humerus (humeral head) tends to dislocate in a forward and downward direction. The most common form of shoulder dislocation is anterior, occurring in 95%–97% of all cases. The incidence of shoulder dislocation in 18–70-year-olds is 1.7%, with males three times more likely to suffer the injury. Shoulder assessment will move through the following stages: look and feel the joint, assess movement and function, assess nerve and vascular supply. Physical assessment should follow a focused history and general health assessment. Establish capacity and gain consent for the examination. The shoulders, clavicles and upper chest should be fully exposed allowing for a visual inspection of both injured and uninjured sides from all planes.

Joint above
- Examine the neck to ensure that there is no restriction of movement or associated discomfort.
- Shoulder pain where there is no history of trauma should always begin with an examination of the neck to rule out a referred pathology (Purcell 2003, p99).
- Extension, side flexion, rotations and flexions should be pain free for the neck to have normal pathology.
- Identify the sternoclavicular joint and check for any deformity.

Look/inspect

- Observe for signs of a 'step' over the acromioclavicular joint (ACJ), sternoclavicular joint (SCJ), scapulothoracic and sub-acromial joints.
- Check for signs of focal trauma, swelling, bruising, redness and fine muscle tremors.
- Check for limb symmetry and compare with uninjured side.
- Check for signs of joint wasting or previous injury/surgery. Ask the patient to point to the painful area as this may give clues to its origin, for example lateral pain radiating towards the deltoid is indicative of a rotator cuff tear.

Feel/palpation

- Gently palpate the major shoulder landmarks (ACJ, SCJ, clavicle, acromion, scapula, humeral head, upper humerus and elbow).

Move

- Active, passive and resisted movement can be carried out to help isolate injuries.
- Synovial joints have a finite range of movement due to the design of the joint capsule.
- Observe for capsular pattern and arcs of pain. Capsular pattern refers to pain or restriction in ROM specific to injury. Arcs of pain refers to the characteristic discomfort felt on moving the joint. This pain is transient depending on ROM. Ask yourself, what could be causing the pain?

Passive and active and resisted movement can be used to isolate muscular from ligament injury (see Table 8.6).

Table 8.6 Muscular and ligament injury

Joint structure	Capsular pattern
Glenohumeral	Pain of lateral rotation, abduction and medial rotation
Sternoclavicular	Pain at extreme ROM
Acromioclavicular	Pain at extreme ROM
Rotator cuff	Pain on lateral adduction following passive 90 degree lateral abduction

Nerves and vessels

- Check for axillary nerve function by checking for sensation at the top of the deltoid muscle.
- Check radial, median and ulnar nerve sensation distally at the hands.

- Check distal pulse at the brachial and radial arteries and compare on both limbs.
- Assess distal perfusion, limb temperature and capillary refill.

Special tests

- *Drop arm test* – This test highlights a rotator cuff tear. The arm is abducted to 90 degrees and the patient slowly lowers the arm. Pain and/or weakness are positive findings.
- *Horizontal flexion* – This test elicits pain from an acromioclavicular sprain. The arm is abducted to 90 degrees and then the arm passes across the chest, putting the hand on the opposite shoulder. Again pain and/or weakness are a positive sign.
- *External rotation against resistance* – The patient's arm is flexed at 90 degrees at the elbow and the arm is internally rotated 20 degrees. The patient is then asked to externally rotate their arm against resistance. Weakness of fatigue is a sign of a *rotator cuff tear.*

Red flags

Referred pain (myocardial infarction, pneumothorax, pneumonia, tumour, aneurysm, gall bladder infection, ruptured spleen, ectopic pregnancy), ACJ injuries, shoulder dislocation, clavicle fractures, humeral head fracture, scapula fracture, bicep tendon rupture, scapula wing, tendonitis, impingement, capsulitis, rheumatoid arthritis, osteoarthritis.

Elbow

The elbow is a synovial hinge joint. It consists of three bones, distal humerus, radial head and proximal ulna. These joints are connected by the radial and ulnar collateral ligament. The joint is susceptible to three types of fracture: supracondylar of the humerus, radial head fracture and olecranon fracture. In addition radial head dislocations, bursitis and epicondylitis (*tennis and golfer's elbow*) are common findings.

Joint above
Examine the shoulder for any abnormal pathology or restrictions in ROM.

Look
Assess for deformity of joint and check for obvious swelling, bruising, signs of previous injury or surgery.

Feel

Palpate bony landmarks and feel for inflammation, heat or boggy swelling over the olecranon (bursitis). Support the patient's forearm so that the elbow is flexed to approximately 70 degrees. Palpate bony prominences of the elbow and record findings.

Move

Passively flex the elbow to 90 degrees and apply a downwards force to the palmar surface of the patient's hand whilst supporting under the elbow. The elbow's range of movements includes flexion and extension of the elbow and pronation/supination of the forearm. Apply varus (*towards midline*) and valgus (*away from midline*) force to joint site. Note any positive findings.

Function

Test for general function of the elbow through all planes of movement as described above.

Nerves/vascular supply

Check for sensation around the joint and check distal pulses.

Red flags

Fractures, dislocations or suspected joint infection.

Forearm, wrist and hand

In the out-of-hospital environment, the occurrence of a fall onto an outstretched hand (FOOSH) is a common cause of injury. The nature of the fall (mechanical or collapse) should be investigated to rule out priority signs. Common patterns of injury of the forearm are shown in Table 8.7.

Table 8.7 Patterns of injury in the forearm

Pattern of injury	Bones
Monteggia pattern	A fracture of the ulna with associated dislocation of the proximal radius.
Galeazzi pattern	A fracture of the radius with an associated dislocation of the distal ulna.
Colles fracture	A fracture of the distal end of the radius which is displaced backwards and upwards to produce a 'dinner fork' deformity. The avulsion of the ulna styloid process also usually occurs.

Joint above

■ Review the joint at the elbow and record any abnormal pathology.

Look

■ Observe the forearm, wrist and hands for obvious signs of deformity, swelling, redness or loss of function.
■ Observe for muscle tremors, bruising or signs of guarding from patient.

Feel

■ Palpate the head of the radius when the arm is in motion. Note any crepitus.
■ Palpate the scaphoid (*anatomical snuff box*).
■ Systematically palpate the carpals and metacarpals of the hand and note any site specific pain, crepitus or deformity.
■ Palpate the phalanges and note any abnormal pathology.

Move

■ Flex elbow to 90 degrees, extend wrist to 90 degrees. Test pronation and supination, note any pain on movement.
■ Test active and passive range of movement of fingers through normal ROM.

Function

■ Observe for loss of function or weakness in forearm, wrist and hand.
■ Compare both limbs.

Nerves/vascular supply

■ Check for sensation, distal pulses and capillary refill.
■ Compare limb temperature with uninjured side.
■ Note any abnormal pathology.

Red flags

Unless trauma is very minor, x-ray is indicated due to risk of permanent disability and loss of function.

Pelvis

The formation of the pelvic bones and associated structure suggests that significant trauma is required to fracture the pelvic girdle itself. A fracture of the femoral head is a more common finding. Multiple fractures of the pelvic girdle are common with significant trauma mechanisms. Suspected pelvic fractures are time critical due to the potential for catastrophic haemorrhage.

Due to the pelvis's close association with the abdominal cavity and its organs it is difficult to isolate pelvic pain outside of a clear trauma history. Significant trauma to the pelvis should prompt the clinician towards analgesia, splinting and the management of internal haemorrhage (*see Trauma Assessment: Chapter 7*).

Joint above

- The pelvis articulates with the femoral head and is continuous with the vertebral column. Due to complex structures, the potential for muscle strains, ligament tears, tendon ruptures and fractures are all possibilities as the pelvis forms a large surface area for attachment to the lower limbs.
- The patient should be able to flex and extend at the hip. Rotation should be unopposed and pain free.
- The patient should be able to carry out passive, active and resisted leg movements within their ROM, again without the reporting of pain.

Look

- Look for a symmetrical pelvic girdle that is continuous on light palpation. Note the presence of incontinence.
- Observe for the open '*book sign*' as legs and feet externally rotate indicating pelvic fracture.
- Watch for abdominal distension and rigidity as a sign of internal haemorrhage.

Feel

- Lightly palpate the iliac crests and note any irregularity.
- Do not 'spring' the pelvis to assess. This will only increase bleeding, elicit pain and break down clot formation.

Move

- If the paramedic/clinician suspects pelvic trauma, splint and immobilise the patient. A high index of suspicion of associated fractures is best practice in these circumstances.

Function

- Observe for loss of power and sensation in the legs.
- Check distal pulses and capillary bed refill.

Nerves/vascular supply

- Due to the nature of the pelvic anatomy suspect neurovascular compromise in the presence of significant pelvic trauma.

Knee

The knee is a complex joint which is often a source of pain and discomfort for patients. The joint suffers from injuries as a result of trauma and degenerative diseases such as arthritis. Knee pain is common amongst all age groups. Reports of knee pain, swelling and locking are common presentations. Ligaments, tendons, cartilage (meniscus) can all produce knee pain and loss of function. In extreme cases, dislocation of the knee joint can occur. The knee joint experiences significant pressure during normal ADLs. Walking up a flight of stairs increases the pressure in the knee by a factor of 4.

Joint above
- Observe the patient's quadriceps for signs of wasting and asymmetry.
- Examine the pelvis and hip joint and report any abnormal pathology.

Look
- Compare both knee joints and observe any signs of obvious inflammation.

Feel
- Palpate the bones of the knee.
- Check for signs of fluid and note any difference in joint temperature.
- Note any crepitus on movement.

Move
- Utilise passive, active and resisted movement to take the joint through its ROM. Note any abnormal pathology.

Special tests
- *Draw test* – tests for anterior cruciate ligament stability. Knee joint is flexed to 90 degrees. The foot is isolated (sit on it) and the tibia is pulled anteriorly to asses excessive joint mobility.
- *Lateral stressing* – tests medial and lateral collateral ligament. Carried out on a straight leg. Pressure is applied laterally and medially against a splinted knee joint.

Function
- If possible the patient should be observed walking, standing and sitting. If possible ask the patient to crouch to fully assess the integrity of the joint.

Nerves/vascular supply
- Check for distal pulses, sensation and power.

Red flags

Fracture/dislocation, septic arthritis and osteomyelitis.

Ankle and foot

Ligament tears, fractures and damage to associated structures are relatively common in this area of the body. On assessment, the patient should be seated to avoid further injury or pain (Caroline 2008).

Joint above
- Palpate the knee and calf.
- Check for signs of inflammation behind the knee and note any swelling or pain in the calf (? deep vein thrombosis).

Look
- Observe for any signs of swelling, redness and/or deformity of the ankle joint.

Listen
- Note any audible noises on joint movement.

Feel
- Palpate the bones of the lower leg, ankle and foot. Include the Achilles tendon, fibula, calf, calcaneum, malleoli and 5th metatarsal.
- Note any abnormal pathology or presence of pain.
- Positive findings may require x-ray (Ottawa ankle rule).

Move
- In the absence of swelling, carry out passive, active and resisted movements.

Special tests
- *Simmonds' calf squeeze* – Patient kneels on a chair with both feet hanging off the end. The feet should sit squarely. The calf is squeezed and the foot should flex. If the foot does not move this is a sign of an Achilles tendon injury.

Function
- Observe for the ability to weight-bear.
- Pain may only occur on lateral or medial movement indicating a ligament injury.

Nerves/vascular supply

■   Check distal pulses and capillary bed refill.

Red flags

The absence of distal pulses. Capillary refill >2 seconds.

OTHER CONSIDERATIONS

Communication

The presence of a musculoskeletal injury is often accompanied by pain. This can be a significant barrier to treatment in the young and old alike. The paramedic/clinician will need to gain the confidence of the patient by demonstrating a clear understanding of concerns of the patient. The use of analgesia leading to effective splinting and immobilisation will have a positive impact on the psychological aspect of the injury. The paramedic/clinician will need to consider the expectations of the patient with regard to healing times and the effect that the MSI may or may not have on their ADLs. Special consideration needs to be given when assessing patients where English is not their first language, or have other barriers to effective communication. It is the responsibility of the paramedic/clinician to explore all avenues of communication (language line, interpreters, phrase books, appropriate family members) to ensure that every patient receives the appropriate standards of care.

Social/family/carer/guardian

When conducting a physical examination in a *minor*, best practice dictates that the parents/guardians are present, but in the absence of these individuals, every effort should be made to ensure the safety and well-being of the patient whilst in the paramedic/clinician's care.

Ethical and legal issues

Informed consent to examine the patient should be gained and revisited throughout the assessment, and the use of chaperones considered, where appropriate. The withdrawal of consent should be noted and the assessment stopped in compliance with a consenting adult/child with capacity. Every effort should be made to ensure the safety, dignity and health of the patient without capacity who is refusing treatment. The paramedic/clinician should comply with current legislation guidelines with regard to the consent and capacity, and simultaneously be aware of the vulnerability of their patient, reporting any areas of concern via the most appropriate pathway (social services, police) (DH 2005).

Destination/receiving specialist units/non-conveyance

The emergence of major trauma centres (MTC), minor injury units and other specialist medical facilities allows the paramedic/clinician to treat and refer MSI appropriately. Current guidelines and referral processes should be accessed by the paramedic/clinician and every effort made to ensure the patient is started down the most appropriate care pathway. Non-conveyance should be followed up with appropriate referral to partnership agencies, GPs, falls referral teams, to ensure a joined up system of care. Documentation of all findings, referrals and decision making processes are vital to mitigate risk and protect the patient and paramedic/clinician.

CHAPTER KEY POINTS

- Musculoskeletal injuries can present significant challenges for the paramedic/clinician.
- Ensure adequate pain relief.
- Remember the joint above, look, listen, feel, move, function approach to assessment.
- Clear histories of MOI should be consistent with injuries sustained.
- Watch for 'red flag' conditions and inconsistent history.
- Consider and utilise appropriate referral to trauma units, minor injury units, or general practitioner.
- If in doubt, refer patient for further assessment and tests.

9 Child assessment

Denise Aspland

This chapter will provide an overview of the principles of assessment of the child. It will follow a **DR ABCDE** approach in the primary survey and will identify aspects of paediatrics to consider within the secondary survey. The primary survey, when followed in a structured manner, will identify areas of concern. As with adults, these problems should be treated as they are found and the primary survey used as an ongoing tool. For the purpose of clarification of ages an infant is a child under 1 year, and a child is between 1 year and puberty (Resuscitation Council (UK) 2010, p99).

SCENE ASSESSMENT

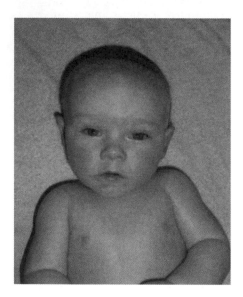

Figure 9.1   Six-month-old male

The scene assessment involving children can and does include injuries which may include a road traffic collision, or playground injury; alternatively the child may have become unwell and the parent/ guardian/carer has called the 999 emergency ambulance service. Assessing the scene of a child who came off their skateboard in a skate-park area would potentially identify different problems to being called to an infant who has become unwell. On arrival to the patient, would his appearance equate him to being: generally unwell, vomiting and lethargic? (See Figure 9.1.)

Is your experience of paediatrics sufficient to assess and make an appropriate management decision? Table 9.1 defines normal paediatric values.

Table 9.1 Normal paediatric values

Age (years)	Heart rate (bpm)	Respiratory rate (RR)	Blood pressure (systolic BP= 80+(agex2))
<1	110–160	30–40	70–90
2–5	95–140	23–30	80–100
5–12	80–120	20–25	90–110
>12	60–100	15–20	100–120

(Source: Advanced Paedriatric Life Support (APLS) 2011.)

PRIMARY SURVEY

The primary survey of the child continues to utilise the DR ABCDE framework. An emergency call to an unwell child can differ from one call to another and situations will vary considerably upon arrival. Often the child will be accompanied by an assortment of relatives and carers with different degrees of composure and offering different levels of assistance. It is imperative that the child remains as your main focus throughout your assessment, but it is also important to mention here that the composed and calm carer will be invaluable to your assessment and management of the child. Communication with carers throughout, particularly in the younger child and infant, will enhance your knowledge of the child and the history surrounding the illness. It is also helpful to note that when dealing with children first impressions are important.

DANGER

Children do not appreciate or see danger in the same way as adults. The child who enters the building site or derelict building and subsequently injures themselves will pose added problems to the attending paramedic/clinician. Entering unfamiliar territory possesses various potential hazards. Therefore every paramedic/clinician should be aware of the precautions to be taken upon entering property and each scene should be assessed for danger.

- Ensure that the scene/site is secure before entering, if appropriate request emergency rescue services.
- Ensure personal protective equipment (PPE) is worn, especially due to the potential of contact with body fluids.

■ Ensure dogs are removed from the working area as they may see you as a threat when dealing with the child.

Possible actions to be taken:

■ Ensure the scene/site is secure before entering
■ Wear PPE as appropriate
■ Request dogs to be removed from the scene

RESPONSE

A child who is alert and aware of their surroundings will inevitably react to a stranger entering their environment. They may well become distressed and upset upon examination. It is important to recognise this and assess each situation on an individual basis. Steps should be taken to calm and reassure in order to avoid a screaming and uncooperative child. It should also be noted that a distressed child will have altered vital signs that may impair your assessment. Assess the level of consciousness by undertaking a quick neurological assessment, AVPU.

A – Alert (GCS 15)
V – Voice, responds to voice command (GCS 13)
P – Pain, responds to painful stimuli (GCS 8)
U – Unconscious (GCS 3).

A child who is P or U on AVPU needs immediate airway management as they are at significant risk of airway compromise due to loss of gag reflex and risk of aspiration. If possible:

■ Refer to the child by their first name rather than he, she or baby.
■ Assess a small child on the parent's/carer's lap or at least with them nearby.
■ In toddlers, kneel down to their level.

Some children, however, may be extremely delighted to see you and be more than willing to allow assessment with the hope of a ride in an ambulance!

Possible actions to be taken:

■ Assess and record the patient's level of consciousness (AVPU)
■ Refer to the child by name, and approach them at their level
■ Do not shake infants or children with suspected cervical spine injuries

---

AIRWAY

A child's airway has significant anatomical and physiological differences to that of an adult and will change with age. Each age will present with a different set of problems at each stage of childhood, these can and may include:

- Nasal breathers below 2 months of age
- Occipital cervical flexion
- Small face – large head
- Anterior larynx
- Short trachea.

Are there any added specific noises? If so, are they inspiratory or expiratory?

- Snoring (stertor) (upper airways). May be present if there is an obstruction in the pharynx (possibly due to swollen inflamed tonsils).
- Stridor (upper airways). May indicate tracheal or laryngeal obstruction and will be heard on inspiration (consider epiglottitis).
- Grunting in infants. This sound is produced when exhaled air goes against a partially closed glottis. It is an attempt to prevent airway collapse by producing positive end-expiratory pressure. It is a sign of severe respiratory distress (ALSG 2011).

A younger child requires a '*sniffing*' position and the older child requires a full head tilt to maintain a good open airway. In the absence of trauma and to obtain an open airway a head tilt/chin lift manoeuvre needs to be applied. When performing a chin lift, care should be given to finger positioning, so as not to press on the soft tissue and occlude the airway further. Fingers should be placed on the bony prominences of the mandible. Due to a large occiput, large tongue and narrow trachea the airway may occlude fairly easily in an unwell and collapsed child. In an infant, a neutral position needs to be maintained. When assessing the child's airway, consider:

- Does the child have a patent airway? If not patent, is the airway compromised . . .
- Do you need to re-position the airway?
- Does the child need advanced airway support and/or ventilation?

Due to the complex differences in the child's airway, intubation and advanced airway management should only be performed by a skilled and competent paramedic/clinician. A short narrow trachea, posterior placed epiglottis and narrowing at the cricoid ring makes intubation extremely difficult and can cause significant oedema and further compromise to the airway if not performed correctly. Correct airway positioning, an oropharangeal airway and bag-valve-mask ventilation with high flow oxygen will be adequate in a compromised airway until further expertise can be sought.

Possible actions to be taken:

- Open the child's mouth and remove any visible obstruction. Do not perform a blind finger sweep
- Consider suction and airway adjuncts if appropriate
- If epiglottitis is possible then exercise extreme caution
- If head tilt and chin lift has not opened the airway, try the jaw thrust method
- Stepwise airway management if appropriate and trained (see Chapter 2)
- Surgical airways should not be performed in a child under 12 (JRALC 2006c)

BREATHING

This area of the primary survey is complex but it is essential to obtain a good clear assessment of how unwell the child is. To obtain a thorough breathing assessment the child's chest should be fully exposed during examination.

In paediatrics *Effort, Efficacy* and the *Effects* of inadequate breathing should be assessed.

Effort

- What is the child's respiratory rate and how does it compare to normal values?
- An increased RR (*at rest*) may be an indication of respiratory compromise or a metabolic acidosis.
- A decreased RR may indicate exhaustion, cerebral impairment or a sign of peri-arrest.

Examine the chest and ascertain if there is evidence of increased work of breathing? Is there:

- Intercostal recession (indrawing is seen between the ribs)
- Subcostal recession (indrawing occurs at the costal margins where the diaphragm attaches)
- Sternal recession (in small babies even the sternum may be drawn in)
- Tracheal tug
- Head bobbing in infants (due to the sternocleidomastoid accessory muscle being used)
- Nasal flaring (indicates significant respiratory distress)

- Tripod positioning in older child
- See-saw abdominal breathing (JRALC 2006c).

If the child is demonstrating multiple respiratory signs there is a greater risk of respiratory compromise and potential respiratory failure and arrest.

- Are there added noises and if so, are they inspiratory or expiratory?
- Is the chest silent? (A pre-terminal sign and needs immediate management)

Efficacy

How efficient is the breathing?

- What are the child's oxygen saturations? (Although this gives a base line, oxygen saturations are unreliable in the acutely ill child due to peripheral shutdown. In air <95% considered abnormal, <85% potentially life-threatening) (ALSG 2011).
- O_2 saturations should be used in correlation with other respiratory signs.
- Observe the chest for degree of expansion. This can indicate how much air is being inspired/expired.
- Are the movements deep and sighing (signs of metabolic acidosis), quick and shallow (respiratory distress) or slow and shallow (exhaustion).

Effects of respiratory inadequacy

Respiratory distress, if left untreated, will rapidly result in respiratory failure which in turn will result in a hypoxic child. 60% of paediatric cardiac arrests are caused by prolonged hypoxia. Survival rates from arrest are poor with figures less than 20% (Anaesthesia UK 2005).

Hypoxia in a child can be seen by assessing the following:

- Heart rate
- Mental status
- Skin colour
- Cyanosis.

Observe the child for cyanosis.

- Central cyanosis in a child is a late sign of respiratory failure and a good indicator of peri-arrest.

It should be noted that there may be situations where there is little or no evidence of increased work of breathing but the child may still be in significant respiratory failure.

These exceptions are:

- A child with cerebral depression caused by such conditions as raised intra-cranial pressure (ICP), poisoning or infection. This is due to an alteration in the respiratory drive
- Children with known neuromuscular disease such as muscular dystrophy
- Prolonged respiratory distress leading to exhaustion and a decrease in respiratory effort.

If the child is showing signs of respiratory compromise all possible attempts should be made to minimise further distress to the child. This can exacerbate the problem and send respiratory distress into respiratory failure and arrest. If appropriate, keep main carers close by to familiarise and settle the infant/child.

Possible actions to be taken:

- Ensure adequate oxygenation
- Ascertain the child's SpO_2 levels and administer oxygen accordingly
- Children with sickle cell disease, suspected carbon monoxide poisoning or cardiac disease should be administered high flow oxygen despite the SpO_2 reading
- Assess the effort, efficacy, and effects of their breathing
- Consider assisted ventilation if they are hypoxic <90%, their RR is <than half their normal, or >than three times their normal rate, or if chest expansion is inadequate (JRALC 2006c)

CIRCULATION

Assessment of the circulatory system should be quick but thorough. Alongside airway and breathing assessment it can assist the paramedic/clinician in ascertaining the severity of the child's illness/injury. A child will compensate well in shock and will have a relatively normal blood pressure even though they may be acutely unwell. Obtaining a blood pressure (BP) early will provide a baseline for assessment.

- What is the child's pulse rate and how does this compare to normal values?
- Initially, a child's pulse rate will rise in shock due to the catecholamine release.
- Tachycardia occurs, but in severe hypoxia the pulse rate and strength will fall pre-empting cardio-respiratory arrest (asystole).

- A child has superior compensatory mechanisms and will maintain a tachycardia for a prolonged period of time before decompensating.
- A rapidly falling pulse rate or a significant bradycardia is a pre-terminal sign and may indicate raised intracranial pressure and is therefore a clinical emergency.
- In an infant the pulse rate should be felt at the brachial or femoral arteries.
- In a child and an older child, carotid or femoral pulses may be sought (consider consent in the older child if there is a need to palpate the femoral pulse).
- What is the child's blood pressure?
- The correct sized blood pressure cuff must be used to obtain an accurate reading.
- Incorrect BP cuff-sizing will give a false reading, too large will lower the blood pressure and too small will give an artificially high blood pressure.

The width of the cuff should be more than 80% of the length of the upper arm and the bladder more than 40% of the arm's circumference (Moses 2009).

Peripheral and central pulses can be checked and compared. An absent peripheral pulse and a weak central pulse indicate severe shock and significant hypotension (see Table 9.2).

Table 9.2 Systolic blood pressure by age (ALSG 2011)

Age (years)	Systolic BP (mmHg) 50th centile	Systolic BP (mmHg) 5th centile
<1	80–90	65–75
1–2	85–95	70–75
2–5	85–100	70–80
5–12	90–110	80–90
>12	100–120	90–105

- How does the child look?
- Examine the child's skin colour, looking for pallor, mottling, and peripheral shutdown.
- Skin colour – due to the catecholamine release caused by hypoxia, vasoconstriction occurs and the child appears pale and mottled (catecholamines, include dopamine, epinephrine (adrenaline), and norepinephrine (noradrenaline)) (*Encyclopaedia Britannica* 2010).

- These signs, if present, along with pulse checks will indicate a significant degree of shock.
- Check the child's central capillary refill.

This can be achieved by pressing on the sternum for 5 seconds. The capillary refill should be less than 2 seconds. This examination should not be used in isolation but with other circulatory assessment checks. This clinical assessment is particularly useful in septic shock where the child is likely to have warm peripheries and look comparatively well, but have a prolonged central capillary refill. This is due to a relatively normal cardiac output (usually bounding on palpation) but poor tissue perfusion due to abnormal distribution of blood in the circulatory system.

If there are signs of hypovolaemic shock which is thought to be due to blood loss you need to look for where the child is bleeding from. These are the anatomical and general areas to examine for blood loss in the hypovolaemic child. A good guide is to assess each area fully including palpation and auscultation:

- Chest
- Abdomen
- Long bones and pelvis
- Floor – at the scene of the incident or from external haemorrhage.

If the patient is an infant do they have abnormal fontanelles? There are two fontanelles, anterior and posterior. The anterior fontanelle closes around 18 months of age and is the fontanelle used for assessment. By examining the fontanelle the following assessment can be made:

- A tense bulging fontanelle will indicate raised intracranial pressure (ICP)
- A markedly sunken, depressed fontanelle will indicate dehydration
- Note – Fontanelles will bulge in the crying infant.

Possible actions to be taken:

- Assess the child's pulse (*is it tachycardic or bradycardic? manage accordingly*)
- Assess the child's skin colour
- Ascertain the signs of circulatory inadequacy early
- Assess and record the blood pressure (*hypotension is a late pre-terminal sign in the child*)
- Manage shock accordingly (*obtain IV or IO access en route*)
- Pre-alert the receiving paediatric unit

DISABILITY

Assessment of the disability element will give an indication of potential central neurological failure. The assessment should include level of consciousness, pupils, posturing and blood glucose levels. There is a modified Glasgow Coma Scale for children that can be used in the secondary survey to give a more comprehensive assessment of level of consciousness and should be used in conjunction with the National Institute for Health and Clinical Excellence (NICE) *Guidelines on Head Injuries* (NICE 2007b).

Level of consciousness

■ To assess the level of consciousness in paediatrics a quick neurological assessment for the primary survey is obtained through AVPU. When assessing painful stimuli in the child either pinch a digit or pull a frontal hair. The child who responds only to painful stimuli has a significant level of coma (JRALC 2006c).

■ Mental status – a child may show signs of agitation or drowsiness and an infant may appear floppy (*hypotonic*) or irritable.

Pupils

Assessment of pupillary response:

■ Assess the pupils and ascertain if they are: Pupils Equal and Round; React to Light and Accommodation (PERRLA).

■ Are they unequal or dilated?

■ Non-reacting pupils may indicate significant neurological impairment due to pressure on the optic nerve.

■ Pupillary size and reactivity may be indicative of certain drugs and/or poisons.

Posture

■ Posture – what is the child's posture?

■ Is there decorticate posture (*flexed arms/extended legs*) (see Figure 9.2).

■ Is there decerebrate posture (*extended arms/extended legs*) (see Figure 9.3).

Either of these positions is indicative of significant neurological impairment. Caution should be given as these postures may be mistaken for the tonic phase of a convulsion.

A good clinical sign that a child is suffering from a serious illness is that they will become hypotonic and listless.

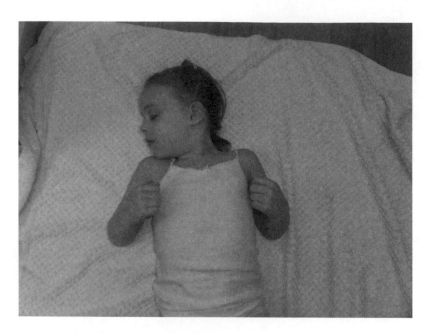

Figure 9.2   Decorticate positioning

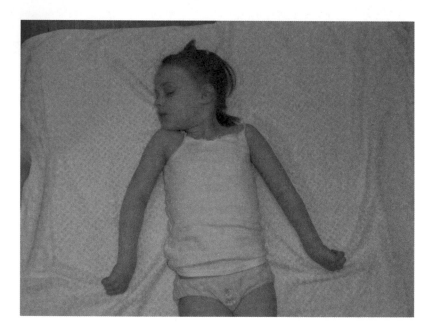

Figure 9.3   Decerebrate positioning

Blood glucose level

- What is the child's blood sugar?
- In a child who is lethargic, floppy and/or unresponsive a blood sugar level must be obtained.
- The paramedic/clinician should consider the Airway, Breathing, Circulation, *DEFG,* utilise the phrase 'Don't Ever Forget Glucose'.
- Due to poor fat reserves and an increased metabolic rate exacerbated by illness the child will use glucose reserves rapidly. Therefore, the child is at increased risk of hypoglycaemia. A blood glucose of <3mmols is classified as '*hypoglycaemia*' in a child and may result in seizures if not treated (ALSG 2011).

Possible actions to be taken:

- Assess and record the child's LOC (AVPU)
- Assess and document size and equality of pupils (PERRLA)
- Assess and record abnormal postures
- Monitor and record blood glucose levels (*manage accordingly*)

EXPOSE/EXAMINE/EVALUATE

Undress the child having obtained the appropriate consent (DH 2009). By exposing and examining the child the paramedic/clinician will obtain further clues to the child's illness. Observe for signs of rashes, unexplained bruising and general skin colour.

What does the rash look like?

- Is there purpura? (appearance of red or purple discolorations on the skin that do not blanch on applying pressure, caused by bleeding underneath the skin and measure 3–10 mm.
- Are there petechiae? (pinpoint flat round red spots under the skin surface caused by bleeding into the skin; petechiae are red because they contain blood that has leaked from the capillaries into the skin. They are quite tiny (less than 3 mm in diameter), and do not blanch when pressed).
- Is there urticaria? (commonly referred to as hives, it appears as raised, well-circumscribed areas of erythema and oedema involving the dermis and epidermis that are very pruritic (**intense sensation of itching**), otherwise has a distinctive appearance, and it blanches completely with pressure).

■ Is there erythema? (redness of the skin caused by dilatation and congestion of the capillaries, often a sign of inflammation or infection).

Rashes and marks can change rapidly in an unwell child; the paramedic/clinician should remember that a few spots of petechiae on initial assessment can rapidly develop into widespread purpura in the case of sepsis.

Consider:

■ If there is a non-blanching rash in an unwell person meningococcal septicaemia must be assumed. If a glass tumbler is pressed firmly against a purpuric rash, the rash will **NOT** fade, and the rash remains visible through the glass.

■ A non-blanching rash is indicative of meningococcal septicaemia but it is not a foolproof technique (*there may be NO rash*); up to 30% of cases start with a blanching pink rash which fades with pressure and then becomes purpuric.

■ Meningococcal septicaemia is a medical emergency where the earliest administration of benzyl penicillin may save life and reduce morbidity; the septicaemic patient needs immediate benzyl penicillin en route to hospital (JRCALC 2006d).

Document carefully any marks found on the child. Bruising noted on assessment may be indicative of sepsis but may also indicate non-accidental injury (NAI) and so therefore documentation is paramount (comply with local and/or national procedures).

■ Is there any unexplained bruising?

Most unwell children will have or have had a raised temperature at some point during their illness. However, in septic shock the child may be normal-thermic or even hypothermic and therefore the absence of raised temperature does not rule out serious illness.

■ Does the child have a temperature?

A child with an underdeveloped hypothalamus (premature or underdeveloped neonate) will have difficulty maintaining thermoregulation. Caution should be given to prolonged exposure as the child will use further energy reserves in an attempt to keep warm. This in turn may exacerbate potential hypoglycaemia as previously mentioned. If a child appears pyrexic then measures need to be taken, as per local procedures, to reduce temperature if significantly high. Further advice can be sought from the NICE (2007d) *Feverish Illness in Children Guidelines*.

Rapid, thorough assessment of the child's primary survey, performed in a structured manner, will identify problems and provide the paramedic/clinician with an indication of the severity of the illness or injury. A useful acronym to identify and evaluate pre-terminal signs in a child is: Bradycardia, Exhaustion, Central cyanosis, Hypotension and a Silent chest:

- ■ B   Bradycardia
- ■ E   Exhaustion
- ■ C   Central cyanosis
- ■ H   Hypotension
- ■ S   Silent chest.

A child who is unwell and presenting with any of the above symptoms should be considered by the paramedic/clinician as time critical (ALSG 2011).

Possible actions to be taken:

- ■ Expose patient and examine (remember appropriate consent)
- ■ Observe for rashes (especially those that do not fade under pressure)
- ■ Assess by pressing a glass against the skin (if present consider bacterial meningitis, manage appropriately)
- ■ Examine the patient for bruising (is it due to illness, or an NAI?)
- ■ Assess and the child's temperature (normal – thermic, pyrexic or hyperpyrexic?)
- ■ Evaluate – If time critical, transfer to the appropriate treatment unit or centre
- ■ Alternatively undertake a secondary survey?

SECONDARY SURVEY

Once the primary survey is complete and in the absence of any life threatening problems, the paramedic/clinician needs to gain further information in order to deal with the child's condition. Caring for a child has multiple areas for consideration; a specific area to be considered is the *age* of the patient. Other areas that are appropriate to the ongoing assessment of the patient would be the ethical and legal aspects. All of these need to be addressed whilst performing a secondary survey and obtaining a comprehensive history and physical examination to ascertain and detect if there are any less immediate threats to the patient (Gausche-Hill *et al.* 2007, p44).

HISTORY

Presenting complaint

The paramedic/clinician needs to clearly identify the reason(s) why the parent, carer or patient (child) has requested their attendance. This may be due to the exacerbation of an existing medical condition (*asthma, epilepsy, diabetes*), or it may be that the child has become unwell and is presenting with symptoms of a specific condition (*appendicitis*). Alternatively the patient may have suffered a trauma injury and the paramedic/clinician will need to ascertain the mechanism of injury (MOI) (Bledsoe and Benner 2006, p196).

- What is the presenting complaint?
- What is the age of the patient? (Infants and small children may require you to address your questions to the parent/carer.)
- What is the nature of the presenting complaint (illness or injury)?
- If illness, does it affect a specific system (abdominal pain – gastro-intestinal)?
- If an injury, does it affect a specific limb (arm or leg)?

History of presenting complaint

What is the history of the presenting complaint? The history of the presenting complaint for a 7-year-old child who is complaining of abdominal pain may have an entirely different diagnosis to the infant who has diarrhoea and vomiting (D and V), and may require the paramedic/clinician to identify the following:

Child

- Exactly where is the pain? (*ask the patient to point to the location*)
- Implement the OPQRSTA framework to assist in gaining a more thorough impression of the presenting complaint.

Infant

- When was the onset of the vomiting and/or diarrhoea? And what is the frequency?
- The amount of oral fluid intake since symptoms commenced?
- The total number of wet nappies during the previous eight hours?
- When did they last urinate or have a wet nappy?

Possible actions to be taken:

- Ascertain the blood glucose level of any child who presents with a history of vomiting, diarrhoea and poor oral fluid intake (Dieckmann 2006, p119)

Past medical history

When ascertaining a child's past medical history, depending upon their age this may need to incorporate information regarding their gestation/birth period, then any childhood illnesses and/or injuries since birth. For the infant/younger child consider the following:

Birth history
- Did the child have a difficult neonatal period?
- Were there special care needs at birth?
- Was the child premature?

These elements can potentially impact on respiratory or neurological systems and the child may have known pre-existing conditions arising from birth complications.

Developmental history
- How is the child developing according to childhood milestones?
- Is this impacting on their current health?

These are particularly helpful questions in the under-2-year-olds, or if the child has a known developmental condition. It will help ascertain the '*norm*' for the child and assist with the child's assessment. For example, a child with cerebral palsy may normally have poor muscle tone and be hypotonic and so therefore, in isolation, not an unduly concerning aspect of the disability assessment of the primary survey. Alternatively the paramedic/clinician can obtain a focused paediatric history by using a paediatric version of the **SAMPLE** framework (see Table 9.3).

Table 9.3   SAMPLE framework

S – Signs/symptoms	Onset and nature of the symptoms of pain or fever? Are there age appropriate related signs of distress?
A – Allergies	Any known drug reactions or allergies (*foods or drugs*)
M – Medications	Exact name/s and dosages of prescribed drugs (*GP/doctor/hospital*) Exact name and dosages of any non-prescribed (*over the counter* (OTC) *drugs*) (*purchased and administered by parent/carer/guardian etc.*) What was the time and amount of the last dose? The time and dose of any analgesics/antipyretics (*Calpol, junior disprin, etc.*)
P – Past medical problems	History of gestation, labour and delivery? Any previous illnesses or injuries

Table 9.3 Continued

	Immunisations: HIB, MMR, etc. (*check their immunisation record book*)
L – Last food or liquid	The time of the child's last food or drink? For infants this could be by breast or bottle
E – Events leading to the injury and/or illness	Ascertain what were the key events leading to this incident. Any history of fever?

Drug/medication history

This provides the paramedic/clinician an opportunity to obtain specific information regarding the actual (*intended*) and potential (*non-intentional/accidental*) administration of the child's drugs/medications.

- Is the child on any current prescribed or over-the-counter medication? If so,
- When was it last given?
- If poisoning is suspected, did the child have access to other medications in the house?

Immunisations and contact with infectious diseases:

- Is the child up to date with their vaccinations or have they been in contact with any infectious diseases?
- Does the child's symptoms correlate to any signs and symptoms of infectious disease?

Family/social history

Family history
Always ask about the health of the rest of the family. The child may have an inherited disorder or may well have been in contact with an infection or ill member of the family who may have contributed to the current problem.

Social history
- Who are the child's main carers and who has parental responsibility?
- Who does the child live with?
- Gaining an understanding of these aspects may help to determine the possibility of a non-accidental injury (NAI) or a child in need.

EXAMINATION

Use the 'Toe to Head' structure when undertaking a physical examination of infants, toddlers and pre-school patients, and the opposite 'head to toe' structure for the older child.

By incorporating this arrangement into your approach it will help to gain opportunity of the child's trust and cooperation, and increase the accuracy of the physical findings obtained. When doing so remember to obtain the assistance of the parent/carer/guardian in the examination process. Explain to the child and parent/carer/guardian what you are about to do, leaving the more unpleasant tasks until last. The examination should include the following:

- General observations (clothing, if wet or soiled, remove). If the child has vomited/does vomit note the presence of bile or blood. Bile suggests an obstruction, blood suggests trauma or GI bleeding.
- Skin (inspect for rashes, bite marks, hand, burns, belt mark bruising).
- Head (infants 9–18 months, assess the anterior fontanelle. Bulging and non-pulsatile may indicate IC bleeding, meningitis or encephalitis. Sunken anterior fontanelle indicates dehydration, look for bruising, swelling and haematomas).
- Eyes (PERRLA).
- Nose (assess for obstructions, foreign bodies, rhinorrhoea).
- Ears (presence of discharge or pus, otorrhoea – infection or perforation).
- Mouth (if a stridor is present, ?epiglottitis. Breath smell, sweet suggests acidosis, drooling suggests upper airway infection).
- Neck (ensure trachea is midline, auscultate over midline of trachea, ascertain if wheezing and stridor are present).
- Chest (assess for bruising, rashes, tenderness, auscultate).
- Back (assess for bruising, rashes, tenderness, deformity, auscultate).
- Pelvis (assess and feel for instability and tenderness).
- Extremities (assess for symmetry, compare limbs for colour, warmth, size and tenderness).
- Neurological – conduct a cranial nerve evaluation:
  - *Ask them to open and close their eyes*
  - *Ask them to smile*
  - *Ask them to stick out their tongue*
  - If cooperative, hold an object in front of their eyes
  - *Assess and track eye movement*
  - *Upwards, downwards, left and right*
  - Assess gross motor function
  - *Ask them to lift their arms and legs*
  - *Shrug their shoulders*

- *Push against resistance (use your hand)*
- *Squeeze your hands*
- If old enough and no injury
- *Ask them to walk (assess gait, balance)* (Gausche-Hill *et al.* 2007, p46–7).

Consent to treatment

It is also vital to determine who at the scene gives consent to care. There are many legal papers regarding children's consent and the subject is not as straightforward as it may seem. Due to the complexity of the subject further information can be found in the Mental Capacity Act, and the Department of Health Reference Guide to Consent for Examination or Treatment (2009, Section 3).

However, the guidance by the General Medical Council (GMC 2007) states that children and young people should be involved as much as possible in decisions about their care, even when they are not able to make decisions on their own.

Ideally, in order to assist with consent to treatment, an adult with parental responsibility should be present. Once again, this is an area of complexity and further guidance can be found at NHS UK, 2011) and from the Department of Health (DH 2009). The Children Act 1989 sets out persons who may have parental responsibility (The Children Act 1989).

Paramedic/clinicians should remember that children/minors who are deemed competent either by Gillick competence or Fraser guidelines cannot have their consent decision overruled by someone with parental responsibility. However, the person with parental responsibility **can** overrule a child's decision if they are refusing life-saving treatment (Woollard *et al.* 2010, p10). In any emergency situation, where you believe it is in the best interests of the child, treatment must be given to the best of your ability in order to prevent further complications, whether consent is forthcoming or not. This must be fully documented and recorded and also witnessed by colleagues. Paramedic/clinicians should familiarise themselves with internal policies surrounding this area.

Child protection

Every child has the right to protection from harm (Unicef UK 2004), and it is the paramedic/clinician's responsibility to ensure that they are up to date and familiar with child protection policies within their area of professional practice. When attending a sick child, child protection should always be present in the paramedic/clinician's thought process. Child abuse may present in many ways but the four classifications are as follows:

- Physical
- Emotional
- Neglect
- Sexual (NSPCC 2009).

Although abuse is not always apparent and evident, there are some helpful indicators:

- late presentation
- history does not correlate with injury/illness
- concern for the child by the carer may be either indifferent and off-hand or
- may present as over the top and/or angry
- the history is inconsistent with each telling
- the child does not interact with carer or appears frightened of carer.

Attention should be given to the child's surroundings whilst at scene and conveyed to appropriate professionals if concerns are present.

If non-accidental injury (NAI) or abuse is suspected by the paramedic/clinician, then good documentation and communication with other agencies is paramount. Policy guidelines should be followed and the paramedic/clinician involved should be at the forefront of this process. It is good practice to complete all documentation at the time of the incident as errors may occur if written in retrospect. In all cases, the primary and secondary surveys should be completed appropriately with the findings recorded.

OTHER CONSIDERATIONS

Communication

Remember that some patients may not yet even have learned how to talk, therefore ensure communication with relatives and carers throughout; particularly if the patient is a younger child or infant, it will enable you to enhance your knowledge of the child and the history surrounding the illness. Involve children and young people as much as possible in decisions about their care, even when they are not able to make decisions on their own, and ensure you obtain the appropriate consent.

Destination/receiving specialist units/non-conveyance

Convey the patient to the appropriate unit of care. The National Institute for Clinical Excellence (NICE) offers specific guidance and are developing guidance in the following areas relevant to out-of-hospital practice:

- Constipation in children and young people
- Diarrhoea and vomiting in children under 5
- Neonatal jaundice (NICE Guidance 2010).

Social/family/carer/guardian

In the majority of situations an appropriate member of the patient's family will be present, and able to provide the history. Ascertain the relationship of the adults present at the incident to the patient. Remember you may on occasions have to convey a patient whose relatives are not with you: use teachers and/or police officers as chaperones.

Ethical and legal

Consider and obtain the appropriate level of consent to treatment ideally from an adult with parental responsibility if the circumstances dictate. The paramedic/ clinician may also in certain situations need to consider the possibility of a non-accidental injury (NAI), completing all relevant documentation, ensuring that this is passed to the appropriate agencies.

COMMON CONDITIONS AFFECTING PAEDIATRIC PATIENTS

Asthma

Asthma is a chronic inflammatory disease of the airways, associated with widespread, variable outflow obstruction which may reverse either spontaneously or with medication. The underlying inflammation is associated with bronchial hyper-responsiveness or airway hyper-reactivity to a variety of stimuli, such as environmental allergens and irritants.

Signs and symptoms
- Cough
- Difficulty breathing
- Chest tightness
- Wheeze.

Laryngotracheobronchitis (croup)

A condition which results from the inflammation or irritation of the larynx and trachea and bronchial passageways, due to a viral infection. It is more prevalent in infants and children between 3 months to 3 years old, the majority of which are males, but may also occur at any age, but is most common in 18-month-old infants.

It is more prevalent during the late autumn and winter months. Croup usually lasts for about five days; the symptoms are more severe at night, and worse during the first two nights.

Signs and symptoms
- Sore throat
- Mild cold (with low grade fever)
- Runny nose
- Loss of appetite
- Cough.

Over a period of one to two days the characteristic signs and symptoms of croup develop:

- Bark-like cough
- Hoarse or croaky voice
- Dyspnoea
- Stridor.

Measles (rubeola)

Is an infection of the respiratory system caused by a virus, it is highly contagious and is spread by respiration (either contact with fluids from the infected person or airborne). The incubation period of the infection has an average of 14 days (range 6–19 days). The infectious period lasts from 2–4 days prior until 2–5 days following the onset of the rash (i.e. 4–9 days infectivity in total).

Signs and symptoms
- Fever (4 days) (may reach 40°C)
- Cough
- Coryza (runny nose)
- Conjunctivitis (red eyes)
- Erythematous (red) rash (begins several days after the fever starts)
- It starts on the head before spreading to cover most of the body (often causing itching)
- The rash is said to 'stain' (changing red to dark brown before disappearing).

Mumps

Is a communicable paramyxovirus disease which attacks either one or both parotid glands (largest of the three pairs of salivary glands – located below the ears), with it classically presenting as swollen parotid glands. It is most common amongst children with the symptoms usually developing 14–25 days after being infected with the virus (the incubation period). The average incubation period is around 17 days.

Signs and symptoms
- Pain and tenderness in the swollen glands
- Pain on swallowing or dysphagia (difficulty swallowing).

Other symptoms of mumps include:

- Headache
- Joint pain
- Nausea
- Dry mouth
- Abdominal pain
- Fatigue
- Loss of appetite
- Pyrexia (fever) of 38°C or above.

CHAPTER KEY POINTS

- Always follow a structured approach to the primary survey.
- Ensure consent is obtained appropriate to the child and the situation.
- Fully assess each area of the primary survey.
- Manage identified problems as they are found.
- Complete a structured secondary survey (*history, physical examination and vital signs*).
- Be aware of the normal values for each stage of childhood.
- Involve carers as much as is reasonable in order to pacify the child.
- Have a clear understanding of child protection policies and procedures.
- Always document clearly your management of the child.

10 Older person assessment

David Kerr

The UK population is growing older with the fastest increase in the over-85-year-olds (approximately 1.3 million in 2008). This increase has been attributed to improvements in medical treatment, housing, living standards and nutrition. In the past 25 years the expected years of good or fairly good health, and the expected years without a limiting illness or disability have increased for both men and women. However, they have not increased at the same rate as overall life expectancy (Office for National Statistics (ONS) 2009).

The conclusion drawn from this is that the paramedic/clinician will encounter increasing numbers of older people presenting with poorer health with limiting illness and/or disability.

This chapter will provide an overview of the clinical skills required for an effective assessment of the older patient in the out-of-hospital environment. It will identify areas of key importance and discuss the considerations required to aid the assessment process.

SCENE ASSESSMENT

When called to the aid of an older person many clues can be gained by a thorough scene assessment as you approach the patient. As a person ages their thermoregulation becomes less efficient making them prone to hypothermia especially if they have a poor diet.

If the patient is outdoors take account of:

- The weather, especially the ambient temperature.
- Clothing that the patient is wearing.
- Due to poor thermoregulation and loss of subcutaneous body fat do not be surprised if the older patient is wearing many layers of clothing even in weather that you might consider quite mild.

If the patient is indoors observe:

■ The general state of the house and its garden. Signs of neglect of a person's dwelling can indicate general neglect of the person themselves either through the person's inability to cope or from a general lack of support for that person.

■ Observe the general condition of the house and the ambient temperature. Many older people resist having the heating at a high enough temperature during cold weather for fear of being unable to pay the bill.

■ Clues such as handrails, walking frames and commodes can provide an insight into the patient's general mobility.

Support can take many forms including friends, neighbours and relatives as well as the more formal social services such as home helps or carers. Many older people choose to live in communities with others of a similar age. These can range from sheltered accommodation with a warden, where the resident retains their privacy and independence, to nursing/care homes, where the person is looked after by a team of nurses and carers. As with the domestic dwelling it is worth noting the general condition of the facilities and the other residents, as people in these facilities are vulnerable and can suffer from neglect even if unintentional.

Remember, as an out-of-hospital practitioner you are ideally placed to identify potentially vulnerable adults and alert the appropriate authorities.

Depending on any specific information and the circumstances of the incident, whether it is winter or summer it may be appropriate to utilise blankets for warmth and/or to maintain the patient's dignity.

PRIMARY SURVEY

Remember that the older patient has a lifetime of knowledge and experience behind them and deserves the honour of being treated with respect. The purpose of the primary survey is to rapidly assess and identify potentially life threatening conditions that require prompt intervention by the paramedic/clinician. Certain conditions are more prevalent in the older population. It is worth remembering that the unwell or traumatised older person may have more than one complaint at the same time. The primary survey provides the opportunity to assess whether the patient is ill, injured or both. The paramedic/clinician should bear in mind that with the older person an underlying medical condition may be the cause of the events leading to an injury or conversely that trauma could exacerbate an existing medical condition.

DANGER

On approaching the patient consider if there is any danger to yourself, colleagues, the patient and bystanders (if present) in this order. Consider the cause of the incident (fall, road traffic collision, epistaxis), and identify actual or potential risks. Once you are satisfied the scene is safe, approach the patient in a friendly yet respectful manner.

> ## Possible actions to be taken:
>
> - Ensure safety of self, colleague(s), and patient
> - Wear appropriate PPE (gloves and/or high visibility)

RESPONSE

Using the AVPU scale to assess the patient's response gives an early indication of the mental state of the older patient. Ageing by itself does not cause mental status changes so NEVER accept confusion as *normal* (Snyder and Christmas 2003). In the conscious older patient who may suffer from an underlying dementia or delirium the possibility of an inaccurate assessment of their current state compared with what is normal for them could arise.

> ## Possible actions to be taken:
>
> - Assess and record the patient's level of consciousness (AVPU)
> - Remember that older patients may have existing conditions which may cause an inaccurate assessment of their level of consciousness (LOC)

AIRWAY

When assessing the older patient's airway, especially in the unconscious patient, check for false teeth (dentures). If the patient has kyphosis (posterior curvature of the spine), this may pose the paramedic/clinician with airway management problems (Snyder and Christmas 2003).

Possible actions to be taken:

- Assess airway and consider the need for dentures to be removed or left in situ ,
- If obstructed manage utilising stepwise airway management (see Chapter 2)
- If the patient has kyphosis consider the need to pad the gaps under the head and neck, if in the supine position
- Ensure airway is patent and secure before proceeding to next element

BREATHING

Many older people suffer from chronic obstructive pulmonary disease (COPD), or other long-term conditions of which the symptoms may be displayed in the respiratory system, such as left ventricular failure (see Chapter 3). As a consequence of these conditions the patient may present with new symptoms or an exacerbation of an existing condition.

- Do they have any shortness of breath, difficulty in breathing? (dyspnoea), if so,
- Is the dyspnoea normal for them?
- Do they have a chronic respiratory condition? If so,
- Ask them if there any associated signs or symptoms?
- Are these new or old?

Possible actions to be taken:

- Assess breathing and ensure that the rate and rhythm is adequate
- Assess the patient's oxygen saturation (SpO_2) level
- Maintain an oxygen saturation of 88%–92% for those with COPD (BTS 2008)
- Ensure the patient is not hypoxic
- Administer oxygen appropriate to patient's illness/injury

CIRCULATION

Assess the patient's circulation, initially checking the pulse for rate, rhythm and volume. The pulse can provide an early indication of the need for further investigation, and is the easiest and least intrusive to initially assess and it also helps to begin the process of physical contact that will be necessary to fully assess the older patient. Assess whether the rhythm is regular or irregular; in the irregular pulse, consider arrhythmias as they are common In the otherwise asymptomatic elderly patient. Orthostatic (postural) hypotension is common in the elderly, and is defined as a drop in blood pressure (usually >20/10 mmHg) within 3 minutes of standing.

- If an injury is there any obvious external haemorrhage?
- Assess the patient's pulse (regular or irregular).
- Does the problem occur when the patient stands? (orthostatic or postural hypotension)
- Assess the blood pressure (if normally hypertensive, and reading is within normal adult parameters, consider internal haemorrhage).
- Ascertain if the patient takes medications for circulatory/cardiac conditions. If so,
- Ascertain what they are (antihypertensives, anticoagulants or glycosides).

Possible actions to be taken:

- If applicable control external haemorrhage (*see Trauma Assessment: Chapter 7*)
- Assess the patient's pulse, if appropriate obtain an ECG trace and manage accordingly
- Ascertain if the problem occurs on standing (consider orthostatic (postural) hypotension)
- Obtain and record the blood pressure (consider internal haemorrhage, manage accordingly, *see Trauma Assessment: Chapter 7*)
- Ascertain if the patient takes medications for any circulatory/cardiac conditions

---

DISABILITY

Having assessed the patient's initial response on your approach to them, take time now to reassess their mental status (AVPU). The older person has an increased risk of a stroke or transient ischaemic attack; undertake a FAST assessment. Check their pupils for equality, reactivity and accommodation (PERRLA), bearing in mind the possibility of the patient having existing conditions, such as cataracts, blindness or even a false eye. Remember that the older patient will have differing metabolic needs. Ensure that their blood glucose levels are assessed as part of this element.

Possible actions to be taken:

- Re-assess and record the patient's LOC
- Assess and document size and equality of the patient's pupils (PERRLA) (consider cataracts, blindness and/or false eyes)
- Obtain and record blood glucose levels (manage accordingly, IV glucose (10%) or appropriate drink or food if conscious)
- Undertake a Face, Arms, Speech Test (FAST) (Nor *et al.* 2004; DH 2007; NICE 2008a; JRCALC 2009a)
- If positive pre-alert and transfer to a hyper-acute stroke unit

EXPOSE/EXAMINE/ENVIRONMENT

Exposing the older patient, whether it is to assess an injury or to begin a more detailed secondary survey, can bring its own challenges as many older patients are often very modest and therefore uncomfortable being exposed, especially by someone they have just met! Explain to the patient exactly what you need to do, and why, and obtain consent. Examine the patient accordingly: the presence of a scar on the median thoracic wall may indicate previous heart (cardiac) or thoracic surgery. Where possible protect their privacy by only exposing where necessary and covering them with appropriate blankets. With respect to the environment, the blankets may help maintain the patient's temperature loss, as their thermoregulatory function is often impaired due to loss of fat reserves, thinning skin and slowing metabolism (Snyder and Christmas 2003).

Possible actions to be taken:

- Expose the patient's affected areas
- Examine and ascertain if there is an existing condition (evidence of median cardiac scars or thoracic injuries, glyceryl trinitrate GTN patches, implantable cardioverter defibrillator ICD)
- Remember patient dignity and consider the environment (possible hypothermia)
- Evaluate – transfer patient to an appropriate unit or move onto secondary survey

SECONDARY SURVEY

The older patient often has more than one complaint and these can be a combination of chronic problems, such as arthritis or chronic obstructive pulmonary disease (COPD), and acute problems, such as sudden chest pain or a fall. Also, there could be an exacerbation of a chronic problem such as COPD due to an acute chest infection. Therefore careful patient questioning will be required to identify the problems and their priority for assessment and treatment. Remember to consider the following:

- Give elderly patients time to respond to your questions
- Speak slowly and clearly but do not shout or raise your voice
- Visual cues may be important, so make sure your face is well lit
- If they wear glasses, make sure they put them on (Bickley and Szilagyi 2009).

Ideally, you want to obtain the history of the chief complaint from the patient, but there are times when the patient will be incapable of answering your questions, such as when suffering from an altered mental status or unconsciousness, and you must rely on the patient's carer.

Presenting complaint

Asking an older patient 'What is wrong?' often results in a lengthy and wide ranging answer, therefore it is important that you get the patient to focus on what their current most important problem is. This is best achieved by asking questions such as 'What made you call us today?' or 'What is different about what is bothering you today?' If the reason for attendance was a fall ascertain if it occurred due to trauma or was due to an underlying medical condition.

Ask yourself the following questions:

- Did the patient really trip, or fall?
- Is there a medical reason for the fall?
  - Dizziness (*may be suggestive of orthostatic (postural) hypotension*)
  - Palpitations (*may be suggestive of cardiac arrhythmias*)
- Is there an environmental hazard that caused the fall? (*loose handrails or carpets*)

Common complaints in the older patient include:

- Shortness of breath
- Chest pain
- Altered mental status
- Abdominal pain
- Dizziness or weakness
- Fever

- Trauma
- Falls
- Generalised pain
- Nausea, vomiting and diarrhoea (Snyder and Christmas 2003).

History of presenting complaint

Whilst the history of the presenting complaint is concerned with the events leading up to the emergency call (*presenting complaint*), the paramedic/clinician will need to consider the fact that the patient may not be able to recall events. The patient who has fainted (*syncope*) may not even be aware that they had passed out prior to the fall. In situations where the incident has occurred in a public place, or the patient lives alone, then information concerning what occurred may have to be obtained from bystanders, carer or relatives. The SAMPLE framework will assist the paramedic/clinician to structure the investigation into the events preceding the history of the presenting complaint, and the OPQRSTA framework should be utilised in assessing pain that the patient presents with. Consider the following:

- Ask the patient, 'What is the last thing you can remember'?
- If applicable ascertain history of the presenting complaint from bystanders, carer or relatives.
- Does the information provided correlate with the mechanism of injury?
- If concerned, question patient regarding specific causes (dyspnoea, chest pain, dizziness, loss of balance, etc.).

Past medical history

A lot of information can be gleaned from the answer to questions regarding an older patient's past medical history but care must be taken to keep the conversation around relevant information. The fact your patient broke their wrist falling from a tree at the age of 10 probably has no bearing on their current complaint! Try and keep your questions open. Asking a patient if they suffer from cardiac problems might get the answer 'no', even though they have such medication as GTN, digoxin, aspirin and frusemide. When questioned further, the patient may well consider themselves free of cardiac problems because they take that medication. Consider asking the following:

- Can you tell me about your past medical history?
- Do you have any other medical conditions?
- Do you have diabetes? If so, what type, I or II?
- Do you suffer with a breathing problem? If so, is it a long-term condition (COPD, emphysema or chronic bronchitis)?
- Do you have a problem with your heart (hypertension, angina, LVF, RVF, CCF)?
- Have you ever been hospitalised or had any operations? If so, what for?

Drug/medication history

This is a vital aspect of the older patient's history and consideration must be given to the normal parameters of drug pharmacology (absorption, distribution, metabolism, excretion and tissue sensitivity). Renal function declines with increasing age and will therefore affect the 'pharmacokinetics' of various drugs, specifically those that are predominantly eliminated by the kidney. Excretion of these drugs will occur more slowly, resulting in their half-lives (duration of action) being prolonged, and they can accumulate to a higher (potentially toxic) concentration even in a well state. Consider the patient's overall hydration (Kane *et al.* 2003, p393). Older people use more prescription medicines than younger people and therefore there is an increased chance of them experiencing side effects. Older people also tend to use more over the counter medications including herbal remedies, so it is important to ask about these as well (Snyder and Christmas 2003). Remember that the older patient with chronic conditions will often have a repeat prescription list which is useful in ascertaining the patient's medication especially if the patient is confused or forgetful. However, it is important to check that the patient is adhering to their medication regimen. It is also worth checking if the patient is taking any prescription medication not prescribed specifically for them (e.g. a spouse's sleeping tablets) (Caroline 2008).

Social/family medical history

When asking about the social aspect of the older patient's history include asking about their activities of daily living (ADLs) and how these have changed over time. Bickley and Szilagyi (2009) tells us there are two standard categories of assessment: physical ADLs and instrumental ADLs (see Table 10.1), and the paramedic/clinician should assess whether the patient can carry out these activities independently, with some help or is entirely dependent.

Table 10.1 Activities of daily living (ADL)

Physical ADL	Instrumental ADL
Bathing	Using the telephone
Dressing	Shopping
Toileting	Preparing food
Transfers	Housekeeping
Continence	Laundry
Feeding	Transportation
Managing money	Taking medicine

Other aspects of the older patient's social history include their diet, exercise, sources of stress, especially bereavements, leisure activities, alcohol and drug use. Check for non-adherence to dietary regimens such as diabetic diets causing hyperglycaemia and restricting salt intake which can worsen congestive heart failure (Snyder and Christmas 2003). It is likely that today an older person will have smoked at some point in their life so try and ascertain how much they smoked and for how long. For cigarettes this is often reported as pack years (number of packs smoked per day × number of years smoking). If they have given up, ascertain how long ago. Alcohol use is on the rise in the older population with a smaller amount using illegal drugs. This can often be in response to a life changing event such as loss of a spouse, declining health or low self-esteem (Caroline 2008). Ascertain if the patient lives alone, in social housing (rented) or if they are homeowners, and if possible their financial position; evidence has shown how the older person is, and feels, excluded due to these (see Table 10.2).

Table 10.2 Social exclusion in people aged 80+

	Severely excluded	**No signs of exclusion**
Weekly income (median)	£131	£142
Health	53% report health problems	20% report health problems
Mental health (mean)	2.9 symptoms of depression	1.4 symptoms of depression
Loneliness	37% feel lonely	19% feel lonely

- Severe exclusion affects people living in all types of housing, but the risk is twice as high for renters (28%) as for homeowners (14%).
- 21% of people living alone are severely excluded, compared to 11% living with a partner (Age Concern 2008).

When asking about the older patient's family medical history you are trying to ascertain a genetic link for common familial diseases such as cancer, cardiovascular diseases, respiratory diseases and neurological diseases so ask about the health and, where appropriate, cause of death of grandparents, parents, siblings, children and grandchildren.

REVIEW OF SYSTEMS AND VITAL SIGNS

This section will review the systems and associated vital signs of the older patient highlighting the most common conditions, illnesses and injuries that you may find.

Respiratory system

Older people have decreased ability to clear secretions, as well as decreased cough and gag reflexes making aspiration and obstruction more likely. Complaining of shortness of breath is common amongst older people with the potential causes being the only symptom of a heart attack, COPD, congestive heart disease (*all cause wheezing*) or other medical reasons such as pain, bleeding or medication interactions (Snyder and Christmas 2003). Consider the following when undertaking the review of the following systems and vital signs:

- Normal range for respiratory rate, character and work of breathing for the older patient is the same as for the younger patient (12–20 breaths per minute).
- Chest stiffness could make it more difficult to assess chest rise.
- Loss of elasticity of the lungs and a decrease in the size and strength of the respiratory muscles.
- The above changes cause decreased vital capacity (50% by age 75) and increased residual volume leading to a progressive decline in the proportion of air usefully used in gas exchange.
- Musculoskeletal changes such as kyphosis (*curvature of spine*) can also impact on respiratory function. The older patient also has a declining partial pressure of oxygen ($pO_2 = 100 - age/3$).
- Dulling of the respiratory drive due to decreased sensitivity to arterial blood gas changes causes older patients to have a slower reaction to hypoxaemia and hypercarbia (Caroline 2008).

Oxygen saturation (SpO₂)
- Due to the increased incidence of COPD in older people the oxygen saturation levels can be lower. Aim for a target saturation of 94% to 98% in the acutely unwell patient or where there is a risk of the patient having a hypoxic drive a target range of 88% to 92% should be aimed for (BTS 2008).
- There may be difficulty in gaining an accurate SpO_2 due to poor peripheral circulation. If in doubt, do not withhold oxygen but monitor the patient closely for changes in breathing rate and level of consciousness. When assessing the respiratory system of the older patient ascertain whether the presentation is an existing chronic problem, a worsening of the chronic problem or a new problem.

Cardiovascular system
Pulse
- The ageing heart is less responsive to nervous stimulation which can lead to a lower heart rate and weaker pulses.

- Always check pulses bilaterally to exclude obstruction rather than a reduced heart function.
- Peripheral pulses can be difficult to find due to vascular changes and poor circulation.
- Palpate the carotid pulse gently to avoid dislodging a thrombus. Alternatively, use a stethoscope to listen to the apical heartbeat (Snyder and Christmas 2003).

One third of patients around 60 years old, and over half who reach 85 years, have had an aortic systolic murmur heard on examination due to a process of fibrosis and calcification known as aortic sclerosis. A similar process affects the mitral valve approximately a decade later leading to a systolic murmur of mitral regurgitation which cannot be discounted due to the extra load placed on the heart by the leaking mitral valve.

- If auscultating the middle or upper carotid arteries and turbulence (*known as a bruit*) is heard it can suggest, but not prove, a partial arterial obstruction secondary to atherosclerosis (Bickley and Szilagyi 2009).
- When assessing the older patient's heart rate and character remember to take account of any medication the patient takes, especially beta blockers. A normal response to shock is a rise in heart rate which beta blockers would prevent, misleading the paramedic/clinician into thinking the patient is not shocked.

Blood pressure
- It is important that you try and ascertain the older patient's normal blood pressure history as it is common for the older person to have hypertension, therefore a recording considered normal for a younger person may indicate shock.
- If the patient has very high blood pressure it may signal an impending stroke or other problem (Snyder and Christmas 2003).
- A blood pressure consistently higher than 140/90 mmHg is considered to be hypertensive and patients will often be prescribed medication for this. However, a single blood pressure reading is largely meaningless on its own, as trends give more information on the cardiovascular status of the patient. Obtain at least three readings.
- If possible, assess the older patient for postural hypotension by taking their blood pressure when supine, semi-recumbent and standing. If the patient's blood pressure drops the more vertical they get this could indicate a cause for symptoms such as dizziness and syncope.
- Remember to factor in the effects of stress and anxiety on your patient's blood pressure.

ECG recordings
- Arrhythmias in older people are generally a result of age-related changes in the heart, existing cardiac disease, adverse drug effects, or a combination of these factors.
- The most common arrhythmia in the older population is atrial fibrillation (AF) which increases the risk of stroke and heart failure.

Neurological system
Glasgow Coma Score (GCS)
- Altered mental status is a common presentation of a number of underlying causes in the older patient which may be due to a malfunction of virtually any body system, therefore it is important to investigate it thoroughly (see Chapter 5).
- It is worth noting that the causes of an altered mental status are the same across the life span but have a higher frequency for older patients (Snyder and Christmas 2003).
- When assessing an older patient with an altered mental status differentiate between delirium and dementia, which are the most common causes of 'confusion' in the older population (Kane *et al.* 2003, p126).
  - Delirium is a symptom with a rapid onset (hours to days) that resolves once the underlying cause has been treated.
  - Dementia is a disease that produces irreversible brain damage.

The two most common degenerative dementias are 'multi-infarct' or 'vascular dementia' and Alzheimer's disease which is one of the fastest growing health care issues. Research suggests that there are approximately 820,000 people in the UK suffering from dementia and that the estimated cost of dementia to society is approximately £23 billion a year (Luengo-Fernandez *et al.* 2010).

Blood glucose levels
- Approximately 10% of over-65-year-olds have type 2 diabetes, which is frequently diet or tablet controlled. These patients are at risk of hypoglycaemia due to such factors as medication, irregular or inadequate dietary intake, failure to recognise the warning signs and/or blunted warning signs.
- Delirium may be the only indication of hypoglycaemia in the older patient. If the patient is hyperglycaemic the presentation is likely to be acute confusion with dehydration.

Pupils

- Decreases in visual acuity are common in older people without underlying diseases.
- Assess pupils – PERRLA, remember the two most common visual disturbances are cataracts (hardening lenses that eventually become opaque) and glaucoma (increased intra-occular pressure that damages the optic nerve).

Temperature

- Thermoregulation in the older patient is impaired due to a slowed endocrine system and can be adversely affected by chronic disease, medications and alcohol use.
- Older people account for half of all deaths and most indoor deaths from hypothermia which can develop in temperatures above freezing from prolonged exposure.
- Hypothermia death rates are more than double for older people with those over 85 years old most at risk (Caroline 2008).

Pain score

- Older patients may not perceive pain normally due to a number of factors such as neuropathy caused by diseases (e.g. diabetes) and the ageing process.
- Remember medications and/or living with chronic pain (e.g. arthritis) can give the patient a higher pain tolerance. It is important to note any changes to the level or location of the pain (Salomone and Pons 2007).
- The standard pain score is still a useful assessment tool with the older patient as it monitors pain levels from a subjective patient viewpoint.

Trauma

- Injuries to the older person should be considered to be more serious than their outward appearance, to have a more profound systemic influence and to have a greater potential for producing rapid decompensation (Salomone and Pons 2007).
- Medication, such as beta blockers, can prevent the normal homeostatic responses to shock.
- Osteoporosis can make the older patient more prone to fractures even from low energy impacts and they can even suffer pathological fractures from sudden movements.

- When assessing the older patient careful questioning about past falls as well as the current incident could highlight an underlying cause. The incidence of falls increases with increasing age and is evenly split between extrinsic causes (slip or trip) and intrinsic causes (dizziness or fainting) (Caroline 2008).
- If the older patient takes blood thinning medication such as warfarin any haemorrhage could be more severe and last longer due to disruption of the clotting process.

Impressions

The key impressions that the paramedic/clinician notes when dealing with the older patient should include the impression of the patient and their condition in addition to the situation:

- What is the state of the patient's living conditions?
- Does the patient have home oxygen?
- Do you think the patient can manage at home?

The paramedic/clinician should ensure that if the patient is taken to hospital, they verbally provide their '*impression*' when handing over the patient, and record on their documentation to prevent this information from being lost.

OTHER CONSIDERATIONS

Communication

- Do not shout at an older patient who has a hearing impairment.
- Ensure they are wearing their hearing aid if available.
- Move closer to the patient and speak into their ear or use a 'reverse stethoscope' technique (the ear pieces of the stethoscope are placed in the patient's ears and the clinician speaks softly into the diaphragm).
- If the patient has a visual impairment do not assume they also have a hearing impairment. It is important that you describe the procedures you wish to carry out and the equipment you are going to use.
- Make sure you are facing the patient and allow your facial expressions to reflect your meaning.
- Use short sentences and avoid technical jargon. This is especially true if the patient does not speak English and you are interviewing the patient through an interpreter.
- If the patient has aphasia, which is the partial or total inability to produce and understand speech as a result of brain damage caused by injury or disease, give them time to talk and encourage all modes of communication.

- If the patient has dementia use simple, clear language conveying only one idea at a time; there is a delayed reaction time in conversation so if repeating yourself use the same words to allow for this.
- If the patient still does not understand then try rephrasing possibly using gestures to augment your communication.

Social/family/carer/guardian

- When assessing the older patient listen to any concerns voiced by the patient's caregiver regarding changes in the patient's health or the ability of the patient to cope.
- If you think the history given by the older patient is unreliable or incomplete use the caregiver to confirm the history.
- It is worth noting any signs of stress or frustration in the caregiver as they may need help as well (Snyder and Christmas 2003).
- Where the patient lives with their spouse consider the ability of the spouse to cope should you take your patient to hospital and give consideration to conveying the spouse as well.
- If there are any suspicions of abuse of the older person then these should be reported to the appropriate authority.
- Remember it is not the paramedic/clinician's place to conduct an investigation but to report any concerns (JRCALC 2006a).

Ethical and legal

- As with all adult patients the older patient has autonomy over their choices in accordance with their own goals and values.
- Where there may be conflict in 'end of life care issues' or the patient has a 'do not resuscitate' order and their family disagree, check documentation.
- As far as possible the patient's wishes must be respected.
- The paramedic/clinician should satisfy themselves that the patient can give informed consent for any proposed treatment and that the patient's decision making capacity is assessed (DH 2005, 2009).
- Utilise the local guidelines of your service when assessing a patient's capacity and make sure the process is documented fully.
- When dealing with end of life issues, consider the patient's beliefs and how they might impact on the care you propose and the needs of the patient and their family. This may involve facilitating the presence of a religious leader.
- It is important not to let your own beliefs influence the treatment of those who hold a different view to yourself but to deliver the most appropriate care in a professional manner.

Destination/receiving specialist units/non-conveyance

- There is an ever-increasing choice of where to refer your patient and local guidelines should be followed.
- Specialist units include acute stroke units for new onset strokes, hospices for palliative care and trauma centres for major trauma.
- A patient may refuse treatment or transportation and a quick assessment of their capacity is required. There can be many reasons for refusal to go to hospital, from a poor past experience to a fear of never getting home again.
- Reassurance and honesty is the best route in these circumstances.
- If the patient is deemed to have capacity, then their wishes must be respected and the appropriate documentation completed.
- If the patient is not deemed to have capacity, then assistance might need to be sought from the patient's doctor or the police in order to treat the patient.

Professional

The Health Professions Council sets out the expected *Standards of Proficiency* (HPC 2007) and the *Standards of Conduct, Performance and Ethics* (HPC 2008) for the registrant paramedic/clinician, and also provides *Guidance on Conduct and Ethics for Students* (HPC 2009) for 'student paramedics' on HPC approved pre-registration courses.

- These are regularly reviewed and updated and it is the paramedic/clinician's responsibility to be fully conversant with the latest version.
- The *National Service Framework for Older People* (DH 2001b) sets down the minimum level of care an older patient should receive.

Facts and figures

- The Office for National Statistics (2009) reports that the population of the UK is growing increasingly older.
- Over the last 25 years the percentage of the population aged 65 and over has increased from 15% in 1983 to 16% in 2008, an increase of 1.5 million people.
- The fastest population increase has been in the number of those aged 85 and over, the 'oldest old', with their numbers more than doubling since 1983, to reach 1.3 million in 2008.
- By 2033 the number of people aged 85 and over is projected to more than double again to reach 3.2 million, and to account for 5% of the total population.
- As a result of these increases in the number of older people, the median age of the UK population is increasing – from 35 years in 1983 to 39 in

2008. It is projected to continue to increase over the next 25 years rising to 40 by 2033.

Older people in the population

■ From the 1950s onwards, the number of centenarians (people aged 100 and over) in England and Wales has increased at a faster rate than any other group to reach 9,600 in 2008.

■ The major contributor to this rise has been an increase in survival of those aged between 80 and 100.

■ Probable factors driving this increase are improvements in medical treatment, housing, living standards and nutrition.

Increases in life expectancy

■ The increase in the size of the older population has largely been driven by increases in life expectancy.

■ Life expectancy at birth in the UK has reached its highest level on record for both males and females.

■ A newborn baby boy could expect to live 77.2 years and a newborn baby girl 81.5 years if mortality rates remain the same as they were in 2005–07. Women continue to live longer than men, but the gap has been closing.

CHAPTER KEY POINTS

■ Older patients will call the ambulance service as a '*last resort*', often apologising for calling the emergency services.

■ The older patient should as with any patient be treated with respect.

■ Ensure consent is obtained appropriate to the older person and the situation.

■ Undertake and follow the structured approach to the primary survey DR ABCDE and manage time critical conditions accordingly.

■ Undertake and follow the structured approach to the secondary survey, and ensure you cover all important aspects, do not negate the patient's social and environmental history.

■ Take your time with your verbal history taking, physical assessment and social assessment. If older people feel rushed, they may omit an important piece of information, if they sense you are in a hurry.

■ Always ascertain the drug/medication history, as many older patients may have added complications due to pharmacokinetics of multiple medications.

- If appropriate utilise bystanders, carers and relatives to ascertain important information.
- As older people are subject to abuse, ensure you have a clear understanding of the vulnerable adult policies and procedures, and always document clearly.

11 Obstetric patient assessment

Graham Harris and Rehan Kahn

Childbirth is a natural event which in itself is not a medical emergency, and which for millions of years has required little medical assistance (McDonald and Ciotola 2009, p463). For paramedic/clinicians however this area of practice has always caused feelings of trepidation even for the experienced practitioner. However, by undertaking a systematic and structured approach when completing a primary and secondary survey of the obstetric patient the paramedic/clinician will remain not only professional, but will ensure they obtain the relevant obstetric history (Woollard *et al.* 2010, p44).

The primary survey is extended in this chapter to include: *F – Fundus* and *G – Get to the point quickly*. The aim of this chapter is to provide the paramedic/clinician with a systematic approach to the assessment of the patient which will enable them to ascertain the key features of the obstetric history. It will identify whether the patient has any potential life threatening conditions, which will require the paramedic/clinician to implement the appropriate management and transfer immediately to an obstetric unit.

SCENE ASSESSMENT

The assessment of the scene and the patient occurs as you approach the patient; the paramedic/clinician should subconsciously undertake a **DR 'C' ABCDEFG** assessment as they scan the scene. D – Danger, R – Response, C – Circulation (obvious external haemorrhage), A – Airway, B – Breathing, C – Circulation, D – Disability, E – Expose/Environment/Evaluate, F – Fundus, and G – Get to the point quickly, undertake a primary survey.

- Are there other children present? (indication of previous pregnancies)
- Is the environment clean and warm?
- Is there a midwife present?

PRIMARY SURVEY

The paramedic/clinician should remember that with the obstetric primary survey there are two patients (sometimes more in multiple pregnancies). If already born, assess the newborn baby (see Chapter 12). The primary survey provides the paramedic/clinician with the first 'hands on' examination of the pregnant patient. If the patient has sustained significant trauma, either blunt or penetrating to the abdomen then they should be referred to hospital for assessment. The primary survey should be modified in accordance with the findings of the element, for example the presence of vaginal bleeding post-trauma is a *'red flag'* and potentially indicates the patient is time critical, until proven otherwise (Woollard *et al.* 2010, p148).

DANGER

Whilst the majority of obstetric emergency calls attended by paramedic/clinicians will not present any substantial dangers, the need to ensure that an assessment of this element has been undertaken is important.

- Always ensure the safety of yourself, your colleague(s), other health care professionals (midwives) and the patient.
- If pets such as dogs are present politely request they be removed to another room.
- Remember that obstetric situations have a high risk of body fluids, and the appropriate personal protective equipment (gloves, aprons) should be worn.

Possible actions to be taken:

- Ensure safety of self, colleague(s), midwives and patient
- Request pets to be removed if present
- Wear appropriate PPE (gloves, aprons)

RESPONSE

The patient who responds clearly to your questions can be deemed to be conscious, however remember that if the patient's level of consciousness is altered this can also have an effect on the unborn foetus.

- Assess the patient's response using the AVPU scale and record appropriately.

■ Remember that alterations in the patient's level of consciousness (LOC) may be due to hypoxia caused by an airway, breathing or circulation problem.

Possible actions to be taken:

■ Assess and record the patient's level of consciousness (AVPU)
■ Remember that obstetric patients have differing oxygen requirements during the pregnancy, which can affect the patient's (level of consciousness)

CIRCULATION (OBVIOUS EXTERNAL HAEMORRHAGE)

This extra element of the primary survey occurs not only because pregnant females increase their blood volume, but also because the placenta and gravid uterus are highly vascular and injuries to these can cause profound haemorrhage. Death due to haemorrhage remains a leading cause of death (Centre for Maternal and Child Enquiries (CMACE) 2011).

■ Is there a significant amount of blood visible on the floor?
■ Is the patient's clothing visibly wet/saturated with blood?
■ Is blood running down the patient's legs?
■ Is there evidence of blood soaked pads? If so, how many?
■ Is the haemorrhage compressible?

Bear in mind that some causes of obstetric haemorrhage, e.g. placenta previa (placenta obstructing the birth canal) lead to REVEALED haemorrhage i.e. visible blood loss in keeping with haemodynamic state, whereas others e.g. placental abruption lead to CONCEALED haemorrhage i.e. visible blood loss less than that suggested by haemodynamic state.

Possible actions to be taken:

■ If compressible manage immediately (pressure dressing(s), tourniquets)
■ If it is an ante-partum haemorrhage (APH), remove to the nearest obstetric unit for surgery
■ Cannulate and administer IV fluids en route
■ Pre-alert the hospital/obstetric unit

AIRWAY

Whilst the airway does not change dramatically due to pregnancy the paramedic needs to be aware of the issues that may affect the airway of the pregnant patient. Obesity can cause airway management problems (Heslehurst *et al.* 2007). Oedema of the airway may occur in patients with a hypertensive condition, and due to a decrease in peristalsis of the gastro-intestinal tract they are at risk of regurgitation and aspiration (Salomone and Pons 2007, p307).

- Is the patient able to talk clearly and does she have an open airway?
- Is she making unusual noises indicating a possible airway obstruction?
- If obstructed manage accordingly (stepwise airway management, see Chapter 2).
- If unresponsive manage the airway with positioning (place the patient in a left lateral tilt 15–30° or manually displace the uterus) to prevent compression of the vena cava.

Possible actions to be taken:

- Ensure airway is patent and secure before proceeding to next element
- If obstructed manage utilising stepwise airway management
- If unresponsive manage the airway (*place the patient in a left lateral tilt 15–30° or manually displace the uterus*)

BREATHING

During pregnancy the shape of the rib cage alters anatomically to accommodate the gravid uterus, the abdominal muscles lose their tone and breathing becomes more diaphragmatic (Panté and Pollak 2010, p262). Throughout pregnancy both the vital capacity and respiratory rate increase, but the residual volume decreases and during late pregnancy the patient may exhibit dyspnoea (Marieb 2009, p565). In late pregnancy the tidal volume increases by 40%, however the tidal increase causes an increase in the minute ventilation by as much as 50%.

- Ascertain the patient's respiratory rate and effort (increased rate without increased work of breathing may be indicative of an attempt to compensate for a circulatory problem) (Woollard *et al.* 2010, p40).
- Ascertain the patient's oxygen saturation levels.
- Administer oxygen only in relation to the clinical findings (administering oxygen to well pregnant patients may cause alarm).
- Auscultate for and clarify if there are adventitious sounds.

Possible actions to be taken:

- Ascertain the patient's oxygen saturation levels
- Administer oxygen only in relation to the clinical findings (BTS 2008, pvi2)
- Manage breathing problems and/or associated hypoxia effectively before moving to the next element

CIRCULATION

Physiological changes occur with the circulatory system as the pregnancy develops; these incorporate an increase in heart rate 15/20 bpm by the 3rd trimester. Blood pressure decreases 5/15 mmHg during the 2nd trimester, but returns to normal by term. Cardiac output increases by 1–1.5 L/min by the tenth week, but by term blood volume increases by approximately 50% (Salomone and Pons 2007, p307; Resuscitation Council (UK) 2011). The paramedic/clinician should remember that a pregnant patient at term can lose 30%–35% of their blood volume before presenting with signs of hypovolaemia.

- Assess the patient's radial pulse to ascertain the rate and rhythm.
- Assess the patient's blood pressure (BP):
  - A systolic BP of 100 mmHg is not uncommon in the healthy pregnant patient
  - A systolic BP of 160 mmHg or over requires urgent further medical assessment (CEMACH 2007, p72).
- Ask the patient if they have had problems with their BP during the pregnancy.
- Always read the patient's hand-held records to assess trends in their blood pressure and judge for the presence of pre-eclampsia (hypertension associated with proteinuria occurring after 20 weeks).
- ECG changes occurring in pregnancy include ectopic beats and supraventricular tachycardia (these are often considered normal).

Possible actions to be taken:

- Assess the patient's heart rate
- Assess the patient's BP (note and record, if hypertensive >160mmHg arrange further assessment)
- Ask to see the patient's hand-held records and ascertain trends or problems with blood pressure

DISABILITY

Pre-eclampsia in late pregnancy is characterised by changes in the patient's mental status, and can result in seizures (eclampsia). Both eclampsia and pre-eclampsia were identified as a cause of death for pregnant patients (major morbidity and mortality ensues from strokes and seizures) (CEMACH 2007, p72). Gestational diabetes is increasing with the rise in obesity, and is more common in Asian women. Approximately 87.5% of pregnancies complicated by diabetes are due to gestational diabetes (CMACE 2010).

- Assess the patient's level of consciousness (LOC) (*utilise AVPU*).
- Assess the patient's blood glucose levels (*ascertain if the patient has pre-existing diabetes? If so, is it type I or type II?*).
- Assess the patient's pupils for both size and reaction, PERRLA.

EXPOSE/ENVIRONMENT/EVALUATE

The paramedic/clinician may or may not be experienced in obstetric situations, however if you have not already done so, briefly expose and examine the introitus. Always ensure you obtain consent first from the patient and that it is recorded (HPC 2008; DH 2009, p5). If the patient is contracting and in apparent labour, consider:

- Have the waters broken? (spontaneous rupture of membranes (SROM))
- Can you see any presenting parts of the baby?
- Environment. Is it warm, and as clean as possible? (especially if considering to deliver on-site)
- Evaluate the findings from the primary survey and if you have identified any time critical problems within any of the elements, then consider the need to transport and transfer immediately to an appropriate obstetric unit, if not then conduct the secondary survey and then transfer the patient to her pre-booked unit.

Possible actions to be taken:

- Expose patient and examine
- Ensure consent and patient dignity
- Evaluate – time critical obstetric emergencies require transfer to an appropriate obstetric unit, pre-alert the hospital/obstetric unit
- Request midwife/skilled assistance if remaining on scene
- Non-time critical – move onto the secondary survey

FUNDUS

When examining make a quick assessment of the fundal height, a fundus at the height of the umbilicus equates approximately to 22 weeks gestation. At full term the fundus is at the xiphoid process.

GET TO THE POINT QUICKLY

The aim of the primary survey is to identify any potential life threatening conditions, which will require the paramedic to implement the appropriate management and transfer immediately to an obstetric unit.

SECONDARY SURVEY

Obstetric history

Paramedic/clinicians may be called to obstetric patients who are either due to undertake, or have undertaken, a home delivery; alternatively they may be booked into a midwifery-led or a consultant-led unit, and in the worst case scenario attend patients who have not pre-booked obstetric maternity care. The majority of patients will however have accessed antenatal care and be in possession of appropriate hand-held maternity notes. Undertaking a complete obstetric history from the patient, in combination with the information provided in the patient's hand-held maternity notes, will enable the paramedic/clinician to identify any potential obstetric or related medical problems that may arise, whilst the patient is in their care. In the first instance ascertain the following information from the patient:

- The patient's name (is she agreeable for you to address her by this name?).
- Date of birth (DOB) or age (this can provide information regarding the possibility of potential obstetric problems, is she young or maternal age >40 years of age?).
- Which hospital is the patient booked in to (if the patent has previously booked)?
- Is she booked into an obstetric or midwife-led unit (the latter normally dictates low-risk antenatal care) (Woollard *et al.* 2010, p44)?
- The gestation of the pregnancy (how many weeks pregnant is the patient?):
  - 1st trimester (1–13 weeks)
  - 2nd trimester (14–27 weeks)
  - 3rd trimester (28–40 weeks).

■ If the patient does not know how many weeks pregnant she is, or is unsure then utilise the estimated date of delivery (EDD) against the last menstrual period (LMP) to ascertain the gestation (*birth normally occurs within 15 days of the EDD, which equates to approximately 280 days from the first day of the patient's LMP*) (Marieb 2009, p566).

■ Remember to look at the patient's hand-held notes (these will provide the paramedic/clinician with information regarding both the current and any previous pregnancies).

Previous medical history

Remember as with any secondary survey the patient's previous medical history will provide evidence that may be relevant, especially with co-morbidity conditions, or if she has any medical problem that may have a relationship with the reason why you are in attendance.

■ Does the patient have hypertension? If so, is this pre-existing hypertension? (hypertension occurring before the 13th week of gestation, a diastolic BP >110 mmHg would be deemed as severe). Or,

■ Is it pregnancy induced hypertension (PIH)? (raised BP which occurs after 20 weeks gestation, with the absence of proteinuria, it is usually mild, with readings normally 140/90).

■ Does the patient have epilepsy? If so, has the patient remained compliant with medication?

■ Is the patient diabetic? (again is this pre-existing (type I or II) or gestational diabetes?).

■ Is the patient asthmatic? (ascertain history of medication compliance and previous attacks).

Past obstetric history

In other chapters this section of the secondary survey relates to '*past medical history*', however in relation to the obstetric patient this is specific to their '*past obstetric history*', therefore the paramedic/clinician will need to clarify and differentiate between '**gravity**' and '**parity**'. Gravity is the total number of pregnancies including the current, whereas parity relates to the number of live births (live or stillborn) (Woollard *et al.* 2010, p47).

■ How many previous pregnancies has the patient had?

■ How many previous deliveries has the patient had?

■ How were these delivered? (naturally or did she have a caesarean section?)

■ Did the patient have any problems in the previous pregnancy(s) (bleeding, BP or pre-term delivery)?

Previous caesarean section is an important risk factor as in labour it carries a 1 in 200 risk of uterine rupture, presenting as constant pain and bleeding.

History of current pregnancy

The information ascertained here is the history that relates to this particular pregnancy, and allows the paramedic/clinician the opportunity to elicit appropriate facts.

- How many weeks pregnant is the patient? Define which trimester the patient is in from this, and consider potential problems.
- Does the patient know her EDD? (are they premature? or overdue?)
- How many babies is she expecting? (single, twins or multiple?)
- Have there been any concerns with the baby? (scans and ante-natal appointments, check notes for information and attendance)
- Has the patient had any problems? (pregnancy induced hypertension, pre-eclampsia, gestational diabetes)

History of current problem

The paramedic/clinician should utilise questions that are aimed at clarifying the patient's current problem. Consider the following structure to assist this format of questions: *Labour, Pains, Discharge, Bleeding, Foetal, and Fits* (Woollard *et al.* 2010, p45).

Labour
- Is the labour at *term* (after 37 weeks) or *preterm?*
- At what stage of labour is the patient in? (first, second or third stage?)
- How many contractions are there in a 10 minute period? (3 or more contractions in 10 minutes is considered established labour).
- Are there more than 5 contractions in a 10 minute period? (if so, consider abruption)
- Have the waters broken? If so, when? (as prolonged rupture of membranes is associated with infection)

Pain
Abdominal pain is a common complaint during pregnancy, being suffered by most women at some stage. Ascertain if it is physiologically normal (muscle stretching or indigestion), or is due to a severe pathological condition (appendicitis or an ectopic pregnancy) (Fraser and Cooper 2009, p334). Ascertain from the patient in the first instance the *location* of the pain, and then obtain a description of the pain, by utilising the OPQRSTA framework:

Onset	Ask the patient: When did the pain start? (was it rapid, over minutes or gradual, over hours?)
Provocation	Ask the patient If anything eases it or makes it worse.
Quality	Ask the patient to describe the pain:

- contractions – does the uterus go hard?
- is it constant?
- is it stabbing?
- does it come and go?
- is it like an ache?

Radiates	Ask the patient if the pain moves anywhere, or does it stay in one place?
Severity	Ask the patient to score the pain? (0–10, where 0 is no pain and 10 is the worst pain ever).
Timing	Ask the patient how long the pain has lasted (is there any history of trauma it may be related to?).
Associated symptoms	Ask the patient if they have any associated symptoms (headache, nausea, vomiting).

Discharge

All women have some vaginal discharge or 'leucorrhoea' (normal discharge is clear, white or creamy and may smell musky but not unpleasant), which normally starts a year or two before puberty and ends after the menopause, and is usually quite harmless. It is quite common for this to increase during pregnancy. In the final weeks of pregnancy the discharge may contain streaks of thick mucus and some blood. This is called a 'show' and happens when the cervical plug (a 'ball' of thick mucus that fills the cervix during pregnancy) comes away. This is a sign that the body is starting to prepare for birth, and the patient may have already had a few small 'shows'. The paramedic/clinician should ascertain from the patient if the discharge is normal or has changed, and consider asking the patient about the colour, odour, consistency and quantity of the discharge.

- Colour – ascertain if the discharge is:
  - Clear and odourless
  - Clear and smells of urine
  - Green
  - Yellow
  - Pink
  - Red
- Odour – does the leucorrhoea have an offensive smell?
- Consistency – ascertain if the discharge is:
  - Watery
  - Thick

      ■ Frothy
      ■ Jelly-like
- Quantity – ask the patient to clarify if the discharge is:
  - A trickle
  - Gushing
  - Still draining.

Bleeding

Whilst approximately 1 in 10 women experience some bleeding during pregnancy, it is usually a terrifying ordeal at the time for those involved (patient and partner alike). It does not necessarily mean a miscarriage will occur. In early pregnancy the patient may have some light bleeding, called *spotting*, when the foetus implants itself into the wall of the uterus. It is also known as *implantation bleeding* and normally occurs at the time when the patient's first period (post-conception) would have been due. In the first three months of pregnancy, vaginal bleeding may be a sign of miscarriage or ectopic pregnancy, whereas in the later stages of pregnancy, vaginal bleeding may be due to different causes. However, bleeding at any stage of the pregnancy from the genital tract is abnormal and needs to be appropriately assessed by a doctor, irrespective of the amount (Stable and Rankin 2010, p 423). Ascertain the following information from the patient:

- Ask the patient: When did it start?
- How much blood is/was there?
  - noticed it when wiping self after going to toilet
  - teaspoon (approximately 5ml)
  - soaked pants/trousers
  - sanitary towel(s) (ascertain how many)
  - visible on legs.
- Ask the patient if she is still bleeding.
- Ask the patient if there were any clots in the blood (size and quantity).
- Ask the patient if there is any mucus mixed in the blood.

Foetal movements

The first movement of the foetus, also known as *quickening*, usually occurs at 20 weeks in a first pregnancy, with the average time of occurrence being between 16 and 20 plus weeks (Fraser and Cooper 2010, p221). By week 28, the patient can expect to feel foetal activity every day, this continues throughout the third trimester. It is crucial to note changes in activity, and any sudden decreases in movements addressed accordingly. Ascertain the following from the patient:

- Ask the patient if the baby is moving normally (after 28 weeks/7 months, 10 movements of any kind in one hour or less is normal).
- The patient may not feel foetal movement if she is contracting.

- Ask the patient if the baby is moving less.
- Ask the patient: When was the last time you felt the baby move?
- No foetal movement, and the patient is presenting with severe pain (with or without haemorrhage – treat as a placental abruption).
- Remember 'dead' babies move (an external movement may cause the baby to move against the uterine wall, and be interpreted as movement) (Woollard *et al.* 2010, p47).

Fitting

The paramedic/clinician should remember that fitting may occur due to complications of the pregnancy – pre-eclampsia (hypertension and associated proteinuria occurring after 20 weeks gestation) and eclampsia (tonic-clonic, grand mal seizure: associated with signs and symptoms of pre-eclampsia). The occurrence of eclampsia in the UK is 2.7 per 10,000 births (Knight 2007, p1072–78). Epilepsy affects 1 in 200 of all pregnant women (Stables and Rankin 2010, p466). Ascertain the following information from the patient, partner or bystanders:

- Does the patient have epilepsy? if so, how is this controlled?
  - Valproate (epilim)
  - Lamotrigine
  - Keppra
  - Carbamazepine, oxcarbazepine or others (Stables and Rankin 2010, p466).
- Does the patient have any previous history of fits? When and why did they occur?
- Was the fit witnessed? if so, ask the witness
  - if there were any tonic-clonic movements
  - for how long they occurred.
- Has the patient suffered any associated problems (incontinence, biting tongue/lips)?
- Check the patient's hand-held notes (ascertain any problems with blood pressure, pregnancy induced hypertension (PIH), pre-eclampsia or eclampsia).

Evaluating the history

On completing the history the paramedic/clinician should evaluate the key components and utilise the findings of the examination to assist in making a diagnosis. Consideration should be given to the following:

- Did the history identify any risk factors? Such as:
  - previous caesarean section (increases the risk of uterine rupture)
  - breech presentation in the transverse lie position (higher risk of prolapse cord)

> ▥ twin pregnancy (increased risk of all obstetric emergencies)
>   (Woollard *et al.* 2010).
> ■ Assess and evaluate the severity of symptoms:
>   ▥ systolic blood pressure >160 mmHg or over (requires further urgent
>   medical assessment)
>   ▥ hypertension (increases risk of abruption)
>   ▥ severe pain
>   ▥ bleeding.

Utilise all of the information obtained during the secondary survey and the findings of the examination to confirm your diagnosis. If appropriate pre-alert the obstetric unit.

HANDOVER OF THE OBSTETRIC PATIENT

At some opportune moment the paramedic/clinician will be required to 'hand over' their patient to another health care professional. It should be structured to ensure that important information regarding the patient is not omitted. The initial stage of a handover may have already occurred with a pre-alert communication being forwarded to the maternity/obstetric receiving unit. For the obstetric patient this should include the following:

- ■ Age
- ■ Signs and symptoms, follow the ABCDEFG framework, include relevant findings (onset of labour, contractions, SROM, omit categories with atypical findings)
- ■ History of the current problem
- ■ History of the current pregnancy (what is the expected date of delivery (EDD), gravidity, number of pregnancies, parity, number of birth events, or any problems identified)
- ■ Interventions (describe any management provided, location of IV/IO sites and doses of drugs)
- ■ Estimated time of arrival (ETA) for those patients with a pre-alert communication (Woollard *et al.* 2010, p50).

OTHER CONSIDERATIONS

Communication

Not only does the problem of communicating with patients of different dialects occur to the paramedic/clinician (English not being the first language). The paramedic/clinician in the worst case scenario may also have to deal with the situation where the baby is born with an unexpected disability, such as cleft lip or clubfoot. In these situations clear, effective and honest communication is considered crucial (Farrell *et al.* 2001).

Destination/receiving specialist units/non-conveyance

Depending on the circumstances of the call and the findings of the primary and secondary surveys, the obstetric patient may not even be required to be conveyed. However, if the patient has an obstetric risk factor, then the receiving unit may need to be an obstetric unit. Alternatively the paramedic/clinician may need to convey the patient to an emergency department due to the dyspnoea associated with life threatening asthma.

Social/family/carer

Childbirth in the 20th century has been transformed from a social, domestic experience into a highly technological medical system. However, evidence clearly shows that there is a link between adverse pregnancy outcomes and vulnerability and social exclusion (CEMACH 2007). Certain groups of patients may be particularly disadvantaged, including women who are asylum seekers, from travelling communities, from black and ethnic minority groups or have a disability (Fraser and Cooper 2010, p24). Support from the family network for the new mother may include partner/husband, parents, grandparents etc., whilst the very young single mother may well have to deal with childbirth entirely alone.

Ethical and legal

As with any patient, the paramedic/clinician has a 'duty of care' to their patient(s), and with obstetric incidents there is the added problem of cultural, religious and gender issues that may affect the ability of conducting a physical examination. Always ask for consent and explain clearly to the patient the need to perform an inspection (document and record this in your notes), maintain the patient's dignity and respect their right to refuse consent.

CHAPTER KEY POINTS

- Fully assess each area of the primary survey DR 'C' ABCDEFG.
- Ensure consent is obtained appropriate to the situation, and is recorded.
- Identify time critical problems within the primary survey.
- Manage time critical problems as they are found, pre-alert the receiving unit.

- Undertake a secondary survey, and evaluate the risks and severity of symptoms.
- Consider cultural, religious and gender issues.
- Provide a structured handover of the patient to other health care professionals.

12 Assessment and care of the neonate

Nandiran Ratnavel

Most baby deliveries occur in hospital. A small number of babies are born as planned home deliveries, a smaller proportion are delivered as unplanned home births. A rather more hazardous situation is the unplanned delivery of a baby in a public place. Roughly 1 in 200 babies will be born unexpectedly outside of hospital without a midwife in attendance (Scott and Esen 2005). This chapter deals with the assessment of the newborn baby and the immediate pre-hospital assessment/ management of the newborn baby requiring resuscitation and subsequent transfer into hospital.

SCENE ASSESSMENT

It is important for the paramedic/clinician to be aware that attending a delivery potentially involves looking after two patients: mother and baby. To that end it may be normal practice for two crews to be despatched to such events. It may be that a community midwife is in attendance and has called for emergency services for transfer into hospital. Alternatively it may be the case that the paramedic/clinician is first to arrive on scene and is subsequently joined by the midwife. It is recommended to take guidance from the birth specialist if she/he is present.

Actions will be determined depending on whether the baby has delivered or not. If not yet born and a midwife is not in attendance it may be necessary for the crew to deliver the baby if there is no opportunity to transfer the mother into hospital first. If the infant has already delivered, it is important to make sure that mother and baby are at the same horizontal level so as to avoid feto-maternal or materno-fetal transfusion until the umbilical cord is clamped and cut. Any visible blood at the scene may indicate acute blood loss from either mother or baby.

Possible actions to be taken:

- If baby has not delivered and birth is imminent, then
  - Request midwife and second vehicle via control (if appropriate)
  - Prepare for delivery utilising Maternity and Paediatric Advanced Life Support (PALS) packs
- If baby is delivered
  - Ensure mother and baby are at same horizontal level until cord is clamped and cut
  - Note the amount of visible blood and ascertain if from mother or baby

PRIMARY SURVEY

The generic process of conducting the primary survey needs to be modified to a more appropriate approach in accordance with the circumstances surrounding the birth of the baby.

DANGER

Circumstances surrounding the delivery of a baby are not usually hazardous to the paramedic/clinician, however, the presence of body fluids mean the paramedic/clinician should wear the appropriate personal protective equipment (PPE). Clamping and cutting the cord will require the paramedic/clinician to be exposed to these fluids. Newborn babies are extremely susceptible to body temperature loss; to that end it may be necessary to close any windows and doors, as well as increase the environmental temperature if it is possible to do so. In the out-of-hospital setting this will usually occur in a domestic environment although this is not always the case. The newborn baby's size means that it has a relatively large surface area to body weight ratio. For this reason heat loss by convection and radiation will be high. The baby will also be wet which means that heat loss via evaporation will be significant. An unexpected delivery outside of hospital will almost certainly be associated with hypothermia as it is far more difficult to control the environmental temperature. It is well recognised that hypothermic babies have significantly increased morbidity and mortality rates compared to normothermic babies (Bhatt *et al.* 2007).

With regard to management of the umbilical cord after delivery of the baby, there are currently two differing schools of thought (represented by the numbers 1 and 2 below):

1   Clamping and cutting the cord gives the clinician a clear time point from which adaptation to postnatal life is required and at the beginning of which effective resuscitation must be commenced (if indicated).

1   It prevents siphoning of blood between the placenta and the infant. There is some evidence to suggest that delayed clamping of the umbilical cord can lead to polycythaemia in the infant if excessive blood passes from mother to baby. Complications associated with hyperviscosity syndrome may then ensue.

2   Not clamping the cord prior to commencing resuscitation centres around allowing the baby to receive whatever residual support from the maternal circulation there may be for as long a time as there is blood flowing from the placenta to the baby.

2   The converse problem of anaemia in the baby can arise from delayed cord clamping due to flow of blood in the opposite direction.

2   There is of course the practical problem of attending to mother and baby as separate patients whilst they are still physically connected.

Possible actions to be taken:

- Ensure that gloves and PPE are worn
- Clamp and cut the cord (as appropriate to situation)
- Close windows and doors and increase environmental temperature

---

RESPONSE – INITIAL ASSESSMENT AT BIRTH

Following initial introductions and assessment it is vital for the paramedic/clinician to establish if any urgent interventions are necessary before ascertaining a complete history. The clinical assessment of the newborn baby immediately after birth allows the paramedic/clinician a quick and informative overview that will direct subsequent resuscitative actions (if required). The continuing assessment of the newborn will be dependent on the following criteria at birth:

- What is the term gestation? Knowing the gestation of the baby will be very helpful both in adjusting the style of respiratory support offered (if this is needed) as well as appreciating the higher rates of heat loss experienced by premature babies. If the mother is unsure then estimate it, based on the first day of her last menstrual period (LMP), particularly if a dating scan was not performed in the first trimester of the pregnancy.
- Is the amniotic fluid clear? (if there was meconium present in the amniotic fluid and a greenish tinge of the baby's skin or fingernails this may indicate foetal distress during labour and the possibility of meconium aspiration syndrome in the newborn).

■ Is the baby breathing or crying?
■ Does the baby have good muscle tone?

If the answer to these is **YES** then routine care should be provided (Resuscitation Council 2006, p98). To that end, make a note of the time.

Possible actions to be taken:

■ Provide warmth
■ Dry and wrap the newborn (see Figure 12.1)
■ Clear airway if necessary
■ Assess colour

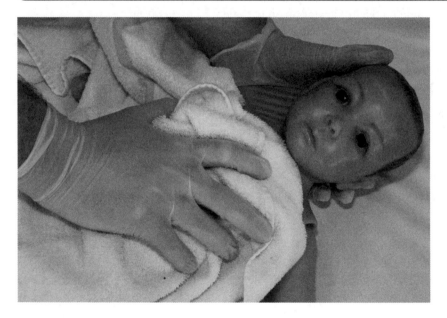

Figure 12.1 Drying a newborn baby

Action: Dry the baby off thoroughly with a warm dry towel. Having done this, discard the wet towel and wrap the newborn up with a new warm dry towel. This will require opening two maternity packs or using domestic towels if in someone's home.

It is important to cover the extremities and the head which is a source of major heat loss. A small triangle of chest may be left exposed in order to assess respiratory effort, chest movement and to listen to the heart rate with a stethoscope. Whilst undertaking the drying and wrapping process, the paramedic/clinician should simultaneously assess and evaluate the following parameters of the newborn: colour, muscle tone, breathing and heart rate.

Colour

Pink	Implies delivery of oxygenated blood to the skin and vital organs
Blue	Implies delivery of deoxygenated blood to the skin and vital organs
White	Implies reduced blood supply to the skin and vital organs

Muscle tone

Normal	Vigorous infant
Abnormal	Some tone but reduced
Absent	Completely floppy and lifeless

Breathing

Normal	Crying infant with regular respirations
Abnormal	Shallow, irregular respirations or gasping
None	No respiratory effort at all

Heart rate

Fast	Above 100 beats per minute
Slow	Between 60 and 100 beats per minute
Very slow	Less than 60 beats per minute
Absent	No audible heart rate

The heart rate should be estimated rather than actually counted so as not to lose time. The paramedic/clinician will more often than not estimate within the correct category and act accordingly with the appropriate action. The most accurate method is ascertained by listening to the left side of the praecordium with a stethoscope. It is difficult in the compromised neonate to palpate the brachial, femoral or carotid pulses particularly in an emergency situation. Experienced midwives may be used to feeling the newborn baby pulse by palpating the base of the umbilical cord, but most paramedic/clinicians will not have this level of expertise. However, not all cardiac pulsations are transmitted to the cord and particularly if the umbilical vessels have gone into spasm these pulsations may not be felt, leading to inaccuracies in heart rate estimation.

After completing the assessment evaluations the newborn baby will fall into one of the following categories:

Pink, vigorous, crying, heart rate >100 bpm

- Keep warm.
- Remain wrapped in dry towels, or skin to skin with mother.
- Take lead from birthing specialist. If no midwife present, await arrival whilst maintaining normothermia.

Blue, reduced or absent tone, irregular or absent breathing, heart rate <100 bpm

■ The stimulation produced during the process of drying is usually sufficient to induce effective breathing. If not, then

■ Place the head into the neutral position (see Figures 12.2, 12.3).

■ Open the airway.

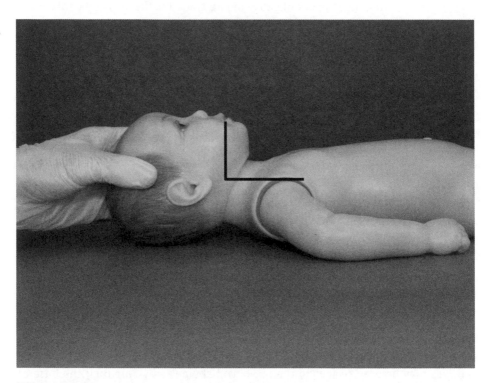

Figure 12.2 Correct neutral head position

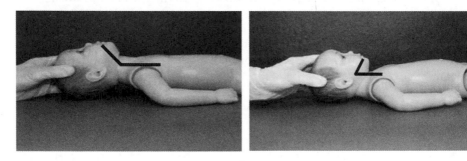

Figure 12.3 Incorrect neutral head positions

- Assess and ascertain if the baby responds. If so, no further resuscitation is needed other than keeping baby warm.
- If there Is no response, then proceed to aerate the baby's lungs (see Breathing below).

Blue or pale, reduced or absent tone, irregular or absent breathing, heart rate slow <60bpm or absent

- Apnoeic babies require resuscitation.
- Place the head into the neutral position.
- Open the airway and aerate the lungs (see Breathing section).
- Reassess and ascertain if there is a heart rate response. If none, then
- Implement circulatory resuscitation accordingly.
- Reassess heart rate and respiration every 30 seconds.

These depend on the newborn baby's condition at the initial assessment following the drying and wrapping process.

Possible actions to be taken:

- Following assessment implement resuscitation measures accordingly
- Airway
- Breathing
- Circulation
- Drugs (consider adrenaline) (Resuscitation Council (UK) 2010, p124)

AIRWAY

The appropriate position to achieve an open airway is a neutral alignment. The prominent occiput of the baby means that the baby will tend to adopt a flexed position to the neck when lying supine. Equally, extension of the neck will also have a tendency to occlude the airway owing to the newborn's anatomy and the relatively collapsible nature of the trachea. Paramedic/clinicians may find it useful to place a folded towel under the baby's neck and shoulders to assist in maintaining the airway in a neutral position (Woollard *et al.* 2010).

Possible actions to be taken:

- Place baby supine on a flat surface, with a folded towel beneath the baby's neck and shoulders
- Position head in neutral position
- Open the airway (if baby is floppy consider applying chin lift)
- Inspect the oral cavity
- Do not attempt blind finger sweeps

BREATHING

The purpose of the initial five breaths is to provide aeration. This is due to the lungs initially being full of fluid. By giving these slow, sustained breaths, the majority of the fluid in the lungs will be driven into the lymphatic system and the alveoli will be inflated and readied for gas exchange with the lung capillaries. These should last two to three seconds each. The aim of these is to inflate the lungs and establish a resting lung volume. It is imperative to visualise the chest to look for chest rise. The aim is to achieve this by the fifth breath. It is not unusual for the initial one or two attempts to fail to give rise to chest expansion. These can be administered with the infant mask carried in the standard paediatric bag which is suitable for the full-term baby. It should be sized to cover the nose and mouth without pressing on the eyes or overlapping the chin and sufficient pressure applied to provide a good seal. Having done this it should be connected to a bag-valve system, which should have a 500ml capacity or more to allow for delivery of a two to three second inflation breath.

The entire capacity of the bag may not need to be used. Smaller bags may not contain the necessary volume to achieve this. Attach face mask to bag-valve device away from the baby's face. Check pressure release valve is working on the bag-valve device. The bag-valve–mask apparatus can be connected to a source of supplemental oxygen but there should be no delay incurred in doing this because achieving lung inflation is far more important than the concentration of inspired oxygen. A newborn baby can be effectively resuscitated with room air. Apply system over the baby's nose and mouth and give five inflation breaths. The paramedic/clinician should simultaneously check for rise of the chest to assess effectiveness. The baby should then be reassessed in terms of colour, tone, breathing and heart rate.

Possible actions to be taken:

- Size mask and attach to 500ml bag-valve device
- Attach supplemental oxygen if available (do not delay resuscitation if not available)
- Administer 5 aerating 'inflation breaths', each of 2–3 seconds duration
- Check for chest rise (remember the initial 1–2 breaths may fail to expand the chest)
- Reassess heart rate and action accordingly

If chest rise has been seen and the heart rate responds lung inflation has been successful. If the baby's colour becomes pink, the tone improves, the infant starts to cry or breathe regularly and the heart rate remains fast he/she must be kept warm. Liaise with midwife/control regarding transferring baby into hospital whilst constant reassessment continues.

Should the baby fail to commence spontaneous breathing

If the baby's colour becomes pink, the tone improves, the heart rate increases but the baby fails to establish regular, effective respirations than ventilation breaths should be administered until he/she is breathing regularly. Reassessment should be performed every 30 seconds to establish whether this has occurred. Ventilation breaths should last 1–2 seconds, a resting lung volume having already been established. The purpose is to maintain continuous alveolar ventilation thus facilitating gas exchange.

The paramedic/clinician should ensure that the chest is rising and falling with the assisted ventilation. If the heart rate increases, one can assume that gas has entered the lungs.

Possible actions to be taken:

- Continue to administer regular breaths at a rate of 30–40 per minute (Resuscitation Council (UK) 2010, p122)
- Reassess every 30 seconds

If the chest does not rise and the heart rate does not improve

- Paramedic/clinicians must assume that the lungs have not been inflated and an alternative airway manoeuvre must be employed.
- Realigning the airway and checking that the neutral position is being maintained may be an appropriate first step with a view to trying the inflation breaths again. If this does not work then applying jaw thrust,

either as a single or two person manoeuvre is often effective. There are three major tasks to be achieved whilst performing the jaw thrust:

1   Ensure a good seal of the mask edge over the baby's nose and mouth
2   Maintain neutral alignment of the airway, and
3   Bring the mandible forward.

■   When performing the single person manoeuvre the mask is held around the firm stem between thumb and index finger such that equal pressure is applied to the face all around the mask edge. This prevents deformation of the soft part of the mask and maintains a good seal. The ring finger can be used to bring the mandible forward by applying pressure along the line of the jaw just proximal to the angle of the mandible. The palm of the same hand can be rested gently on the baby's forehead to keep the airway in a neutral position and to prevent flexion or hypertension of the neck.

■   In the two person manoeuvre the mask can be held onto the face by holding the stem of the mask with the thumb and index fingers of each hand on either side with ring fingers on each side providing the jaw thrust and the palms of the hands keeping the neutral position. If the paramedic/clinician's hands are small then the mask can be held on by both thumbs placed over the soft part of the mask on each side whilst the jaw thrust is achieved with the third finger on each side.

■   Insertion of an appropriately sized oropharyngeal airway under direct vision may help to open the airway. Such airways come in different sizes and it is vital that the paramedic/clinician correctly sizes the airway prior to insertion. This is done by aligning one end with the angle of the mandible and the other with the middle of the lower lip. The airway that most closely spans these two landmarks is the one that should be used. Insertion should never be performed blind and should always be done under direct vision. This minimises the risk of the tongue or foreign material being lodged further down the airway.

■   Five further inflation breaths can then be administered followed by a reassessment of the baby's colour, tone, breathing and heart rate.

Possible actions to be taken:

■   Realign the airway and ensure the head is in the neutral position
■   Apply a jaw thrust (ensure effective seal, neutral alignment and bring mandible forward)
■   Ensure that the aspirator is set to the lowest setting
■   Remove visible obstructions/secretions using suction under direct vision
■   Insert correctly sized oropharyngeal airway under direct vision
■   Administer 5 further 'inflation breaths', each of 2–3 seconds duration

■ Check for chest rise (remember the initial 1–2 breaths may fail to expand the chest)
■ Reassess heart rate and action accordingly

If the heart rate remains slow <60 bpm or absent despite good chest movement during the 5 inflation breaths, commence chest compression.

CIRCULATION

If there has been chest movement then it is likely that the myocardium has become compromised due to hypoxia and needs help to start. This help is provided by giving chest compressions in combination with ventilation breaths at a ratio of three compressions to one ventilation (3:1 ratio). The purpose of the chest compressions is to push oxygenated blood from the lungs forward to the heart to perfuse the oxygen starved myocardium via the coronary arteries. The coronary arteries are branches of the ascending aorta and are perfused during diastole. The relaxation phase of the chest compressions is therefore equally important. The encircling technique is the most efficient method of chest compression on a baby.

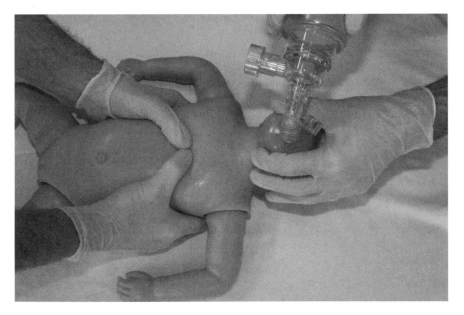

Figure 12.4 Compression technique to be used on a neonate

Chest compression technique (see Figure 12.4):

- The preferred method is to encircle the chest with both hands and press on the sternum with both thumbs.
- The thumbs can be placed either side by side or on top of one another.
- The point of application of pressure for the compressions should be on the lower third of the sternum, just below an imaginary line joining the nipples (Richmond 2006, p23).

Sufficient pressure should be applied to compress the sternum to one third of the depth of the chest. The speed with which this sequence should be carried out is to achieve a rate of 120 events per minute (i.e. 90 compressions to 30 ventilations per minute). This should actually be carried out for 30 seconds following which the baby should be reassessed. This will therefore allow time for 45 compressions and 15 ventilations to be delivered.

Possible actions to be taken:

- Only commence chest compressions when the lungs have been aerated successfully
- Grip the baby's chest in both hands, position thumbs on sternum and ensure fingers support the spine
- Compress the chest and ventilate the lungs at a ratio of 3:1
- Reassess after 30 seconds
- Once the heart rate is >60 bpm and increasing then chest compressions can be stopped
- Consider drugs if the heart rate does not respond despite effective inflation of the lungs and effective chest compressions

---

DRUGS

These are usually unnecessary in the pre-hospital scenario, because effective management of the airway, breathing and circulation is usually sufficient to resuscitate the newborn baby. However, if there is no significant improvement of the baby's cardiac output despite effective lung inflation and chest compressions then the following drugs are needed:

- Adrenaline 1:10,000
- Dextrose 10%, and,
- Sodium bicarbonate 4.2%.

The doses are weight dependent and are ideally administered centrally via either an umbilical venous catheter or an infant intra-osseous needle. Paramedic/clinicians will be proficient in the latter. Recommended doses are:

- *Adrenaline:* 10 microgram/kg (0.1 ml/kg, 1:10,000). If ineffective then a dose of up to 30 microgram/kg (0.3 ml/kg, 1:10,000) may be administered on repeat after 5 minutes.
- *Sodium bicarbonate:* 1–2 mmol/kg (2–4 ml/kg, 4.2% bicarbonate solution). (This drug is not routinely available to paramedics in the pre-hospital environment and needs to be administered intravenously.)
- *Dextrose:* 250 ml/kg (2.5ml/kg, 10% dextrose). On rare occasions the heart rate may not be able to increase due to loss of blood volume.
   On such occasions the use of an isotonic crystalloid for emergency volume replacement is preferred.
- *Saline 0.9%:* 10ml/kg of 0.9% saline bolus administered over 10–20 seconds (may be safely repeated if required after 5 minutes).

Possible actions to be taken:

- Obtain intra-osseous access and administer drugs accordingly
- Consider hypovolaemia
- Consider when to move to hospital
- Notify receiving unit via control with appropriate history/information

---

OTHER CONSIDERATIONS

Premature babies

Fortunately, the same principles apply to the resuscitation of preterm infants as to full-term babies. The important additional considerations are that both inflation and ventilation breaths may need to be done more gently. However, it is vital that the chest is seen to move with these insufflations. Secondly, thermal control is even more important. The premature baby's skin is often thin with a reduced epidermal layer and less subcutaneous fat. The practice of delivering babies at 28 weeks gestation or less into plastic bags is only indicated if they are simultaneously placed under a radiant heat source which is not usually available outside of hospital. Therefore for premature babies who are born outside hospital they should be dried off and wrapped in a fresh towel, as described above for the full-term infant.

Departure to hospital

Most neonates will respond to simple measures during resuscitation at birth. It is important to institute these promptly and effectively on scene rather than simply transfer a compromised baby into hospital without the proper initial actions. Unnecessary hypoxic injury can then be avoided which may not have been sustained if the correct manoeuvres were employed in the first place. It is, however, also important to recognise the window to move the patient. If regular spontaneous respirations and a fast heart rate have been found on reassessment then the baby can be transferred with close monitoring. If the baby's condition has improved but not to normality then another cycle of resuscitation appropriate to the infant's current condition can be employed followed by the reassessment. If the baby's condition is approaching normality then he/she can be transferred. If the clinical condition remains the same or is worsening despite effective technical manoeuvres then this plateau phase should be recognised and the patient moved into hospital without further delay. Whatever the level of resuscitation, this should be continued until arrival and handover in the hospital setting. A decision will need to be made regarding transfer of the mother into hospital either with the baby if he/she has stabilised or separately if ongoing resuscitation of either patient is necessary. Once the baby is in hospital an experienced paediatrician or neonatologist can make the decision to discontinue resuscitation armed with the appropriate facts and background if the baby shows no response to good quality ongoing resuscitation in the hospital setting.

Calling ahead via ambulance control to the local accident and emergency department or labour ward to inform them of the imminent arrival of a potentially critically unwell baby will allow the appropriate staff (i.e. paediatrician or neonatologist and neonatal nurse) to attend the baby on arrival at the hospital as well as the accident and emergency staff.

Apgar score

Four of the clinical parameters assessed above during the resuscitation are also found in the Apgar score (see Table 12.1)

Table 12.1   Apgar scoring

Sign	Score 0	Score 1	Score 2
Heart rate	Absent	<100 per minute	>100 per minute
Breathing	Absent	Weak cry or hypoventilation	Good
Colour	Pale/blue	Body pink, limbs blue	Pink
Tone	Limp	Some flexion	Normal
Reflex response	None/nil	Some movement	Cries

(Source: Richmond 2006, p50).

This score was devised to evaluate a newborn baby's adaptation to extra-uterine life. It was created by Virginia Apgar, Professor of Anaesthetics at Columbia University, USA in 1949. Whilst a useful tool in describing a baby's condition shortly after birth it is best utilised as a retrospective scoring system rather than being used to guide the resuscitation.

Communication

Remember that the birth of a child is an important event for parents, and in situations involving the resuscitation of the newborn this can be an extremely anxious time for them; paramedic/clinicians should be objective with the information they give regarding possible outcomes. In situations where communication with the parents is a problem the paramedic/clinician should request an interpreter via language line; remember the use of friends or relatives as an interpreter is considered poor practice (Richmond 2006, p42). Handover of the patient in the accident and emergency department or on the labour ward of the local hospital is very important. A succinct description of the time of birth and condition of the baby as well as details of the resuscitation will be key to ongoing management. The timing of the infant's responses to resuscitation and the retrospective Apgar scores applied will help to guide the subsequent management of the baby. It will also help the paediatrician in making later decisions regarding prognosis which will of course be central to any discussions with the parents.

CHAPTER KEY POINTS

- Control the environmental temperature.
- Minimise heat loss by drying the baby off and wrapping in a fresh dry towel.
- Most babies will respond well to basic manoeuvres performed effectively.
- Reassess the baby's condition at intervals described above.
- Decide on the opportune time to move the patient into hospital.
- Communicate with parents, control and other health care professionals.
- Give a good quality handover that accurately describes the timeline of events, particularly treatments given and the baby's response to these.

13 Mental health assessment

Graham Harris and Mathew Millman

The assessment of people with mental health issues is a common occurence for all hospital care providers. Evidence indicates that one in four people experience a mental health problem at some point in their life and one in six adults has a mental health problem at any one time. The problem is not restricted to adults, with one in ten children aged between 5 and 16 years also having a mental health problem, and many of these continue to have mental health problems into adulthood (DH 2011).

The DH provides considerable evidence of and guidance for the spectrum of presenting mental health problems of patients which paramedic/clinicians may come into contact with:

- Depression, bipolar disease, postnatal depression, schizophrenia
- Obsessive compulsive disorders, post-traumatic stress disorder
- Self-harming or attempted suicide
- Alcohol or drug misuse (DH 1999, 2001b, 2002a, 2002b, 2004; NICE 2004c, 2005, 2006, 2007e, 2008, 2008b, 2009, 2010).

More often than not, prior information is provided before arrival at a scene; however, the incidental occurrence requires paramedic/clinicians to be fully versed with the necessary tools for the correct assessment of each patient. The purpose of this chapter is to illustrate relevant key issues the paramedic/clinician may find helpful when dealing with patients with mental health issues.

SCENE ASSESSMENT

The scene itself may provide information to the paramedic/clinician. When approaching any scene where the patient has (or potentially may have) a mental health issue then consider the following aspects of the scene:

- Physical environment
    - Type of micro environment – domestic two-storey house, multi-storey apartments, industrial garage space (chaotic living conditions)

250

- ▦ Access and egress routes – narrow passageways, stairs, open spaces
- ▦ Potential hazards – poor lighting, obvious obstructions
- ▦ Paraphernalia like spoons, tin foil, matches, syringes and makeshift tourniquets
- ▦ Smells (particularly alcohol, cannabis or smoked cocaine).
- ■ Personnel already in attendance
  - ▦ Police
  - ▦ Relatives/friends
  - ▦ Social service personnel
  - ▦ GPs
  - ▦ Ambulance personnel.
- ■ Patient presentation
  - ▦ Stance – sitting, withdrawn posture, standing, incessant pacing
  - ▦ Verbal communication – silence, inappropriate language, aggression, shouting
  - ▦ Alcohol – visible evidence, smell
  - ▦ Drug usage – both prescription and illicit
  - ▦ Appearance – dishevelled, unwashed, state of undress.

PRIMARY SURVEY

The purpose of any primary survey is to ascertain if the patient has any *time critical* conditions which require immediate lifesaving attention. The primary survey of the patient with a mental health issue continues the ethos of the DR ABCDE framework; however, the paramedic/clinician should understand that a distressed patient may react extremely to being hurried. Consider and utilise the following approach:

- ■ Do not rush
- ■ Take your time (explain your actions, to patient and relatives)
- ■ Take every effort to be honest
- ■ Explain what is likely to happen (obtain consent, ensure patient has capacity, GP, assessment, hospital, potential admission) (JRCALC 2006f).

Information regarding the patient may have to be obtained from concerned family, partners and/or friends, and in certain instances an Approved Mental Health Professional (AMHP) and the police. The presentation of the patient will vary considerably depending on the condition and the severity of their symptoms. A common symptom, *psychosis* affects the patient's mind and causes them to change the way that they think, feel and behave, resulting in them being unable to distinguish between reality and their imagination. The symptom(s) may be due to:

- Mental health conditions, such as schizophrenia, bipolar disorder (manic depression)
- Physical conditions (Parkinson's disease, meningitis), or as a result of:
- Drug or alcohol misuse.

Psychosis due to drug or alcohol misuse may only last for a few days. However, the psychosis that results from schizophrenia or bipolar disorder may last indefinitely unless it is treated, hence the importance of obtaining the appropriate care. Ascertain if the patient presents with or has suffered from either:

- Hallucinations – the patient may see or hear things that are not there
- Delusions – the patient believes things that are untrue.

DANGER

Most people who suffer from mental illnesses are vulnerable and present no threat to anyone but themselves (DH 1999, p2). Patients with schizophrenia and related disorders may be intensely distressed, especially during the acute phases, which may manifest as fear, agitation, suspicion or anger. Consider the patient's needs but always ensure the safety of self, colleagues, bystanders and the patient at all times. Never place yourself in a situation where you cannot readily exit. Remember the value of an open, non-judgemental approach and the use of a calming voice to assist in easing the situation and in achieving a conversation with the patient and then explaining that you are there to help.

Possible actions to be taken:

- Always ensure safety to yourself, your colleague(s) and then to the patient – in that order
- Ensure a viable escape route
- Obtain consent, and ensure patient has capacity
- Utilise a calming voice and an open, non-judgemental approach
- Remember the value of good verbal and non-verbal communication
- If applicable, ensure that appropriate PPE is worn

Be particularly aware that performing any assessment may have the opposite effect of creating more worry and anxiety for the patient, so describe all of your intended actions.

RESPONSE

Remember to exclude all probable medical or drug related reasons for any patient presenting with altered mental status (hypoglycaemia, head injuries, alcohol or drugs) before considering psychological causes. Obtain the patient's level of consciousness (LOC), and remember that schizophrenic patients often appear emotionless, flat and apathetic.

- Ascertain if possible the patient's LOC (AVPU).
- Ascertain if the patient responds to a calm reassuring voice.
- Does the patient present with *incessant pacing* (*akathisia* – a movement disorder characterised by a feeling of restlessness and the need to be in constant motion).
- Ascertain if the patient has a history of long-term use of antipsychotic drugs (akathisia is a side effect).
- Have they used cannabis or cocaine? The latter is associated with a variety of movement disorders, including akathisia (crack dancers).

Possible actions to be taken:

- Ascertain and record the patient's level of consciousness (LOC)
- Ascertain if the patient responds to a calm reassuring voice
- Ascertain the cause, if present, of 'incessant pacing' (antipsychotic or cocaine use) (NICE 2010, p27)

AIRWAY

The patient who is talking incessantly may initially appear to have a patent airway, however remember that the patient who has misused alcohol or drugs may have an airway problem. Alternatively, the patient may present with tardive dyskinesia, another effect of long-term use of antipsychotic drugs. The patient may present with involuntary movements which normally commence with the face: mouth, lips and tongue, and include grimacing, lip-smacking, tongue and chewing movements (MIND 2011).

- Does the patient appear to have excess salivation (likely to occur with second generation antipsychotics)?
- Is the airway patent?
- Is the patient able to maintain their own airway?
- Correct any airway deficits immediately by stepwise airway management.

Possible actions to be taken:

- Ensure the patient has a patent airway
- Utilise stepwise airway management as appropriate (*see Chapter 2*)

- Identify if the patient has any involuntary movements of mouth, lips and tongue (ascertain the use of 1st generation (FGA) or 2nd generation (2nd GA) antipsychotic drugs)
- Ensure airway is secure before moving to the next element

BREATHING

The patient may be intensely distressed and agitated, and their emotional responses and/or medications may potentially have a direct influence on the respiratory system. These elevated anxiety levels may be the cause of an adrenergic response, resulting in an increase in respiration and other symptoms. Remember that a considerable number of individuals with mental health problems also misuse substances (cocaine 'smoked or snorted', cannabis) (DH 2002a; 2011). Patients who use these substances may present with:

- Shortness of breath
- Productive cough
- Chronic rhinitis (intra-nasal use of cocaine – snorting)
- Oropharyngeal ulcers
- Wheezing
- Chest pain
- Haemoptysis
- Exacerbation of asthma.

Assess and manage any of the above conditions appropriately.

- Listen to the patient talking and assess if their speech is:
    - Disorganised (frequent derailment or incoherent, also known as *word salad*)
    - Disjointed or rambling monologues (patient appears to be talking to themselves or imagined people or voices)
    - Alogia – lessening of fluent speech and productivity (patient may either speak very little or with a lack of spontaneous content). This is also known as *poverty of speech*.
- Identify the presence of either normal or abnormal breathing patterns.
- If possible, obtain a SpO_2 reading, manage accordingly.
- Note any particular odour that may lead you to identify differential complications (alcohol, sweet or pear drop odour).
- Ascertain if the patient has asthma.

Possible actions to be taken:

- Ascertain the patient's breathing pattern (normal or abnormal)
- Identify acute respiratory symptoms (manage accordingly; ensure the patient is not hypoxic)
- Obtain an SpO$_2$ reading
- Note abnormal odours
- Identify if their speech is disorganised, disjointed or if they have alogia
- If *time critical* conditions are identified, manage and transfer in relation to condition

---

CIRCULATION

Patients with schizophrenia have an increased risk of cardiovascular disease, including myocardial infarction (Osborn *et al.* 2007; NICE 2010, p20). Some antipsychotic medications have been shown to induce cardiovascular side effects (lengthening of the QT interval on ECG) (NICE 2010, p21), whilst trycylcic drugs may cause postural hypotension, tachycardia, and ECG changes (BNF (online) 2011).

Remember that patients who use cocaine are also at risk of cocaine-induced myocardial infarction (MI) (Burnett, 2010). Various pharmacologically active substances have reportedly been used with cocaine; with alcohol and nicotine being the most common. Alternatively, the effects of the patient's medication or the fact that they are agitated and distressed may have resulted in elevated anxiety levels and be the cause of an adrenergic response, directly causing an increased pulse rate and blood pressure. The patient however may present with injury as a result of self-harm or failed suicide attempt. Assess the following aspects of circulation:

- Ensure the immediate control of obvious external bleeding
- Assess and record the patient's pulse (bradycardic, normal or tachycardic)
- Assess and record the patient's blood pressure (BP) (hypo- or hypertension may occur as a side effect of the patient's medication)
- Does the patient appear diaphoretic?
- Obtain an ECG trace and ascertain if there is lengthening of the QT interval (measured from the beginning of the QRS to the end of the 'T' wave)
- Ask the patient if they smoke (including cannabis and cocaine) or use other illicit drugs. If so, ascertain frequency and quantity.

Possible actions to be taken:

- Ensure the immediate control of obvious external haemorrhage (*see Chapter 7*)
- Assess and record the patient's pulse and BP
- Obtain an ECG trace and assess for lengthening of the QT interval
- Ascertain if they use illicit drugs
- If a 'time critical' condition is identified, manage and transfer as appropriate

DISABILITY

As with any patient, the assessment of disability includes assessing their neurological function and reassessing their level of consciousness. It also includes assessing and recording their blood glucose levels and conducting an assessment of their pupils. In a patient with mental health issues, these may all potentially be affected. A patient who has catatonic schizophrenia may present with:

- Bizarre posture
- Muscle immobility, or
- Stupor (semi-consciousness due to mental illness, wherein the patient does not move or speak, and does not respond to stimuli).

Alternatively the patient may present with other effects of tardive dyskinesia (MIND 2011). These include involuntary movements which affect other parts of the body, resulting in gestures, tics and writhing movements. It may include the fingers making it look as if the patient is playing an invisible guitar or piano. It can also cause rapid blinking, making the assessment of the patient's pupils more difficult for the attending paramedic/clinician. Unfortunately for the patient, another side effect of antipsychotic medication is the onset of diabetes (NICE 2010, p21, 27). Assess and record the patient's level of consciousness, blood glucose level and pupils.

Possible actions to be taken:

- Assess and record the patient's level of consciousness (AVPU)
- Record any abnormal posture(s)
- Do they present with any other involuntary movements (note and record)
- Assess and record the patient's blood glucose level (manage accordingly)
- Assess the patient's pupils (PERRLA)
- If a *time critical* condition is identified, manage and transfer as appropriate

EXPOSE/EXAMINE/ENVIRONMENT

All reasonable steps should be taken to engage individual patients in meaningful discussion about issues relating to consent, remembering that exposing any patient will require their consent. Ensure that the patient has *capacity*, specific guidance is provided regarding the patient with mental health problems (Department of Constitutional Affairs 2007; DH 2009, p5). Due consideration must be given to the results of a physical examination of any patient with mental health issues as their emotional responses and/or medication may have a direct influence. The paramedic/ clinician will have evaluated all of the information obtained from the elements of the primary survey and the patient's environment, and linked this to their presenting disorder. This should be appraised and the need to remove the patient (time critical conditions) from the scene considered and, if appropriate, action taken, alternatively a secondary survey should be completed.

Possible actions to be taken:

- Consider the effects of the patient's emotional response and/or medication
- Expose patient and examine (remember appropriate consent, and ensure the patient has capacity)
- Evaluate the findings of the primary survey
- If time critical, transfer to the appropriate treatment unit or centre
- Alternatively undertake a secondary survey

SECONDARY SURVEY

Presenting complaint

In relation to attending emergency calls involving mental health issues, the paramedic/clinician may be called to patients who present for various reasons. Whilst the call may have been received as '*person having hallucinations*' or '*hearing voices*', there are specific mental disorders which paramedic/clinicians will be called to attend, which include:

- Mood, stress-related and anxiety disorders
- Psychosis
- Mania/hypomania
- Schizophrenia
- Paranoia (JRCALC 2006f).

A patient who is in the initial phase of schizophrenia may present with symptoms of unusual and uncharacteristic behaviour, disturbed communication, bizarre ideas, poor personal hygiene, and reduced interest in and motivation for day-to-day activities, and may explain that they feel that their world has changed. However, their family and friends may advise that the patient has changed *in themselves*. Alternatively, the presenting complaint may be due to either a self-harm or suicide attempt. Continue the ethos commenced in the primary survey (not rushing, being open and non-judgemental), as misinterpretation due to the paramedic/clinician's view of the events or perceived problems may lead to an incorrect starting point. This can affect the history obtained and potentially have consequences for the patient's care.

- Ascertain the exact cause(s) of the presenting complaint (from patient if possible, alternatively from family, partner or friends).
- Ascertain if this is the first time the problem has occurred.
- Use the patient's own words when detailing and documenting the presenting complaint.
- Undertake a suicide and self-harm risk assessment (see Table 13.1).

Table 13.1 Suicide and self-harm risk assessment

Item	Value	Patient Score
Gender: Female	0	
Gender: Male	1	
Age: <19 years old	1	
Age: >45 years old	1	
Depression/hopelessness	1	
Previous self-harm attempts	1	
Evidence of excess alcohol/use of illicit drugs	1	
Absence of rational thinking	1	
Separated/divorced/widowed	1	
Organised or serious attempt	1	
Absence of close/reliable family or job or active religious affiliation	1	
Determined to repeat attempt or ambivalent	1	
Total patient score		

(Source: JRCALC 2006f)

In emergency situations, it is important to address whether the patient is at immediate risk of self-harm or suicidal intent. The use of this risk assessment scoring system can identify key markers regarding the patient's risk of repeating the self-harm/suicide attempt.

- Score <3 indicates low risk.
- Score 3–6 indicates medium risk.
- Score >6 indicates high risk.

> ## Possible actions to be taken:
>
> - Ascertain the presentiny complaint
> - Undertake a suicide and self-harm risk assessment (record and document low risk as part of history)
> - Medium/high risk patient should be referred/conveyed to an appropriate unit for further assessment)

History of presenting complaint

The actual history of the presenting complaint will specifically vary depending on the *reason* of the presenting complaint. The history of a patient whose presenting complaint is *self-harm* may be due to the fact that they are depressed due to either child or domestic abuse (NICE 2004c). Alternatively, another patient may have a history of suffering from schizophrenia for several years and is suffering an acute exacerbation or relapse and requires additional intervention (NICE 2010, p16). Remember that not all patients that present with indicators for mental health illness will have a definitive diagnosis prior to the time of your assessment. Particular consideration should be made to particular demographic groups:

- Current or ex-military personnel (who may be suffering from post-traumatic stress disorder (PTSD) (Pedrott, 2011)
- New mothers (who may be suffering from postnatal depression (PND) (NICE 2007e).

Endeavour to ascertain any triggering or exacerbating factors that may have led to the patient's present situation. Remember that patients may suffer from more than one mental health problem simultaneously; as well as potentially being drug/alcohol dependent, with specific groups being particularly at risk:

- Young people
- Homeless people
- Offenders
- Women
- Ethnic minority groups (DH 2002a, p18, 19).
- Ascertain the history of the presenting complaint(s).
- Confirm the findings from relatives and friends (time period, symptoms etc.).
- Information obtained regarding vulnerable persons (record and complete documentation as per local guidelines, refer to the appropriate agency).
- Depending on the patient's age/gender consider the need of a chaperone.

Possible actions to be taken:

■ Record and document information obtained regarding vulnerable persons (comply with local guidelines and refer to appropriate agencies)

Past medical history

A full account of a patient's past medical history is invaluable when deciding on an appropriate course of treatment for the individual; these are not normally decided by the paramedic/clinician for patients with mental health problems. However, a patient's past medical history and any pre-existing mental health problems should be obtained by the paramedic/clinician. Ascertain the nature of pre-existing mental health condition(s):

■ Depression, manic depression (bipolar disorder), postnatal depression
■ Schizophrenia
■ Obsessive compulsory disorders, post-traumatic stress disorder
■ Self-harming or attempted suicide
■ Alcohol or drug misuse.

Patients will and do have other co-morbidity conditions that, as with any patient, may be relevant to the existing problem; these can include endocrine (diabetes), cardiovascular (hypertension, lipid levels, heart attack – myocardial infarction), or respiratory conditions (asthma). Evidence suggests that psychiatrists and the patient's GP are particularly poor at recognising and treating physical conditions in patients who suffer from a mental health problem (Roberts *et al.* 2007).

Drug/medication history

A precise notation of all the medications taken by the patient should be obtained wherever possible; although the paramedic/clinician must always be aware that any underlying mental health issues can preclude an accurate list. Also, drug regime compliance and regular concordance must always be taken into consideration. Be cautious of the accuracy of this information from other parties, as emotion may cloud accuracy issues. The use of illegal, illicit or herbal drugs must also be considered as these can interact with prescription medications.

Specifically St. John's wort (*Hypericum perforatum*), which is a popular herbal remedy and available to the public for mild depression. It has drug metabolising enzymes, which differ with the strength of the preparation. Care must be taken to avoid toxicity due to drug interactions between prescribed and alternative (e.g. herbal) or over the counter remedies (BNF 2011).

Patients with mental health problems are prescribed antidepressants, antipsychotic and anxiolytic medications. Antidepressant drugs relieve the symptoms of depression and include four main types:

- Monoamine oxidase inhibitors (MAOIs)
- Selective serotonin reuptake inhibitors (SSRIs)
- Serotonin and noradrenaline reuptake inhibitors (SNRIs)
- Noradrenaline and specific serotonergic antidepressants (NASSAs) (Royal College of Psychiatrists 2011a).

Antipsychotic drugs, also known as neuroleptics and which, affect various chemicals in the brain, tend to be classified into two specific groups:

- Typical – first generation antipsychotics (FGAs) (see Table 13.2)
- Atypical – second generation antipsychotics (2nd GA) (see Table 13.3).

Table 13.2 Typical antipsychotics (FGAs)

Medication	Trade name
Chlorpromazine	*Largactil*
Haloperidol	*Haldol*
Pimozide	*Orap*
Trifluoperazine	*Stelazine*
Sulperide	*Dolmatil*

Table 13.3 Atypical antipsychotics (2nd GAs)

Medication	Trade Name
Amisulpiride	*Solian*
Ariprazole	*Abilify*
Clozapine	*Clozaril*
Olanzapine	*Zyprexa*
Quetiapine	*Seroquel*
Risperidone	*Risperdal*
Sertindole	*Serdolect*
Zotepine	*Zoleptil*

(Source: Royal College of Psychiatrists 2011b.)

Anxiolytics are used for the short-term relief of severe anxiety. Table 13.4 includes some of the common anxiolytics.

Table 13.4	Common anxiolytic drugs
Medication	**Trade name**
Ativan	*Lorazepam*
Valium	*Diazepam*
Librium	*Chlordiazepoxide*
Serax	*Oxazepam*
Xanax	*Alprazolam*
Dalmane	*Flurazepam*
Halcion	*Triazolam*
Klonopin/rivotril	*Clonazepam*

(Source: BNF (online) 2011)

Social/family medical history

Consideration needs to be given to a patient's social and family history, which may have an influence upon a patient's state of mind and therefore thought processes. In the out-of-hospital setting, acquiring an accurate and detailed social and family medical history may not always be possible; however, when treating a patient with acute mental health issues, extended on-scene time may allow for a more detailed questioning regimen. Evidence suggests that various factors may cause mental health problems:

- Physical
- Environmental
- Psychological
- Social (Rethink 2011).

Alternative evidence explains these factors as biological, sociocultural and psychosocial issues (see Table 13.5).

Table 13.5	Biological, sociocultural and psychosocial factors	
Biological	**Sociocultural**	**Psychosocial**
Genetic factors	Personal relationships	Childhood trauma
Pre- and postnatal factors	Family stability	Childhood abuse/neglect
Neuro-biochemical imbalance	Economic status	Dysfunctional family structure
	Social cohesion	Biological disorders
	Work environment	
	Personal belief values	

(Source: Gregory and Ward 2010)

Remember that relatives, families and carers of patients suffering mental health problems may also need support; they may be emotionally and psychologically affected by caring for someone with a mental health problem. They may have been coping with this for days, weeks or even years and be feeling distressed, fearful and isolated, which can have a significant impact on their quality of life (NICE 2010).

REVIEW OF SYSTEMS AND VITAL SIGNS

As mentioned earlier, the exclusion of any physical or medical conditions is important when formulating a treatment plan. Therefore acquiring a set of vital sign observations will not only assist the paramedic/clinician, but may also provide the patient with reassurance that they are receiving treatment and thereby help to reduce their anxieties. The vital signs ascertained if possible should include:

- Respiratory rate, character and work of breathing
- Heart rate, character
- Blood pressure
- ECG
- Blood glucose levels
- GCS/neurological status, including pupillary reaction
- Temperature
- SpO_2.

Consideration, however, must be given to the acquisition and results of any physical examination of patients with a mental health problem, as their emotional response and/or medication may have a direct influence.

- Be particularly aware that performing these assessments may also have the opposite effect of creating more worry and anxiety for a patient, so describe all of your intended actions, and obtain appropriate consent prior to examining.

MENTAL CAPACITY ACT 2005

The Mental Capacity Act 2005 relates to patients over the age of 16 in England and Wales. If the patient has a mental disorder in Scotland or Northern Ireland the paramedic/clinician should note the exceptions in the Mental Health Act 2003 (as amended by the Mental Health Act 2006), the Mental Health (NI) Order 1986, and the Mental Health (Care and Treatment) (Scotland) Act 2003 (GMC 2011). The paramedic/clinician should therefore understand what the Act defines as *a lack of capacity*: 'a person lacks capacity in relation to a matter if at the material time he is unable to make a decision for himself in relation to the matter because of an impairment of, or a disturbance in the functioning of, the mind or brain' (DH 2005; Mental Capacity Act 2005, 4.3, section 2(1)).

This means that a person lacks capacity if they cannot do one or more of the following four things, known as *inability to make a decision*:

- Understand information given to them
- Retain that information long enough to be able to make a decision
- Use or weigh up the information available to make a decision
- Communicate their decision.

An assessment of a person's capacity must be based on their ability to make a specific decision at the time it needs to be made, and not their ability to make decisions in general. This incorporates the five statutory principles included within section 1 of the Act:

- A person must be assumed to have capacity unless it is established that he or she lacks capacity.
- A person is not to be treated as unable to make a decision unless all practicable steps to help him or her to do so have been taken without success.
- A person is not to be treated as unable to make a decision merely because he or she makes an unwise decision.
- An act done, or decision made, under this Act for or on behalf of a person who lacks capacity must be done, or made, in his best interests.
- Before the act is done, or the decision is made, regard must be had to whether the purpose for which it is needed can be as effectively achieved in a way that is less restrictive of the person's rights and freedom of action (DH 2005; Mental Capacity Act 2005, Section 1).

MENTAL HEALTH ACT 1983 (AMENDED 2007)

The Mental Health Act of 1983 provides special legal provision for any person displaying any disorder or disability of the mind and who is considered a danger to either themselves or others, and who refuses to accept treatment that they require. They may be detained under the Mental Health Act 1983 (amended 2007) for a limited time, in order to be assessed or treated accordingly. An application for assessment can be made by an Approved Mental Health Professional (AMHP) (previously known as Approved Social Worker, ASW), or the patient's nearest relative who has cause for concern over their welfare.

The duration and circumstances of the compulsory admission (commonly termed as *being sectioned*) can be broken down into three main sections that are more pertinent to paramedic out-of-hospital practice (Table 13.6).

Table 13.6 Compulsory admission to hospital

Mental Health Act	Purpose	Duration	Decision Direction
Section 2	Compulsory admission for assessment or assessment followed by treatment	Up to 28 days	Application must be made by AHMP, or nearest relative who has seen the patient in the past 14 days. Also seen (examined) by two separate doctors (one of which must be approved under the Mental Health Act) within 5 days of each other. Admission must be within 14 days of last examination.
Section 3	Compulsory admission for treatment	Up to 6 months (may be renewed for further 6 months, and after that 12 monthly)	Application must be made by AHMP, or nearest relative who has seen the patient in the past 14 days. Also seen (examined) by two separate doctors (one of which must be approved under the Mental Health Act) within 5 days of each other. Admission must be within 14 days of last examination.
Section 4	Enables admission in an emergency	Up to 72 hours (can be converted to another section (usually 2) if required)	Application must be made by AHMP, or nearest relative. Must be seen by a doctor (preferably one that knows the patient or one that has been approved under the Mental Health Act). The doctor and the applicant must have seen the patient within the previous 24 hours and the patient must be admitted to hospital within 24 hours of being examined by the doctor or from when the application was made.

(Source: Mental Capacity Act 2007)

There may be times when the paramedic/clinician comes into contact with patients who are at risk to themselves or others and require to be placed into a place of safety. Section 136 of the Mental Health Act 1983 covers this (see Table 13.7).

Table 13.7 Section 136: Mentally disordered people found in public places	
Mental Health Act Code of Practice	**Section 136: mentally disordered people found in public places**
Chapter 10 section 10.12	Section 136 allows for the removal to a place of safety of any person found in a place to which the public have access (by payment or otherwise) who appears to a police officer to be suffering from mental disorder and to be in immediate need of care or control.
Chapter 10 section 10.13	Removal to a place of safety may take place if the police officer believes it necessary in the interests of that person, or for the protection of others.
Chapter 10 section 10.14	The purpose of removing a person to a place of safety in these circumstances is only to enable the person to be examined by a doctor and interviewed by an AMHP, so that the necessary arrangements can be made for the person's care and treatment. It is not a substitute for an application for detention under the Act, even if it is thought that the person will need to be detained in hospital only for a short time. It is also not intended to substitute for or affect the use of other police powers.
Chapter 10 section 10.15	The maximum period a person may be detained under section 136 is 72 hours. The imposition of consecutive periods of detention under section 136 is unlawful.

(Source: DH 2008b, p74)

The paramedic/clinician may also come across patients who have been discharged following a period of compulsory hospital admission (section 3). Depending on the circumstances they may be discharged with aftercare (section 117). The local social services authority (LSSA) is required to provide the patient with the aftercare services, which may include: accommodation, psychological, physical health care, daytime activities or employment needs arising from drug, alcohol or substance misuse.

OTHER CONSIDERATIONS

Communication

Consideration should be given to patients whose first language is not English or who have a visual or hearing impairment as misinterpretation and confusion can lead to an escalation of the patient's symptoms. Consider if the information could be explained or presented in a way that is easier for the patient to understand (visual aids). Endeavour to utilise alternative methods (non-verbal) or other people to aid communication:

- Interpreter (language line)
- Family member
- Support worker
- Speech and language therapists
- Advocate.

Social/family/carer/guardian

Never forget the distress and emotional pressure that can be experienced by relatives of any patient suffering a mental health illness, especially if they have had to instigate a compulsory admission. Remember to fully explain any actions or interventions undertaken in the patient's best interest to any family members present to help avoid misunderstanding and therefore undue distress.

Ethical and legal

Mental illness is not a condition affecting adults alone. Patients under 16 years of age can be subjected to acute episode(s) of mental illness and therefore due consideration must be given to how to manage a young patient accordingly. Compliance with The Children Act 1989 (amended 2004) must be maintained wherever possible. The Act's starting point is to confirm in legislation that it should be assumed that an adult (aged 16 or over) has full legal capacity to make decisions for themselves (the right to autonomy) unless it can be shown that they lack capacity to make a decision for themselves at the time the decision needs to be made. This is known as the presumption of capacity.

Destination/receiving specialist

Always ensure that all documentation appertaining to any patient's compulsory admission to hospital under the Mental Health Act 2007 is transferred to an appropriate receiving professional (Approved Mental Health Professional, nurse or doctor) on their arrival.

Mental health – facts/figures

The World Health Organization's Global Burden of Disease study estimated that depression will be second only to cardiovascular disease in the proportion of disability that it creates in the world (Murray and Lopez 1997). In the year 2000, one in four adults in the United Kingdom were identified as suffering with some form of mental health problem within their lifetime, with one in six having a neurological disorder such as depression or anxiety (ONS 2003).

Mental health problems – 2011 statistics.

- At least one in four people will experience a mental health problem at some point in their life and one in six adults have a mental health problem at any one time.
- One in ten children aged between 5 and 16 years has a mental health problem, and many continue to have mental health problems into adulthood.
- Half of those with lifetime mental health problems first experience symptoms by the age of 14, and three-quarters before their mid-20s.
- Self-harming in young people is not uncommon (10–13% of 15–16-year-olds have self-harmed).
- Almost half of all adults will experience at least one episode of depression during their lifetime.
- One in ten new mothers experiences postnatal depression.
- About one in 100 people has a severe mental health problem.
- Some 60% of adults living in hostels have a personality disorder.
- Some 90% of all prisoners are estimated to have a diagnosable mental health problem (including personality disorder) and/or a substance misuse problem (DH 2011).

CHAPTER KEY POINTS

- The safety of both yourself and your colleagues is paramount when managing any situation involving patients with mental health illness.
- Where possible and safe, allow any patient suffering from a mental health illness to be involved in their assessment and management.
- Ensure consent is obtained, and if required/appropriate assess the patient's capacity.
- Remember the value of effective verbal and non-verbal communication.
- Be careful to exclude any physical and medical causes of altered mental status before considering psychological causes.

■ If the patient is being compulsory admitted to hospital ensure that the appropriate documentation has been completed.

■ Current legislation must always be complied with when dealing with any patient with a mental health issue, especially regarding consent and capacity.

References

Adam, S.K. and Osbourne, S. (2005) *Critical Care Nursing Science and Practice*. 2nd edn. Oxford: Oxford University Press.

Advanced Life Support Group (2011) *Advanced Paediatric Life Support: The Practical Approach*. 5th edn. London: Blackwell Publishing.

Age Concern (2008) *Out of Sight, Out of Mind: Social Exclusion Behind Closed Doors*. London: Age Concern.

American Heart Association (1990). Framingham criteria for assessing LVH: *Circulation* 81: 815–20. Available at: http://www.ecglibrary.com/lvhlah.html (accessed 11th April 2011).

Anaesthesia UK (2005) *Cardiorespiratory Arrest in Children (online)*. Available at: http://www.frca.co.uk/article.aspx?articleid=100380 (accessed 22nd February 2010).

Asthma UK (2009) *What is Asthma?* Available at: http://www.asthma.org.uk/all_about_asthma/asthma_basics/index.html (accessed 15th January 2010).

Astin, F. and Atkin, K. (2010) Ethnicity and coronary heart disease: making sense of risk and improving care. A Race Equality Briefing Paper. London: Race Equality Foundation.

Ballinger, A. and Patchett, P. (2007) *Pocket Essentials of Clinical Medicine*. 4th edn. Edinburgh: Saunders Elsevier.

Banit, D.M., Grau, G. and Fisher, J.R. (2000) Evaluation of the acute cervical spine: a management algorithm. *Journal of Trauma-Injury Infection & Critical Care*, 49(3): 450–6.

Bath, T. and Lord, B. (2010) The risk/benefit of paramedic initiated shoulder reduction, *Journal of Paramedic Practice*, 1(6).

BBC News (2009) Asian heart disease gene found. Available at: http://news.bbc.co.uk/1/hi/health/7833753.stm (accessed 3rd October 2010).

Bhadriraju, S., Ray, K.K., DeFranco, K.M., Bhadriraju, P., Murphy, S.A. *et al.* (2006) Association between blood glucose and long-term mortality in patients with acute coronary syndromes in the OPUS-TIMI 16 trial. *American Journal of* Cardiology, 97(11): 1573–7.

Bhatt, D.R., White, R., Martin, G., Van Marter, L.J., Finer, M. I (2007) Transitional hypothermia in preterm newborns. *Journal of Perinatology*, 27: 45–7.

Bickley, L.S. (2003). *Bates' Guide to Physical Examination and History Taking*. 8th edn. Philadelphia, PA: Lippincott Williams & Wilkins.

Bickley, L.S. and Szilagyi, P.G. (2007) *BATES' Pocket Guide to Physical Examination and History Taking*. 5th edn. Philadelphia, PA: Lippincott Williams & Wilkins.

Bickley, L.S. and Szilagyi, P.G. (2009) *Bates' Guide to Physical Examination and History Taking*. 10th edn. Philadelphia, PA: Lippincott Williams & Wilkins.

Bledsoe, B.E. and Benner, R.W. (2006) *BRADY – Critical Care Paramedic*. Upper Saddle River, NJ: Pearson, Prentice Hall.

British Heart Foundation (2009). *Inherited Heart Conditions*. Available at: http://www.cardiomyopathy.org/assets/files/BHF_HCM_FINAL_28_Sept_09.pdf (accessed 17th October 2010).

British National Formulary (BNF) (2011) Available at: http://bnf.org/ (accessed 3rd May 2011).

British National Formulary [online] (2011) ed. London: British Medical Association and Royal Pharmaceutical Society. Available at: http://bnf.org/bnf/bnf/current/ (accessed 3rd May 2011).

British Thoracic Society (2008) Guideline for emergency oxygen use in adult patients. *Thorax: An International Journal of Respiratory Medicine*, 63: 1–81.

British Thoracic Society (2009) *Guidelines for the Management of Community Acquired Pneumonia in Adults: Update 2009*. London: British Thoracic Society.

British Thoracic Society: *Scottish Intercollegiate Guidelines Network (2011) British Guideline on the Management of Asthma. Quick Reference Guide*. London: British Thoracic Society.

Brooker, C. (2008) *Medical Dictionary*. 16th edn. USA. London: Churchill Livingstone.

Buist, M., Bernard, S., Nguyen, T.V., Moore, G. and Anderson, J. (2004) Association between clinically abnormal observations and subsequent in-hospital mortality: a prospective study. *Journal of Resuscitation*, 62: 137–41.

Burnett, L.B. (2010) *Cocaine Toxicity in Emergency Medicine*. Available at; http://emedicine.medscape.com/article/813959-overview (accessed 1st May 2011).

Burton, H., Alberg, C. and Stewart, A. (2009) Heart to Heart. Inherited Cardiovascular Conditions Services: A needs assessment and service review. Available at. www.phgfoundation.org/file/4668/ (accessed 11th October 2010).

Caroline, N. (2008) *Emergency Care in the Street*. 6th edn. London: Jones & Bartlett.

Centre for Maternal and Child Enquiries (2010) *Post Project Review Report Diabetes in Pregnancy*. London: CEMACH.

Centre for Maternal and Child Enquiries (2011) *Saving Mothers' Lives: Reviewing maternal deaths to make motherhood safer: 2006–2008. Eighth Report of the Confidential Enquiry into Maternal and Child Health*. London: CEMACH.

Clarke, C. Neurological Disease. In P. Kumar and M. Clark (eds) (2005) *Clinical Medicine*. 6th edn. London: Elsevier.

Clubb, R. (2007) Delayed diagnosis of a patient with cervical spine injury resulting in complete cervical spine dislocation without serious or lingering neurological signs: a case report. *The Internet Journal of Emergency Medicine,* 4(1). Available at. www.ispub.com/ostia/index.php?xmlFilePath. . ./ijem/. . ./spine. . .(accessed 22nd August 2010).

Confidential Enquiry into Maternal and Child Health (CEMACH) (2007) *Why Mothers Die 2003–2005. Report on confidential enquiries into maternal deaths in the United Kingdom.* London: CEMACH.

Cox, C. L. (2010) *Physical Assessment for Nurses.* 2nd edn. Oxford: Blackwell Publishing.

Dieckmann, R.A. (2006) *Pediatric Education for Pre-hospital Professionals.* 2nd edn. Sudbury, MA: Jones and Bartlett Publishers.

Department of Constitutional Affairs (2007) *Mental Capacity Act 2005: Code of Practice.* London: The Stationary Office.

Department of Health (1999) *The National Service Framework for Mental Health.* London: Department of Health Publications.

Department of Health (2001a) *Consent – What You Have a Right to Expect. A Guide for Adults.* London: Department of Health Publications.

Department of Health (2001b) *National Service Framework for Older People.* London: The Stationery Office.

Department of Health (2002a) *The Mental Health Policy Implementation Guide: Dual Diagnosis Good Practice Guide.* London: Department of Health Publications.

Department of Health (2002b) *National Suicide Prevention Strategy for England.* London: Department of Health Publications.

Department of Health (2004) *The National Service Framework for Mental Health – Five Years On.* London: Department of Health Publications.

Department of Health. (2005) *Mental Capacity Act.* London: The Stationery Office.

Department of Health (2005a) National Service Framework for Coronary Heart Disease. Chapter 8 of *Arrhythmias and Sudden Cardiac Death.* London: Department of Health Publications.

Department of Health (2005b) *The National Service Framework for Long-term Conditions.* London: Department of Health Publications.

Department of Health. (2007) *National Stroke Strategy.* London: Department of Health.

Department of Health (2008a) *Treatment of Heart Attack; National Guidance.* London: Department of Health Publications.

Department of Health (2008b) Code of Practice. *Mental Health Act 1983.* London: The Stationary Office.

Department of Health (2009) *Reference Guide to Consent for Examination or Treatment.* 2nd edn. London: Department of Health publications.

Department of Health (2010) *Essence of Care 2010.* London: The Stationary Office.

Department of Health (2011) *No Health Without Mental Health: A Cross-Government Mental Health Outcomes Strategy for People of all Ages. Mental Health and Disability.* London: Department of Health Publications.

Dizon, J.M. (2011) *Brugada Syndrome.* Available at: http://emedicine.medscape. com/article/163751-overview (accessed 24th June 2011).

Ekundayo, O., Howard, V.J., Safford, M.M., McClure, L.A., Arnett, D. *et al.* (2009) Value of orthopnea, paroxysmal nocturnal dyspnea, and medications in prospective population studies of incident heart failure. *American Journal of Cardiology,* 104(2): 259–64.

Encyclopaedia Britannica (2010) Online. Available at: http://www.britannica.com/ EBchecked/topic/99345/catecholamine (accessed 16th February 2010).

Elst, M. (2009) *Twelve of the Worst Soccer Injuries of all Time.* Available at: http://www.oddee.com/item_96906.aspx (accessed 12th April 2011).

Epstein, O., Perkin, D.G., Cookson, J. and De Bono, D.P. (2008) *Clinical Examination.* 4th edn. London: Mosby.

Farrel, M., Ryan, S. and Langrick, B. (2001) 'Breaking bad news' within a paediatric setting: an evaluation report of a collaborative education workshop to support health professionals. *Journal of Advanced Nursing,* 36(6): 765–75.

Fraser, D.M. and Cooper, M.A. (2009) *Myles Textbook for Midwives.* 15th edn. Edinburgh: Churchill Livingstone, Elsevier.

Fuller, G. (2004) *Neurological Examination Made Easy.* 3rd edn. London: Churchill Livingstone.

Gausche-Hill, M., Fuchs, S. and Yamamoto, L. (eds) (2007) *The Pediatric Emergency Medicine Resource.* Revised 4th edn. Boston: Jones and Bartlett Publishers.

General Medical Council (2007) *0–18 Years: Guidance for all Doctors,* GMC (online) at http://www.gmc-uk.org/guidance/ethical_guidance/children_guidance_index.asp (accessed 21st February 2010).

General Medical Council (GMC) (2011) *Consent Guidance: Endnotes.* Available at: http://www.gmc-uk.org/guidance/ethical_guidance/consent_guidance_ endnotes.asp (accessed 5th May 2011).

Goldman, L. and Ausiello, D.A. (2008) *Cecil Medicine.* 23rd edn. Philadelphia, PA: Saunders Elsevier.

Gray, J.T. and Gavin C.M. (2005) The ABC of community emergency care: 14 – Assessment and management of neurological problems (1). *Emergency Medicine Journal,* 22: 440–5.

Greaves, I., Hodgetts, T. and Porter, K. (2004) *Emergency Care – A Textbook for Paramedics.* Philadelphia, PA: Saunders.

Greaves, I. and Porter, K. (1999) *Pre-Hospital Medicine. The Principles and Practice of Immediate Care.* London: Arnold.

Greaves, I., Porter, K. and Garner, J. (2009) *Trauma Care Manual.* 2nd edn. London: Arnold.

Greaves, I., Porter, K., Hodgetts, T. and Woollard, M. (2008). *Emergency Care: A Textbook for Paramedics.* London: Elsevier.

Greaves, I., Porter, K. and Smith, J.E. (2003) consensus statement on the early management of crush injury and prevention of crush syndrome. *Journal of the Royal Army Medical Corps,* 149: 255–9.

Gregory, P. and Mursell, I. (2010). *Manual of Clinical Paramedic Procedures.* Oxford: Wiley-Blackwell

Gregory, P. and Ward, A. (Eds) (2010) *Sanders' Paramedic Textbook.* London. Elsevier Health Sciences.

Guly, H.R., Bouamra, O. and Lecky, F.E. (2007) The incidence of neurogenic shock in patients with isolated spinal cord injury in the emergency department. *Resuscitation,* 76: 57–62.

Health and Safety Executive (1999) *Control of Major Accident Hazards Regulations.* Available at: http://www.hse.gov.uk/comah/background/consultcomments.htm (accessed 20th August 2010).

Health Care for London (2009). New stroke and major trauma centres to 'radically improve' care for Londoners (2009) Available at: www.healthcareforlondon.nhs. uk/new-stroke-and-major-trauma-centres-to-radically-improve-care-for-londoners (accessed 26th February 2011).

Health Professions Council (2007) *Standards of Proficiency-Paramedics.* London: Health Professions Council.

Health Professions Council (2008) *Standards of Conduct, Performance and Ethics.* London: Health Professions Council.

Health Professions Council (2009) *Guidance on Conduct and Ethics for Students.* London: Health Professions Council.

Heslehurst, N., Ells, L.J., Batterham, A., Wilkinson, J. and Summerbell, C.D. (2007) Trends in maternal obesity incidence rates, demographic predictors and health inequalities in 36,821 women over 15 years. *British Journal of Obstetrics and Gynaecology,* 114: 187–94.

Hodgetts, T. and Turner, L. (2006) *Trauma Rules 2: Incorporating Military Trauma Rules.* London: Blackwell Publishing

Hodgetts, T., Mahoney, P., Russell, M. and Byers, M. (2006) ABC to <C>ABC: redefining the military trauma paradigm. *Emergency Medical Journal,* 23: 745–6.

Hodkinson, H.M. (1972) Evaluation of a mental test score for assessment of mental impairment in the elderly. *Age Ageing,* 1(4): 233–8.

House of Commons Health Committee. (2005) *The Prevention of Venous Thromboembolism in Hospitalised Patients.* HC 99. London: The Stationery Office.

Hubble, M.W. Richards, M.E., Jarvis, R., Millikan, T. And Young, D. (2006) Effectiveness of pre-hospital continuous positive airway pressure in the management of acute pulmonary oedema. *Pre-hospital Emergency Care,* 10(4): 430–9.

International Spinal Injuries & Rehabilitation Centre (2010) *Spinal Injuries.* Available at: http://www.royalbucks.co.uk/rehabilitation.htm (accessed 25th August 2010).

Jevon, P. (2008) Neurological Assessment Part 1 – Assessing level of Consciousness. *Nursing Times,* 104(27): 26–7.

Joint Royal Colleges Ambulance Liaison Committee (2006) Asthma in Adults: Joint Royal Colleges Ambulance Liaison Committee (ref 1).

Joint Royal Colleges Ambulance Liaison Committee (2006) *Chemical, Biological, Radiological and Nuclear Incidents.* London: Joint Royal Colleges Ambulance Liaison Committee (ref 2).

Joint Royal Colleges Ambulance Liaison Committee (2006) *Dyspnoea,* London: Joint Royal Colleges Ambulance Liaison Committee (ref 3).

Joint Royal Colleges Ambulance Liaison Committee (2006) *Glycaemic Emergencies in Adults,* London: Joint Royal Colleges Ambulance Liaison Committee (ref 4).

Joint Royal Colleges Ambulance Liaison Committee (2006) *Pulmonary Embolism,* London: Joint Royal Colleges Ambulance Liaison Committee (ref 5).

Joint Royal Colleges Ambulance Liaison Committee (2006) *Pulmonary Oedema.* London: Joint Royal Colleges Ambulance Liaison Committee (ref 6).

Joint Royal Colleges Ambulance Liaison Committee (2006) *Thoracic Trauma.* London: Joint Royal Colleges Ambulance Liaison Committee (ref 7).

Joint Royal Colleges Ambulance Liaison Committee (2006a) *Medical Emergencies in Adults: Abdominal Pain.* London: Joint Royal Colleges Ambulance Liaison Committee.

Joint Royal Colleges Ambulance Liaison Committee (2006b) *Drug Protocols: IV Sodium Chloride (SCP)–Sodium Lactate (SLP)* London: Joint Royal Colleges Ambulance Liaison Committee.

Joint Royal Colleges Ambulance Liaison Committee (2006c) *Medical Emergencies in Children: Overview.* London: Joint Royal Colleges Ambulance Liaison Committee.

Joint Royal Colleges Ambulance Liaison Committee (2006d) *Drug Protocols: Benzylpenicillin (Penicillin G)* London: Joint Royal Colleges Ambulance Liaison Committee.

Joint Royal Colleges Ambulance Liaison Committee (2006e) *Treatment and Management of Assault and Abuse: Suspected Abuse of vulnerable adults and Recognition of Abuse.* London: Joint Royal Colleges Ambulance Liaison Committee.

Joint Royal Colleges Ambulance Liaison Committee (2006f) *Medical Emergencies in Adults: Mental Disorder.* London: Joint Royal Colleges Ambulance Liaison Committee.

Joint Royal Colleges Ambulance Liaison Committee (2009a) *Stroke/Transient Ischaemic Attack (TIA): Updated Guidance.* London: Joint Royal Colleges Ambulance Liaison Committee.

Joint Royal Colleges Ambulance Liaison Committee (2009b) *Major Pelvic Trauma: Updated Guidance*. London: Joint Royal Colleges Ambulance Liaison Committee.

Joint Royal Colleges Ambulance Liaison Committee (2009c) *Oxygen – update: Updated Guidance*. London: Joint Royal Colleges Ambulance Liaison Committee.

Kane, R.L. Ouslander, J.G. and Abrass, I.B. (2003) *Essentials of Clinical Geriatrics*. 5th edn. New York: McGraw-Hill.

Kaneshiro, N.K. (2009) *Clubbed Fingers*. Available at: http://www.healthline.com/adamcontent/clubbing-of-the-fingers-or-toes (accessed 21st September 2010).

Kaplan, L.J. and Roesler, D.M. (2008) *Critical Care Considerations in Trauma*. Available at: http://emedicine.medscape.com/article/434445-overview (accessed 16th July 2010).

Kase, C.S., Mohr, J.P. and Caplan, L.R. (2004) Intracerebral haemorrhage. In J.P. Mohr *et al.* (eds) *Stroke: Pathophysiology, Diagnosis and Management*. West Philadelphia, PA: Churchill Livingstone.

Knight, M. (2007) Eclampsia in the United Kingdom. *British Journal of Obstetrics and Gynaecology*, 114(9): 1072–8.

Kupnik, D. and Skok, P. (2007) Capnometry in the pre-hospital setting: Are we using its potential? *Emergency Medical Journal*, 24(1): 614–17.

Lee, C., Revell, M., Porter, K. and Steyn, R. (2007) The pre-hospital management of chest injuries: A consensus statement. Faculty of Pre-hospital Care, Royal College of Surgeons of Edinburgh. *Emergency Medicine Journal*, 24(1): 220–4.

Limmer, D. and O'Keefe, M.F. (2009) *BRADY – Emergency Care*. 11th edn. (Pearson International Edition) London: Pearson Education.

Longmore, M., Wilkinson, I.B. and Rajagopalan, S. (2004) *Oxford Handbook of Clinical Medicine*. 6th edn. Oxford: Oxford University Press.

Lord, B. and Woollard, M. (2011) The reliability of vital signs in estimating pain severity among adult patients treated by paramedics. *Emergency Medical Journal*, 28(32): 147–50.

Luengo-Fernandez, R., Leal, J. and Gray, A. (2010) *Dementia 2010 The Prevalence, Economic Cost and Research Funding of Dementia Compared with Other Major Diseases*. Oxford: University of Oxford.

Manza, L. (2002) Right ventricular myocardial infarction: When the power fails. *Dimensions of Critical Care Nursing*, 21(4): 122–4.

Marieb, E.N. (2009) *Essentials of Human Anatomy and Physiology*. 10th edn. (Pearson International Edition) Boston: Pearson.

McDonald, J. and Ciotola, J.A. (2009) *ALS Skills Review*. Sudbury, MA: Jones and Bartlett Publishers.

Mental Health Act (2007) Chapter 12: Amendments to the Mental Health Act 1983. Legislation.gov.uk. Available at: http://www.legislation.gov.uk/ukpga/2007/12/contents (accessed 30th April 2011).

MIND For better mental health (2011) *Tardive Dyskinesia (TD)*. Available at: http://www.mind.org.uk/help/diagnoses_and_conditions/tardive_dyskinesia (accessed 30th April 2011).

Moore, M. *Daily Telegraph* (published: 7:30 am GMT, 11th January 2010).

Moore, T. (2007) Respiratory assessment in adults. *Nursing Times,* 21(49): 48–56.

Morris, F., Edhouse, J., Brady, W.J. and Camm, J. (2003) *ABC of Clinical Electrocardiography.* London: BMJ Books.

Moses, S. (2009) Blood pressure. *Family Practice Notebook* (online). Available at: http://www.fpnotebook.com/CV/Exam/BldPrsr.htm (accessed 14th February2010).

Moyle, J. (2002) *Pulse Oximetry.* London: BMJ Books.

Murray, C.J. and Lopez, A.D. (1997) Alternative projections of mortality and disability by cause 1990–2020: Global Burden of Disease Study. *Lancet,* 349: 1498–504.

Nader, K. and Shahriar, P. (2009) *Diaphragmatic Paralysis.* Available at: http://emedicine.medscape.com/article/298200-overview (accessed: 20th August 2010).

National Audit Office (2010) *Major Trauma Care in England.* Report by the Comptroller and Auditor General HC213. London. The Stationary Office.

National Confidential Enquiry into Patient Outcome and Death (NCEPOD) (2007) *Trauma: Who Cares?* Bristol: NCEPOD.

National Digestive Diseases Information Clearinghouse (2006) *Smoking and Your Digestive System.* Available at: http://digestive.niddk.nih.gov/ddiseases/pubs/smoking/ (accessed 7th September 2010).

NHS UK (2011) *Does My Child Have the Right to Refuse Treatment?* Available at: http://www.nhs.uk/chq/pages/900.aspx?categoryid=62&subcategoryid=66 (accessed 25th June 2011).

National Institute for Clinical Excellence (2004a) *Chronic Obstructive Pulmonary Disease: Management of Chronic Obstructive Pulmonary Disease in Adults in Primary and Secondary Care.* London: National Institute for Clinical Excellence.

National Institute for Clinical Excellence (2004b) *Trauma: Fluid Replacement Therapy.* TA 74. London: National Institute for Clinical Excellence.

National Institute for Health and Clinical Excellence (2004c) *Self-harm: The Short-Term Physical and Psychological Management and Secondary Prevention of Self-Harm in Primary and Secondary Care.* National Clinical Guideline No. 16. London: The British Psychological Society.

National Institute for Health and Clinical Excellence (2005) *Post-Traumatic Stress Disorder: The Management of PTSD in Adults and Children in Primary and Secondary Care.* National Clinical Guideline No. 26. London: Gaskell and the British Psychological Society.

National Institute for Health and Clinical Excellence (2006) *Core Interventions in the Treatment of Obsessive Compulsive Disorder and Body Dysmorphic Disorder.* National Clinical Guideline No. 31. London: The British Psychological Society and The Royal College of Psychiatrists.

National Institute for Health and Clinical Excellence (2007a) *Venous Thromboembolism – Reducing the Risk*. London: National Institute for Health and Clinical Excellence.

National Institute for Health and Clinical Excellence (2007b) *Head Injury Guidelines*. London: The Stationery Office .

National Institute for Health and Clinical Excellence (2007c) *Head Injury: Triage, Assessment, Investigation and Early Management of Head Injury in Infants, Children and Adults*. London: National Institute for Health and Clinical Excellence.

National Institute for Health and Clinical Excellence (2007d) *Feverish Illness in Children*. NICE (online). Available at: http://www.nice.org.uk/nicemedia/pdf/CG47Guidance.pdf (accessed 21st February 2010).

National Institute for Health and Clinical Excellence (2007e) *Antenatal and Postnatal Mental Health: Clinical Management and Service Guidance*. National Clinical Guideline No. 45. London: National Institute for Health and Clinical Excellence.

National Institute for Health and Clinical Excellence (2008a) *Stroke: The Diagnosis And Initial Management of Acute Stroke and Transient Ischaemic Attack*. London: National Institute for Health and Clinical Excellence.

National Institute for Health and Clinical Excellence (2008b) *Drug Misuse: Psychosocial Interventions*. National Clinical Guideline No. 51. London: The British Psychological Society and The Royal College of Psychiatrists.

National Institute for Health and Clinical Excellence (2009) *Depression: The NICE Guideline on the Treatment and Management of Depression in Adults* (Updated edition). National Clinical Practice Guideline No. 90. London: The British Psychological Society and The Royal College of Psychiatrists.

National Institute for Health and Clinical Excellence (2010) *The NICE Guideline on Core Interventions in the Treatment and Management of Schizophrenia in Adults in Primary and Secondary Care* (Updated edition). National Clinical Guideline No. 82. London: The British Psychological Society and The Royal College of Psychiatrists.

National Institute for Health and Clinical Excellence (2010) *Guidance*. Available at: http://guidance.nice.org.uk/Topic/DigestiveSystem (accessed 23rd August 2010).

National Society for the Prevention of Cruelty to Children (2009) *What is Child Abuse?* NSPCC (online). Available at: http://www.nspcc.org.uk/helpandadvice/whatchildabuse/whatischildabuse_wda36500.html (accessed 21st February 2010).

Nor, A.M, McAllister, C., Louw, S.J., Dyker, A.G., Davis, M. and Jenkinson, D. (2004) Agreement between ambulance paramedic- and physician-recorded neurological signs with face arm speech test (FAST) in Acute Stroke Patients. *Stroke*, 35(6): 1355–9.

Office of National Statistics (2003) *Better or Worse: A Longitudinal Study of the Mental Health of Adults Living in Private Households in Great Britain*. London: ONS.

Office of National Statistics (2009) *Statistical Bulletin: Older Peoples' Day 2009*. London: Office for National Statistics.

Olshansky, B. (2010) *Atrioventricular Nodal Re-entry Tachycardia (AVNRT): Treatment and Medication*. Available at: http://cmedicine.medscape.com/article/160215-treatment (accessed 26th July 2010).

Osborn, D.P.J., Levy, G. and Nazareth, I. (2007) Relative risk of cardiovascular and cancer mortality in people with severe mental illness from the United Kingdom's General Practice Research Database. *Archives of General Psychiatry*, 64: 242–9.

Palatnik, A. and Kates, R. (2002) Could that medication cause bradycardia? *Nursing*, 32(8): 32–4.

Panté, M.D. and Pollak, A.N. (2010) *Advanced Assessment and Treatment of Trauma*. American Academy of Orthopaedic Surgeons. Sudbury, MA: Jones and Bartlett.

Pedrotti, D. (2011) Heroes to Hometown: When Veterans Come Home. *Journal of Emergency Medical Services*, 36(3): 64–72.

Purcell, D. (2003) *Minor Injuries – A Clinical Guide for Nurses*. Edinburgh: Churchill Livingstone.

Raftery, A.T. and Lim, E. (2005) *Churchill's Pocketbook of Differential Diagnosis*. London: Elsevier.

Rathe, R. (2000) *Physical Exam Study Guides: Examination of the Chest and Lungs*. Available at: http://medinfo.ufl.edu/year1/bcs/clist/chest.html) (accessed 2nd March 2010).

Rees, J.P. (2003) Respiratory diseases: symptoms and signs. *Medicine*, 31(11): 1–7.

Reiser, R.C. (2006) Seizures. In Aghababian *et al.* (eds) *Essentials of Emergency Medicine*. Sudbury, MA: Jones & Bartlett.

Resuscitation Council (UK) (2008) *Emergency Treatment of Anaphylactic Reactions – Guidelines for Healthcare Providers*. London: Resuscitation Council (UK).

Resuscitation Council (UK) (2009) *British Thoracic Society Guideline for Emergency Oxygen Use in Adult Patients*. Available at: http://www.resus.org.uk/pages/BTSglOap.htm (accessed 27th July 2010).

Resuscitation Council (UK) (2010) *Resuscitation Guidelines 2010*. Available at: http://www.resus.org.uk/pages/guide.htm (accessed 28th February 2011).

Resuscitation Council (UK) (2011) *Advanced Life Support*. 6th edn. London: Resuscitation Council (UK).

Rethink (2011) *What Causes Mental Illness?* Available at: http://www.rethink.org/about_mental_illness/what_causes_mental_illness/index.html (accessed 4th May 2011).

Richmond, S. (2006) *Newborn Life Support – Resuscitation at Birth*. 2nd edn. London: Resuscitation Council (UK).

Roberts, L., Roalfe, A. and Wilson, S. (2007) Physical health care of patients with schizophrenia in primary care: a comparative study. *Family Practice*, 24: 34–40.

Royal College of Psychiatrists (2011a) *Antidepressants.* Available at: http://www.rcpsych.ac.uk/mentalhealthinfoforall/problems/depression/antidepressants.aspx (accessed 3rd May 2011).

Royal College of Psychiatrists (2011b) *Antipsychotic Medication.* Available at: http://www.rcpsych.ac.uk/mentalhealthinfo/treatments/antipsychoticmedication.aspx (accessed 3rd May 2011).

Royal College of Surgeons of England (2009) *Regional Trauma Systems: Interim Guidance for Commissioners: The Intercollegiate Group on Trauma Standards.* London: The Royal College of Surgeons of England.

Salomone, J.P. and Pons, P.T. (2007) *PHTLS: Pre-Hospital Trauma Life Support.* 6th edn. Maryland Heights, MO: Mosby Elsevier.

Scarborough, P., Peto, V., Bhatnagar, P., Kaur, A., Leal, J. *et al.* (2009) *Stroke Statistics.* London: British Heart Foundation and Stroke Association.

Schilling McCann, J.A. (2008) *Assessment Made Incredibly Easy.* 4th edn. Philadelphia, PA: Lippincott Williams and Wilkins.

Scott, T. and Esen, U.I. (2005) Unplanned out of hospital: who delivers the babies? *Irish Medical Journal,* 98(3): 70–2.

Smith, S.F., Duell, D.J. and Martin, B.C. (2008) *Clinical Nursing Skills – Basic to Advanced Skills.* 7th edn. (Pearson International Edition) London: Pearson Education Ltd.

Snyder, D.R. and Christmas, C. (2003) *Geriatric Education for Emergency Medical Services.* Sudbury, MA: Jones and Bartlett.

Sommargren, C.E. (2002) Electrocardiographic Abnormalities in Patients with Subarachnoid Hemorrhage. *American Journal of Critical Care,* 11: 48–56.

Stables, D. and Rankin, J. (2010) *Physiology in Childbearing: With Anatomy and Related Biosciences.* 3rd edn. Edinburgh: Bailliere Tindall, Elsevier.

Stiell, I.G., Clement, C., Grimshaw, J.M., Brison, R.J., Rowe, B.H. *et al.* (2003) The Canadian C-Spine Rule versus the NEXUS Low-Risk Criteria In Patients With Trauma. *New England Journal of Medicine,* 349(26): 2510.

Swanton, R.H. (2003) *Pocket Consultant: Cardiology.* 5th edn. Boston, MA:. Blackwell Publishing.

Terkelsen, C.J. and Lassen, J.F. (2008) Treatment delays in ST elevation myocardial infarction. *British Medical Journal,* 336: 401 doi: 10.1136/bmj.39475.482419.80 (Published 21 February 2008).

The Children Act (1989) online. Available at: http://www.legislation.gov.uk/ukpga/1989/41/introduction (accessed 12th October 2010).

Thomas, D., Wee, M., Clyburn, P., Walker, I., Brohi, K. *et al.* (2010) Guidelines: Blood transfusion and the anaesthetist: management of massive haemorrhage. *Anaesthesia,* 65(11): 1153–61.

Thompson, M.J., Ninis, N., Perera, R., Mayon-White, R., Phillips, C. *et al.* (2006) Clinical recognition of meningococcal disease in children and adolescents. *The Lancet,* 367(9508): 397–403.

Tidy, C. (2008) *Meningitis* (online). Available at: http://www.patient.co.uk/doctor/ Meningitis.htm (accessed 28th January 2010).

Tortora, G. and Derrickson, B. (2007) *Principles of Anatomy and Physiology*. 11th edn. New York: Wiley.

Trauma Audit and Research Network (TARN) (2010) Available at: https://www. tarn.ac.uk (accessed 17th September 2010).

Trauma.org. (2002) *Initial Assessment of Spinal Injury*. Available at: http://www. trauma.org/index.php/main/article/380/ (accessed 27th April 2011).

UNICEF (2004) *Rights for Every Child* UNICEF (online) at. http://www.unicef. org.uk/tz/resources/resource_item.asp?id=31 (accessed 21st February 2010].

Wardrope, J. and English, B. (2003) *Musculoskeletal Problems in Emergency Medicine*. Oxford: University Press.

Wardrope, J. and Mackenzie, R. (2004) The ABC of community emergency care: 2 The System of assessment and care of the primary survey positive patient. *Emergency Medicine Journal*, 21: 216–25.

Wardrope, J., Ravichandran, G. and Locker, T. (BMJ.com) (2004) *Risk Assessment for Spinal Injury After Trauma*. Available at: http://www.bmj.com/cgi/content/ full/328/7442/721 (accessed: 24th August 2010).

Watson, W., Sinclair, E., Bjelogrlic, P. and Cruickshank, R. (2006) *Cardiovascular Exam – Examining the Heart and Circulatory System*. Available at: www.n3wt. nildram.co.uk/exam/cardio/ (accessed 25th September 2010).

Woollard, M., Hinshaw, K., Simpson, H. and Wieteska, S. (2010) *Pre-hospital Obstetric Emergency Training – The Practical Approach*. Advanced Life Support Group. Oxford: Wiley-Blackwell.

World Health Organization (2008) *The Top Ten Causes of Death*. Available at: http://www.who.int/mediacentre/factsheets/fs310_2008.pdf (accessed 3rd October 2010).

Wyatt, J.P, Illingworth, R.N., Clancy, M.J., Munro, P.T. and Robertson, C.E. (1999) *Oxford Handbook of Accident & Emergency Medicine*. Oxford: Oxford University Press.

Yaseen, S. and Thomas, C.P. (2009) *Metabolic Alkalosis*. Available at: http:// emedicine.medscape.com/article/243160-overview (accessed 28th October 2010).

Zieve, D. and Hoch, D.B. (2010). *Spinal Cord Trauma*. Available at: http://www. nlm.nih.gov/medlineplus/ency/article/001066.htm (accessed 20th August 2010).

USEFUL WEBSITES

www.ageUK.org.uk
Age UK incorporates both Age Concern and Help the Aged. Information and advice for the elderly on benefits, care and age discrimination.

www.asthma.org.uk
Website for Asthma UK is the charity dedicated to improving the health and well-being of the 5.4 million people in the UK whose lives are affected by asthma.

www.alzheimers.org.uk
The leading UK care and research charity for people with this disease and other dementias, their families and carers. It provides a network of support and local information, including England, Scotland and Wales.

www.bcs.com/
British Cardiovascular Society. Professional association for those involved in cardiac care. Provides information on members, meetings, publications.

www.brit-thoracic.org.uk
Website for the official body of respiratory specialists, including medical practitioners, nurses and scientists. Publications are listed on the site.

www.collegeofparamedics.co.uk
Website for the (UK) College of Paramedics. Provides information on continuing professional development workshops, membership, and how the College of Paramedics is currently developing the paramedic profession.

www.dcsf.gov.uk/everychildmatters
An in-depth website examining multiple aspects of child health and wellbeing. Contains chapters on safeguarding children and child protection issues.

www.direct.gov.uk/en/Parents/ParentsRights/DG_4002954
Detailed website on information surrounding the law and parental responsibility.

www.dh.gov.uk
Official website of the UK Department of Health, the government department responsible for public health issues. Provides material which is primarily for use by health care professionals. Free access without registration.

www.easyauscultation.com/
This website presents heart sound and lung sound lessons along with phonocardiograms and cardiac animations. Easy auscultation – heart sounds, murmurs and lung sounds.

www.fphc.info
Website of the Faculty of Pre-Hospital Care, provides information about membership to the faculty and examinations for the Diploma in Immediate Care.

www.gpnotebook.co.uk/
Another excellent website providing accurate information on many conditions and assessment techniques. Free access without registration.

www.hpc-uk.org
Website of the Health Professions Council (HPC) which is a UK-wide regulatory body. Free access for Paramedic Standards of Proficiency, Codes of Conduct, and CPD documents.

www.jrcalc.org.uk
Provides free access to all of the JRCALC guidelines utilised by UK Paramedics, and links to the NHS national library.

www.library.nhs.uk/neurological/
This website signposts NHS professionals to information and evidence in the field of neurology; the section on journals will direct the reader to respected journals, many of which are free to access

www.medicalprotection.org
A legal website giving health care professionals guidance on consent and children and young people.

www.ncepod.org.uk
Website of the National Confidential Enquiry into Patient Outcome and Death. Provides reports and is currently undertaking studies in cardiac arrest procedures.

www.nice.org.uk/
National Institute for Health and Clinical Excellence. Provides access to the latest versions of a series of national clinical guidelines to secure consistent, high quality, evidence based care for patients using the National Health Service.

www.nmc-uk.org/
Website for the Nursing and Midwifery Council. Provides information about the code of conduct for Nurses and Midwives, registration, how to make a complaint, and the standards expected of nurses and midwives.

www.patient.co.uk/
This is an excellent website which provides well referenced articles on many conditions and injuries. It is free of charge with no registration necessary.

www.patient.co.uk/doctor/Mental-Capacity-Act.htm
An easy to follow guide to the Mental Capacity Act and the consent to treatment in children.

www.ramcjournal.com
Website of the *Journal of the Royal Army Medical Corps*. Journal articles published since 1999 are available in .pdf. (downloads of the recent issues are made available six months after the due publication date).

www.rcog.org.uk/
The website if the Royal College of Obstetricians and Gynaecologists (RCOG). Provides a list of publications by the RCOG. Many can be downloaded as PDF files.

www.resus.org.uk/
Resuscitation Council (UK) provider of the (2010) UK Resuscitation Guidelines (free to download). Facilitates education of both lay and health care professional members of the population in the United Kingdom.

www.spinal.co.uk/
The Spinal Injuries Association (UK) is a user-led, national charity, providing support and information for the spinal cord injured community.

www.statistics.gov.uk
Home of the UK National Statistics Publication. Provides data on economy, population and society at national and local level. Summaries and detailed data releases are published free of charge.

www.tarn.ac.uk/
Website of the Trauma Audit and Research Network (TARN), a password will be required please contact support@tarn.ac.uk.

www.trauma.org/
Largest internet trauma care site – covers all aspects of injury prevention, evaluation and management. includes an email discussion group.

Index

muscle strength, assessment of 107
neurological system in older people 213
olfactory nerve 105
onset of pain 102
opisthotonus positioning 98
optic nerve 105
pain 102–4
palliation of pain 102
patient position, observation of 94
photophobia 99
point-to-point coordination 107–8
primary survey 95
professional obligations 116
pronator drift 107
provocation of pain 102
pupil examination 99
quality of pain 103
radiating pain 103
rapidly alternating movements, testing ability in 108
response 95
review of system in trauma assessment 139
review of system and vital signs 102–8
Romberg test 107
scene assessment 94
secondary survey 101
seizures 96, 113–14
sensory assessment 106
severity of pain 103
shoulders, accessory nerve and 106
smell, olfactory nerve and 105
social considerations 115
spinal injuries assessment 122
stroke 108–9
sub-arachnoid haemorrhage 110
temperature 99
timing of pain 103
tonic clonic seizure 113, 114
transient ischaemic attack 109
trigeminal nerve 105–6
unconsciousness 95–6
vagus nerve 106
vestibocochlear nerve 106
vision, optic nerve and 105
neutral head position in neonate care 241
NHS UK 196
non-accidental injury (NAI) 190, 191, 194, 197, 198
non-blanching rash 190
non-cardiac pain 49
non-conveyance implications 11
non-steroidal anti-inflammatory drugs (NSAIDs) 75, 80
Nor, A.M. *et al.* 109, 206
normal paediatric values 179
nose examination in child assessment 195
NSPCC 197

obesity 42
obstetric patient assessment 220–34
airway 223
breathing 223–4
circulation 224
circulation (obvious external haemorrhage) 222
communication 232–3
danger 221
destination decision 233
disability 225
DR 'C' ABCDEFG assessment 220
environment 225
ethical considerations 233
expose/examine/evaluate 225
fundus 220, 226
get to the point quickly 220, 226
handover of obstetric patient 232
history 226–32
bleeding 230
current pregnancy, history of 228
discharge 229–30
eclampsia (and pre-eclampsia) 225, 228, 231
evaluation of 231–2
fitting 231
foetal movements 230–31
gestation of pregnancy 226–7
labour 228
obstetric history 226–7
OPQRSTA framefork 228–9
pain 228–9
past medical history (PMH) 227
past obstetric history 227–8
problem currently presenting, history of 228–31
quickening 230–31
risk factors, identification of 231–2
severity of symptoms, assessment of 232
key points 233–4
legal considerations 233
primary survey 221
response 221–2
scene assessment 220
secondary survey 226–32
social considerations 233
oedema 49, 60
Office of National Statistics (ONS) 201, 217, 268
older person assessment 201–19
airway 203–4
Alzheimer's disease 213
aortic systolic murmer 212
blood glucose levels 213
blood pressure 212
breathing 204
cardiovascular system 211–13
chronic obstructive pulmonary disease (COPD) 207, 211

circulation 204–5
communication 215–16
danger 203
delirium 213
dementia 213
destination decisions 217
diabetes 213
disability 205–6
ECG recordings 213
environment 206
ethical considerations 216
expose/examine/evaluate 206
facts and figures 201, 217–18
Glasgow Coma Score (GCS) 213
history 207–10
activities of daily living (ADLs) 209
dietary regimens 210
drug/medication history (DMH) 209
history of presenting complaint (HPC) 208
past medical history (PMH) 208
presenting complaint (PC) 207–8
social exclusion 210
social/family medical history (S/FMH) 209–10
hypertension 212
impressions 215
indoor assessment 202
JRCALC 206, 216
key points 218–19
legal considerations 216
life expectancy 218
neurological system 213
older people in population 218
orthostatic hypotension 205
osteoporosis 214–15
outdoor assessment 201
oxygen saturation (SpO$_2$) 211
pain score 214
PERRLA framework 214
primary survey 202
professional standards 217
pulse 211–12
pupils 214
respiratory system 211
response 203
resuscitation 216
reverse stethoscope technique 215
review of systems and vital signs 210–15
scene assessment 201–2
secondary survey 207
social considerations 216
support, forms of 202
systolic murmer 212
temperature 214
trauma 214–15
vulnerability, identification of 202